Contrary Native Other

Backward Bears, Berdache, Buffoons, Bluejays, Beings

Jay Miller, PhD, ed

© 2020

Others

Humans differ among themselves as a continuum across the world. These are differences of scale, kind, and degree, depending on culture, regional, and global patterns. Often margins are set by antithesis, of which the most striking that of the "contrary", who lives and responds in reverse of usual "normal" routines. Often known by their Lakota name of *Heyoka*, they engage in reverse, obverse, topsy-turvy behavior that is countering, contending, inversing against usually activities, patterns and flowings in human societies and cultures. Frequently they speak 'backwards' so usual 'yes' is 'no' to them, agreeing is actually rejecting, and denying food hunger is asking to be fed. Understanding these conditions is especially important at sexual proposals and encounters, often at public rites, intended to reconfirm moral parameters.

Editorial changes have sought consistency in citations, while freeing up punctuation as much as possible, but retaining the single most functional mark when there were multiples.

The major adjustment concerns the Aa'ni (technically ʔɔɔʔɔ́ɔ́niinénɔh), the eponym that has replaced or joined references throughout herein to Algonkian speaking Gros Ventre to avoid multiple confusions since this French term for 'big bellies' was also applied to Siouan Hidatsa, though they were distinguished respectively as Gros Ventre of the Prairie or Gros Ventre of the Missouri, while the popular term Atsina derives from Algonkian allied Blackfoot via enemy Plains and Woods Cree. Minitaree 'water people' was also used for both for a time. Aa'ni is often said to mean 'white clay people', though some Aa'ni say it refers to 'mounds of earth used to turn bison when driving them into a corral'.[1]

Throughout we are concerned with these studies and examples of the contrary or counter-human behavior, or 'life style', often sanctioned by hostile, military, or war fraught environments. We begin with my own studies of human variation, which embraces more human like mammals such as bears, then turn to a series of studies of versa persons in North America.

---

[1] Douglas Parks Gros Ventre Synonymy, Smithsonian Handbook Plains 13 part 2: 692 2001.

Contents

4   People, Berdache, and Left-Handed Bears

18   Masks and Matrilineality

21   Indien Personhood I

38   Indien Personhood II ~ Baby

43   Indien Personhood III ~ Water Burial

46   Indien Personhood IV ~ Ashes

60   Bluejay ~ Harry Turney High

64   Bluejay ~ Verne Ray

71   Contrary ~ Verne Ray

95   Clowns ~ John Plant

128   Arapaho

131   Aa'ni

149   Buffoons ~ Julian Steward
161   Steward bio

163   index 167

633 footnotes

People, Berdache, and Left-Handed Bears:
Human Variation in Native America

Abstract

The Native cultures of North America recognize a bewilderingly large range of people, only some of whom are human. Focusing on four widely scattered tribes (Nootka, Keres, Kootenay, Winnebago) with examples from several others (Blackfeet, Pomo, Ojibwa, Tsimshian, Lenape Delaware), this paper examines :he mediating role played by berdaches, bears, and others in these cultures. Consideration is also given to variations in the psychological, categorical, and symbolic aspects of gender and of the culture + nature continuum.

AN INTRIGUING FEATURE of Native American conversation is the frequent reference to "people" of various sorts, who are not usually human in European terms. Underlying these references, it seems, is a common view of the universe as anthropomorphic − if not in form then in emotions and personality − in keeping with what Mary Douglas[2] has called a pre-Coperanican, or anthropocentric universe.

Over and over again, elders make reference to animal people, plant people, water people, spirit people, rock people, and many others, while at the same time recognizing the unique position of human people at the center of the overall plan of the cosmos. All of these cosmologies are based upon a pervasive belief in humanoid beings, suggesting that Amerind tribes use a flexible definition of what constitutes humanity in order to justify such a great range of people. As a preliminary attempt to grasp this definition, this paper will look at a few interrelated examples within particular tribes, which bear on the generalities involved. The related, inverse topic, of the contrary, often known by its Lakota reference as Heyoka, is considered elsewhere.

Miller[3] discussed several universal categories that are important for efficiently articulating the structural configuration (abbreviated as *struckon*) of a culture. In rank order from the most confined to the most extensive, these categories involve handedness, gender, and biota. In light of these categories, we will consider complex interactions involving the symbolic importance of left priority, the berdache ~ transexual, and bears, especially grizzlies. While information on these topics from each of the tribes is not always complete, such data do exist for the Nootka (West Coast People) of Vancouver Island, the Keres Pueblos of New Mexico, the Kootenay of British Columbia, and the Winnebago of Wisconsin. Because it has some bearing on the overall argument, we will also consider Delaware data relative to these categories, so as to suggest why the berdache role, so common elsewhere in Native America, was singularly lacking in the Northeast, among the Iroquois and the Coastal Algonkians.

From all of the available evidence, it appears that the Nootka, Keres, Kootenay, Winnebago, and Delaware use gender as the organizing, most pervasive tenet of their cultures. Complementarity of the sexes is, therefore, the dominant metaphor for expressing the tension that unifies and diversifies these cultures. Within the context of mythology, such a tension

---

[2] Mary Douglas Purity and Danger, London: Pelican Books 1970: 98, 104.

[3] Jay Miller A Struckon Model of Delaware Culture and the Positioning of Mediators, American Ethnologist 6: 791-802 1979.

serving as the keystone of a culture has been variously called a *paiduma* by Leo Frobenius[4] and an armature by Claude Levi-Strauss.[5] In practice, however, it is more like an echo reverberating throughout a culture, at all levels and times.

These reverberations have different forms in different cultures, depending upon the way in which the components of the gender echo are defined in the format. Basically, the format has three components, serially defined in terms of a notion of concentric degrees of confinement, or limitation. The echo itself consists of a dominant pair, one member of which is defined as exclusive (inside, closed, and positioned) within the other member, which is inclusive (outside, open). For example, in almost all human cultures, gender is defined such that Woman is the demarcated, exclusive category within the inclusive category of Man.

Further integrating these pairs is the notion of mediation, in which mediators are defined as inclosive, partaking of the attributes of each member of a pair as well as of qualities from a third dimension unique to mediators, making them inclosive of the entire system. Such inclosiveness is a constant in all cultures, although the hierarchical position of individual mediators will vary from culture to culture. For those with a Man/Woman tension, the most universal mediator is that of Mind (consciousness, thought, memory), variously represented as a high god, water, fire, or other sacred centers permeating the cosmos.[6] Mind itself shares with other mediators the quality of being a permeating nexus of channels, or webbing, for the reverberations of the cultural echo throughout the organization.

While the universal equation seems to be Man-(Mind)-Woman as inclusive / inclusive /exclusive, certain cultures have deliberately manipulated this analogy to establish their own distinctive configuration. Hence, while the Delaware follow this norm (as the Nootka and Winnebago also seem to), the Keres and Kootenay have reversed it so that Man is exclusive and Woman inclusive.[7] In fact enough comparative data already exists to propose that the pan-human norm is an equation of the inclusive with the dominant, the right side, Man, animals, and winter; or of the exclusive with the subordinate, the left side. Woman, plants, and summer. While exceptions do occur, they often appear to be intended to reinforce the tribal identity by emphasizing intercultural differences.[8] Other examples of this process appearing below are the left priority found in revitalization or nativistic movements such as the Delaware Big House Cult or the Great Lakes Midewiwin instituted by the mythic Bear. As right / left, Man / Woman, and animal / plant are obvious and rich polarities for coding the word and for relating to neighbors through similarity and reversals, so are some other natural phenomena appropriate for serving as mediators. In addition to the ones listed above, the following analysis will show that berdaches and bears also function as important mediators.

Throughout Native America, the bear is viewed as the great healer, patron of herbalists and shamans, because its large size, many human characteristics, and frequent grubbing for roots and plants encourages such links with medicines and supernatural power. Further, being

---

[4] J Miller A Struckon Model 1979.

[5] Claude Levi-Strauss The Raw and the Cooked, New York: Harper and Row 1969.

[6] J Miller The Matter of the (Thoughtful) Heart: Centrality, Focality, or Overlap; Journal of Anthropological Research 36: 338-42 1980a; High-Minded High Gods in North America. Anthropos 75: 916-19 1980b.

[7] J Miller The Priority of the Left, Man 7: 646-47 1972

[8] J Miller The Delaware As Women: A Symbolic Solution, American Ethnologist 1: 507-14 1974.

omnivorous, bears are often in competition with humans for the same foods, and thus have been much in human awareness. It seems probable, therefore, that bears came to be regarded as left-handed, as a means of distinguishing them specifically from humans. As has been frequently noted, bears are often regarded as pseudo-human or humanoid, much as apes arc by many cultures; unlike apes, known to most Americans only from zoo cages, Native Americans correctly viewed bears as dangerous and unpredictable, sometimes equating them with the worst aspects of Nature. There is, moreover, the possibility that bears are regarded as left-handed because their harvesting of plant foods links them with women. For example, out of great respect for the power of bears, most tribes never use the species name directly, but instead insist on the use of circumlocutions that often include a version of terms like "auntie" or "female affine" for addressing bears when they are encountered.

The justification for this seems to relate to a widespread belief in a special affinal relationship between hunter and prey in the Americas. Tales abound in references to the courtship and marriage between humans and other "people" who are often sources of food, with the right to kill and eat these species derived from a mythic charter setting up reciprocities as a result of the original marriage. Of note in this regard are the widely distributed stories about Star, Bear, Frog, Maize, Salmon, and other spouses. These marriages can be consummated and produce viable offspring because under the robe of each species the males and females are really humanoid. While this is implied for all species, it is most obvious in the case of the large mammals, most especially bears. In this way, bears have come to symbolize relations with the entire animal kingdom, making bears particularly suitable for spouses in myths chartering economic and ritual relations of reciprocity.

While this seems to be the context of generalized bear beliefs in America, specific tribes have developed their own versions within the framework of their own culture. In addition, bear beliefs can be compared with those associated with the berdache, since both of them seem to relate to the overall definition of humanness. Because they are regarded as intermediate between Man and Woman in some sense, berdaches also serve to mediate many aspects of culture. It is actually only the formal, institutionalized berdache role that has bearing here, not the effeminate characteristics, relating more to personality than to social structure.[9]

The four cultures about to be considered represent four different languages and culture areas, suggesting that these relations are much more widespread in America than available evidence would indicate. The Nootka, now usually called West Coast People, comprised about a dozen political divisions along the western shore of Vancouver Island. With the Kwakiutl (*Kwakwala*), they make up the Wakashan stock and belong to the central province of the Northwest Coast, or North Pacific culture area. The Keres inhabit seven pueblos in central New Mexico, belong to the Southwest, or Oasis area, and speak a language classified as an isolate, although their participation in the Oshara archaeological continuum suggests an ultimate ancestry in the Hokan stock. The Kootenay also speak a language classed as an isolate, and are scattered in several bands along the river and lake of the same name, on either side of the British Columbia and Idaho-Montana border. While placed in the Plateau, or Intermontane culture area, the Upper (Eastern) Kootenay, along the river, were strongly influenced by the Plains area, while the Lower (Western) Kootenay, along the lake, were more of the Plateau type. Much Kootenay research remains unpublished, so the citations found below are all the more remarkable. Among

---

[9] H Broch A Note on Berdache Among the Hare Indians of Northwestern Canada, Western Canadian Journal of Anthropology 7 (3): 95-101 1977.

the most recent revisions, to our understanding is the work of Lawrence Morgan,[10] indicating that Kootenay and Proto-Salishan are collaterals of an earlier parent language. The Winnebago have largely remained in their homeland around Green Bay, Wisconsin, speak a Macro-Siouan language, and have been placed in the Great Lakes province of the East culture area. Yet for all these differences, each of these four cultures shares beliefs about left-handed bears and berdache, within a general context of gender symbolism.

Nootka

like that of other Northwest Coast societies, Nootka social structure emphasizes rank and class within the ambilateral descent system common to the central province. In practice it happened that rank was a prerogative of the noble class, in contrast to commoners, the other freeborn class; both freeborn classes were distinct from that of slavery. Gender echoed through this society in terms of complementarity in economics, the inheritance of rank and privileges, marriage arrangements, and seating at feasts, potlatches, and shamanic dancing,[11] Fixed seating at public events was the prime expression of rank and class, so it is significant that at one potlatch chiefs sat at one end of the house, with men on the right and women on the left.[12] More importantly, during the initiation of new members into the Shamans' Dance, "the most important ceremonial of the Nootkan tribes" and key privilege of high rank,[13] seating ignored distinctions of rank and used only that of gender. Based on the elaborate rituals and patterns of female seclusion and the prohibition of women from ocean travel. Woman is the exclusive gender; the lack of any comparable restrictions suggest that Man is the inclusive one.

According to Drucker,[14] both male and female transvestites were known among the Nootka, but they were few in number, generally characterized by a preference for the work of the opposite sex. Such women were famous warrior leaders who had been given supernatural sanction successfully to undertake such a career, while the men performed female tasks like berdaches elsewhere. As most tribes recognize only male berdaches, these females in male roles indicate the full complementarity of the sexes found elsewhere among the Nootka.

The Nootkans gave priority to the right, as indicated by the fact that eating with the left hand was considered a deliberate insult to everyone present. The only physical punishment Drucker[15] noted was striking a child's left hand with a warm stick, to encourage him or her to be right-handed. While in quest of a guardian spirit, children were told they could receive shamanistic power from a right hand sticking from the ground and shaking a rattle, but to flee from a similar disembodied left hand, since it would confer only death.[16]

Nonetheless, bears were considered to be left-handed by the Nootka. In his study of

---

[10] L Morgan Kootenay-Salish Linguistic Comparison: A Preliminary Study, Vancouver: University of British Columbia MA 1980.

[11] Philip Drucker 1951 The Northern and Central Nootkan Tribes. Bureau of American Ethnology, Bulletin 144: 28ff, 36ff, 267.

[12] Drucker Nootkans 1951: 263.

[13] Drucker Nootkans 1951: 439.

[14] Drucker Nootkans 1951: 331.

[15] Drucker Nootkans 1951: 130.

[16] Drucker Nootkans 1951: 153, 185.

social dialects among the Nootka, Sapir[17] noted that in stories and jokes bears speak using left-handed speech forms. Northern Nootka bear hunters ate with the left hand so as to identify more closely with their quarry. Bears were killed to supply meat and grease, while the skin was used to make shirts for ritual bathers to warm themselves in after a chilly ordeal.

Once killed, the bear was brought home from the trap and tied into an upright posture at the rear of the house, with four white mats holding dried salmon in front of it. A chief or other important person sprinkled eagle down on its head, such as was done for any ranking guest, and issued formal greetings. Later the bear was taken to another part of the house and butchered, while chiefs ate the dried salmon from the mats, since it was said to be a gift to them from the bear. Drucker[18] was impressed by this ritual attention, but perplexed because bears were of such minor economic importance. The point of this ritual, however, is not economic but ideological; to borrow arguments from a characterization of totemism, bears are much better to think with than to eat,[19] because of all the animal people they are the most similar to humans.

In a collection of tales written by a contemporary Nootka author and artist, we learn that "During the berry season Momma Bear would pick berries with her left hand. It is said that all bears are left handed. They do everything with their left hands".[20] According to another story, a famous bear trapper named *Liaik* once came upon a person with very white skin fasting, praying, scurbbing, and plunging at a remote pond in order to gain the power to defeat the two traps owned by Liaik. The trapper learned from his hidden observations and began to use the same procedures, vastly increasing his own hunting success because he had learned the techniques used by bears.[21] The point of the story is that bears without their skin robes are just like humans – able to speak, share the same ritual, and recognize a moral world. When women and others were frightened by bears in the berry patches, they shout to warn them away, calling bears by a title translated as "noble lady, wife of a chief, queen," regardless of the actual sex of the bear. The same title is also used for whales, which were courageously hunted by Nootkan nobles in the recent past. The implication is that by evoking these affinal relationships, eaters and eaten were reminded of their existing mutual respect and reciprocity. While the Nootka were fully aware that bear people have the same two genders as humans, their overall might and ambiguity made bears natural mediators between humans and other kinds of people, as will be more fully explored in the conclusion.

Keres

In the Southwest, the Keres Pueblos make much of the doctoring abilities of bears in keeping with the more widespread belief, but as with all other Pueblo cultures, they have formalized this belief into a number of institutionalized priesthoods working for the benefit of the whole community. Individual power is considered to be selfish and distrusted; only power channeled through a priesthood is ever acceptable. The remarkable aspect of this systemization,

---

[17] Edward Sapir 1915 Abnormal Types of Speech in Nootka, Canada Department of Mines, Geological Survey, Anthropology Series 62 (5): 7.

[18] Drucker Nootkans 1951: 180.

[19] Levi-Strauss Totemism, R Needham, translator, Boston: Beacon Press 1962.

[20] George Clutesi Son of Raven, Son of Deer, Sidney, BC: Grays. 1967: 65.

[21] Drucker Nootkans 1951: 166.

however, is that while each priesthood taps a particular power source, all of the priests as a group are known as bears, and accordingly use the left hand while curing. At the pueblo of Sia[22] (White 1962), which in this regard is typical of all seven towns. Bear is the patron of all the curing priesthoods, the guardian of the west, sponsor of the Bear matriclan; a masked deity among the Katsina, and expressly left-handed. An individual who kills a bear must channel his success for the public good by joining a minor priesthood that constitutes a vestige of the warrior, or enemy-slayer cult. In this last regard, the killing of a bear is specifically equated with the killing of a human.

When a Keres medicine man, or priest, performs a cure, he wears a bear-claw necklace and bear-paw skins on the left or both hands.[23] This use of the left is not limited to doctoring, however, since the Keres are one of the few cultures in the world who have a left priority[24] as the general rule. In the theocracy governing each town, a leader is succeeded by his left-hand man, who had previously served as assistant. The second assistant is the right-hand man, and he then moves up to become the heir and left-hand man. The most senior initiate then becomes the right-hand man. In all, then, men arc associated with left, priesthoods, animals, and death, because they are killers; women are associated with right, matriclans, plants, and birth. Moreover, Man is exclusive and Woman inclusive in the Keresan scheme of things, reversing the nearly universal pattern of gender and concentric attributes.

Male berdaches occur among the Keres, talking, dressing, and acting like women. White[25] provides a particularly detailed account of the way in which a boy was pressured and manipulated into becoming a berdache, indicating that the role represents a structural need in society. His data derive from an 1851 examination of an Acoma berdache by a surgeon, William Hammond. Female berdaches are not reported, although Curtis[26] did learn of two women who became ill in 1910 and insisted on initiation into the Giant priesthood. After community uproar and sadness, they were initiated into this lesser priesthood on the stipulation that they act and dress like men during cures. From this account, it appears that the women did not become berdaches, intermediate between the sexes, but rather became men by a cultural fiction. This is much the same way in which the priest in charge of each town is said to become a woman after installation, even though he maintains a married, family life outside the office. Similarly, in northern California, where most shamans were biologically women, they were known by a term meaning "real men," indicating that their long period of disciplined training had turned them culturally into men.[27] These examples indicate the wide cultural range permissible to gender roles, including not only other physiological species, but also individuals with a physiological make-up more appropriate to one category, who through determination and training assume the other form. They transpose themselves between the genders, but do not blur these distinctions as does the berdache.

---

[22] Leslie White The Pueblo of Sia, New Mexico, Bureau of American Ethnology, Bulletin 184 1962.

[23] Charles Lange Cochiti, Carbondale: Southern Illinois University Press 1968: 195.

[24] Miller, The Priority of the Left 1972.

[25] White, New Material From Acoma. Bureau of American Ethnology, Bulletin 136: 301-59 1943: 325.

[26] Curtis Cochiti, Laguna, and Acoma; The North American Indian # 16, Norwood, Mass: Plimpton Press 1926: 134.

[27] Thomas Buckley, personal communication (pc).

From this perspective, the berdache can be seen even more clearly as occupying a separate status, belonging to neither gender but standing somewhere between them. If individuals can choose or be made to switch their gender identity for reasons of personality, ritual, and ideology, the berdache must be regarded as having had a similar option to assume a third position mediating between the other two. This implies that there is not so much a continuum of human variation in Native America, as there is a set of cultural categories with which individuals can affiliate at will or via supernatural sanctions.

The Keres provide a telling case for the argument, since they have a left priority for humans and bears, male berdaches, and a highly structured society based on the tension between male cults and matriclans. After being killed, bears are welcomed into the household and community with the same regard as slain deer and other large mammals, much as honored guests are also greeted and feted. The affinal connection between humans and bear people seems to apply among the Keres as elsewhere, and bears and doctors are both considered nurturant and, thereby, Womanly in the Keres context.

The reasoning behind the left priority is based on the observation that the left hand is closer to the heart, the locus of both thought and emotions. Among the Keres, social class are based on access to knowledge of an esoteric sort, so that a closer association with the left and the heart for men serves to indicate that they are more knowledgeable. This reversal of the right / left polarity is, furthermore, in keeping with several other reversals in the association of the sexes and seasons that help to distinguish the Keres from close Pueblo neighbors such as the Tewa.[28]

Keres boys can become berdaches, but girls cannot, because the semantic categories already assert that men are only Manly, while women have the qualities of both genders because Woman is inclusive. A woman attempting to become a categorical Man would be losing much of her self-esteem, while a man becoming a woman-like berdache would be enhancing his own status to some extent, allowing for some personal opposition from friends or relatives who had their own plans for the individual. It is fitting that in the reported instance of women seeking male privileges they were attempting to become priests rather than ordinary men, although in consequence they had become like other men who had gone through a more natural initiation into the priesthood. As will be considered in the conclusion, these concentric attributes have much bearing on the handedness, genders, and biological solutions utilized in different cultures.

Kootenay

The Kootenay,[29] like the Keres, use the concentric attributes of gender to link men with the inside and exclusive, women with the outside and inclusive. For example, when a man died the frame of the tipi was destroyed; for a woman, the floor and lodge coverings were destroyed. Unlike the Keres, however, the Kootenay associated men with right priority – the right side of the lodge was the honored section where men sat.[30] The left side was associated with women and considered harmless.

____

[28] J Miller The Delaware As Women 1974.
[29] Curtis The Kutenai, The North American Indian # 7: 117-54, Norwood, Mass: Plimpton Press 1911.
[30] Harry H Turney-High Ethnography of the Kutenai. Memoirs of the American Anthropological Association 56 1941.

Bear hunters identified with their prey by using the left hand, because "the grizzly bear is regarded as left-handed".[31] As myths make clear, animals are basically humans or humanoids wearing the cloak of their species. As Boas[32] noted, "the coat of Grizzly Bear is a skin. He put it on and became a grizzly bear." Both grizzly and black bears were hunted for their grease, meat, and hides, while the grizzly was also sought after as a very powerful, if dangerous, guardian spirit.

A special Grizzly Bear Rite was formerly held (before the tribe's conversion to Catholicism) in early March, when medicine bundles were unfolded and renewed while songs were sung on behalf of men and women bears. During the rite, everyone used the left hand. The culmination of the rite was an offering of pipestems buried in honor of the bears, who then judged the sincerity of the person making each gift and accordingly benefited, harmed, or killed the individual. From this we can judge that the supernatural power of bears was such that they could and did influence the life and death of humans. This is in keeping with their position as mediators between such vital categories as life / death, woman / man, human / supernatural, and so forth. Interestingly, the chartering myth for this rite involves a young boy who lived for two years with a bear mother and her cubs. After his return, he instituted the rite based on his observations of this bear woman. This association of bears with the Womanly is also implied by the story of a man who angered the bears by saying that the grizzly was his wife and ordering her to come to him immediately. When she did so, the man was greatly frightened and asked forgiveness.[33]

The Kootenay recognized with special terms both male and female berdaches, although the males were much more numerous. The females acted like amazons in that they became important war and diplomatic leaders. In the most famous instance, a Kootenay woman assumed a full range of male roles in marriage, military, political, and religious areas. She was widely known during the early historic period in the Northwest, until she was killed by the Blackfeet in 1837 for covering the escape, of some Flathead during diplomatic negotiations. Based on this and other cases provided by Schaeffer,[34] it appears that such women were physically large, tall, and robust to begin with and matched this size and strength with assertive personalities like those of the manly hearted women best known for the Blackfeet.

Once again, the Kootenay provide evidence of the co-occurance of male berdaches, left-handed bears, and the possibility for individuals to jump gender roles with sufficient provocation. The evidence of Man as the segregated and of Woman as the integrative categories, however, together with the mediation of the berdaches, make the Kootenay consistent with the same pattern among the Keres. A man gained additional dimensions by becoming a berdache, but a woman lost qualities by such a decision, whether personally or supernaturally sanctioned.

---

[31] Claude Schaeffer Bear Ceremonialism of the Kutenai Indians. Browning, Montana: Museum of the Plains Indian, Studies in Plains Anthropology and History 4 (6) 1966: 50 #22).

[32] Franz Boas Kutenai Tales. Washington, DC: Bureau of American Ethnology, Bulletin 59 1918: 93.

[33] Schaeffer Bear Ceremonialism of the Kutenai Indians, Browning, Montana: Museum of the Plains Indian, Studies in Plains Anthropology and History 4 (6) 1966: 6, 45-47.

[34] Schaeffer The Kutenai Female Berdache: Courier, Guide, Prophetess, and Warrior. Ethnohistory 12: 193-236 1965.

HoChunk ~ Winnebago

The HoChunk played upon this difference in psychological desires and categorical sanctions as revealed by their own ambiguous treatment of berdaches. This society was founded upon a thoroughgoing regard for the opposition between Sky and Earth, formalized in the two moieties of the same names. According to the origin myth, Earthmaker created four worlds, with the sky representing the last man created and the earth the last woman.[35] From this, we can deduce that Man is open and inclusive, while Woman, like the earth, is closed and exclusive. Mediation is represented by Earthmaker himself, a wise and mindful being with the appearance of a man and the creative abilities of a woman.

The patrimoieties consisted of twelve named sibs, with four named for birds belonging to the Sky moiety, but with four named for land mammals and another four named for water creatures, in the Earth moiety. Of these twelve, the Thunderbird sib led those of the Sky, as the Bear led those of the Earth. When the Bear sib held a feast, the members ate with the left hand, out of respect for their eponym.[36] In other situations, the right hand had priority – this use of the left was a peculiarity of bears. Bear clansmen acted as tribal soldiers and police, in addition to holding a special curing dance, given them by bears. Moreover, bears were hunted for food, quested after as guardian spirits, and generally respected by all. Those blessed by a grizzly guardian formed a secret organization, like that of others gifted by a particular spirit.[37] As the Thunderbird sib represented the right, males, and the cosmos, so the Bear represented left, women, and the earth.

Data on HoChunk berdaches are sparse because Christian missionaries have taught them to be embarrassed by the subject, at least in public. Nonetheless, Lurie[38] learned that men who had received power from the moon, a female spirit, were obliged to become berdaches, performing tasks appropriate to women in addition to acquiring a special ability for prophecy. These berdaches were respected and highly honored, sometimes marrying a husband. In addition to this supernatural sanction, however, war captives and dishonored Winnebago men were sometimes humiliated by making them assume a female role in lieu of being killed. Women berdaches as such seem to have been unknown. The indications for the Winnebago, therefore, are that while some unfortunate men were forced to assume the female role, the only true berdaches were those who had a supernatural sanction to compensate for the loss of their integrative position as men and for assuming the mediating role of the berdache.

Other Examples

While other data have been sought to expand this comparison to other tribes, only tantalizing hints have been found. While it seems likely that left-handed bears and berdaches were much more common in aboriginal times, there are only the following scattered data to lend support to this.

---

[35] Paul Radin The Winnebago Tribe, Lincoln: University of Nebraska Press 1970: 329.

[36] Sapir 1915 Abnormal Types of Speech in Nootka, Canada Department of Mines, Geological Survey, Anthropology Series 62 (5) 1915: 7 #1; Radin The Winnebago Tribe 1970: 180, 274.

[37] Radin Winnebago Tribe 1970: 63, 180, 299.

[38] Nancy O Lurie Winnebago Berdache, American Anthropologist 55: 708-12 1953.

Among Plains tribes, Schaeffer[39] refers to Blackfeet myth where a man with bear power became a bear by having a companion scratch his left foot with a bear claw. Elsewhere, Schaeffer[40] also noted the presence of two male berdaches among the Southern Piegan division of the Blackfeet confederation, suggesting that the Blackfeet shared in the pattern found elsewhere with greater documentation.

In California, which was formerly populated by several species of grizzly bears now memorialized on the state flag, the Pomo had a class of ruthless shamans called Bear Doctors, widely distributed in other societies of western Native America. Among the Pomo, they would don full bearskin costumes, using the left hand.[41] While female shamans are well known for the Pomo, there is only a vague reference to berdaches among them,[42] making this example dubious.

A particularly telling case that suggests that belief in left-handed bears was very widespread relates to the *Midéwiwin,* or Shamanic Academy, reformulated about 1700 by the Ojibwa and diffused to other Great Lakes tribes. According to its origin myth, deities instructed Bear (or sometimes Otter, in other versions) to institute the cult among the Ojibwa by training a man named Cutfoot in the lore and ritual. While none of the sources specifies that Bear was left-handed, some of the birchbark mnemonic scrolls used in cult training and the memorizing of the details of myth, ritual, and song, indicate an importance to the left hand. Although many of the figures in the scrolls are armless, Dewdney[43] shows a master scroll from Ontario and a copy of it from Minnesota with twenty-four deities (*manito*), each holding a pouch insignia in the left hand; Landes[44] reproduces a scroll with many armless figures and four others holding rattles in the left hand. This use of the left is clearly related to the general respect shown to bears in America. One Midé (*Midéwiwin*) master went so far as to say "the Bear is the strongest animal, so it came to represent God. A bear can do anything".[45] Once initiated, the members, or Midé priests, were believed to become actual deities and to take on the qualities of Bear. The more selfish and dangerous ones were sometimes accused of wandering at night, dressed in bearskins, to harm people or take revenge.[46]

This association of bears with the left and the Midé does not, however, mean that they had priority. In one version of the origin mythic saga, the Underwater Panther created Man in his right hand and Woman in his left, giving females an inferior, if more flexible position. The implication, by no means substantiated by the data, is that the right hand was associated with chiefs, while the left one was emphasized by Midé shamans. The link between left and Midéwiwin was quite strong even when diffused, since among the Omaha, where the Midé was called the Shell (Cowry) Society and the white swan was a patron, "the down near the left wing

---

[39] Schaeffer Bear Ceremonialism of the Kutenai Indians 1966: 50 #19.

[40] Schaeffer The Kutenai Female Berdache 1965: 221.

[41] Samuel Barrett Pomo Bear Doctors, University of California Publications in American Archaeology and Ethnology 12 (11): 443-65 1917: 458ff.

[42] NC Willoughby Division of Labor Among the Indians of California, Reports of the University of California Archaeological Survey 60: 7-79 1963: 59, Table 6.

[43] Dewdney The Sacred Scrolls of the Southern Ojibway, Toronto: University of Toronto Press 1975: 95.

[44] Ruth Landes Ojibwa Religion and the Midewiwin, Madison: University of Wisconsin Press 1968: 82.

[45] Dewdney, S The Sacred Scrolls of the Southern Ojibway 1975: 25.

[46] Landes Ojibwa Religion and the Midewiwin 1968: 63.

should be worn on the head. The left wing of the bird would be a symbol of its power".[47]

Delaware: A Negative Example

Lastly we turn to a consideration of data from the Delaware of the Northeast, where the berdache role appears to have been singularly absent. Repeated questioning among modern Delaware has convinced me that there is no evidence for a formalized berdache role in this culture. The nearest equivalent is the term *malxkwe*, which is used to refer to a womanish, whiney man, but only in terms of personality characteristics, not social role. For the Delaware, Man was inclusive and Woman exclusive, with mediation supplied by a concept of mind-memory.[48] Priority shifted to the left, under much the same influences and reactions as those behind the Midé. Here the stimulus was a mid-1700 reformist movement called the Big House Cult, which codified traditional culture so that it could better withstand Christianity with its emphasis on the right hand of God. In addition, the Delaware had an elaborate Bear Rite and several other bear observances which indicate that bears held important roles in the cosmology.[49] Unfortunately, there is no evidence as to which paw might have been given priority in this belief system.

From what data do exist, however, we can surmise that bears probably were considered left-handed, because the left hand was used in all rituals. Bears did serve as mediators, with their humanity, strength, herbal lore, and supernatural powers expressed in the Delaware practice of calling them "grandparent" or specifically addressing them as "grandfather" or "grandmother" if the sex were known. This kin term served to emphasize the attitude toward bears as old, wise, and respected.

The lack of berdaches among the Delaware, and by extension the culturally very similar Iroquois, seems to derive from two features of the culture. First, the definitions of concentricity made it unlikely that men would assume a womanlike, berdache role and lose their wider attributes of inclusivity. Second, both Delaware and Iroquois women had extremely high social status as compared to " women elsewhere in Native America, because their identification with the earth included extensive farming and reliable food surpluses. Unlike the Keres, where Woman is inclusive and the clans arc matrilineal, with both male and female members, the Delaware exclusive Woman suggests that their clans were matrilineal, because blood ($humuk^w$)[50] as a Womanly substance was closely circumscribed and the subject of special concern during the transmission of cultural continuity. Delaware women played important roles in the less public negotiations and in matters of home and kinship, while men managed the public and external aspects of the society and had considerable freedom to travel long and far. In this context of greater personal fulfillment, the lack of a berdache role or of any supernatural justification for it

---

[47] Alice Fletcher and Frances La Flesche The Omaha Tribe, vol 2, Lincoln: University of Nebraska Press. 1972: 514.

[48] Miller A Struckon Model of Delaware Culture 1979.

[49] Anthony FC Wallace The Role of the Bear in Delaware Society. Pennsylvania Archaeologist 19 (1-2): 37-46 1949; Tantaquidgeon, Gladys Folk Medicines of the Delaware and Related Algonkian Indians, Harrisburg: Pennsylvania Historical and Museum Commission, Anthropology Series 3 1972; Speck, F Oklahoma Delaware Ceremonies, Feasts and Dances, Philadelphia: Memoirs of the American Philosophical Society 7 1937.

[50] Jay Miller Delaware Anatomy: With Linguistic, Social, and Medical Aspects, *Anthropological Linguistics* 19 (4), 144-166 1977.

seems to be particularly revealing of the psychodynamics behind the berdache position.

Of the tribes cited above, only the Keres and Delaware practiced extensive farming, but among the Keres the men tilled the fields. The Nootka, Kootenay, and HoChunk had foraging economies with local specialities – whaling for the Nootka, bison for the Kootenay, and wild rice for the Winnebago. These economies were clearly expressed in the degree of complimentarity between the sexes and the categorical genders, but they by no means explain the gender definitions within these cultures. At best they are merely congruent with the conceptual logic and intertribal relations that provide the molding influences for a culture.

Conclusion

It remains for us to assess the overall significance of left-handed bears in the cultures of Native America. In his classic study of circumpolar bear ceremonialism, Hallowell[51] specifically discounted from consideration the bear rites of the Delaware, Kootenay, and Ute, as radically different from the hunting observances that were the focus of his comparisons. In doing so he missed the most important feature of bear ceremonialism. In trying to explain why slain bears were welcomed into a home and given special treatment, he went through three possible theories. The economic one held that the propitiation was proportional to the usefulness of bears, but this proved inappropriate when it became clear that bears were economically important in an area larger than that where the ritual was observed. The psychological theory held that bears were so humanoid that their killing would cause some regret, if not guilt, and call for some ritual of propitiation. Here again, however, bears occur in a wider area than that of the ritual, so this supposed regret was not universal. Even within the area of the ritual, regard for bears varied greatly, from slight regard to serious reverence. Lastly, the historic-geographical theory held that the observances began in the Paleolithic, as seen by caches of cave bear skulls in Neanderthal sites, and has been gradually diffusing since that time throughout the northern hemisphere, from Scandinavia through arctic America. This theory accounts well for the facts, but only because it is post hoc.

Bear ceremonialism is part of a larger complex of hunting rituals emphasizing respect for animals so that their immortal souls will continue to be reborn and supply humans with protein. Often, the animal that is the focus of such rites is the staple in that habitat, either as the primary food and/or a dominant species. The First Salmon Ceremony of the Northwest, Deer Greeting of the Southwest, Bear Ceremonialism of the boreal forest, First Roots and Seeds of the Intermontane, and Acorn Rites of Native California are therefore all aspects of this same complex.

Ignored by Hallowell, the Bear Rites of the Delaware and Kootenay are really an intensification of this respect for animals, but involve bears because of the cultural role that bears play as mediators in many cultures. Bear spouses and child adoptions that are the subjects of myth are another aspect of such intensification.

Bears are people in the same sense that other species are people. They are anthropomorphic under their species robes, exist in complimentary genders, and conduct themselves in a moral fashion through language, etiquette, and ritual. Yet bears are also left-handed in the cultures considered above, and probably in many others. While the Keres, Delaware, and Midéwiwin members do have left priority, data strongly suggest a universal right priority for humans, except in cases of deliberate reversal, having to do with asserting a distinct identity, as among Big House adherents. This universal right priority has been linked to male

---

51   A Irving Hallowell   Bear Ceremonialism in the Northern Hemisphere.   American Anthropologist 28: 1-175   1926: 67, 73 #292, 77   1926.

dominance, so that left is associated with females.[52]

From the available evidence, therefore, it seems that bears are left-handed because they are in some sense like women, in addition to being strong and terrifying like men, and being mediators because they share in both of these attributes. To grasp the sense in which they are women, we must turn to the important article by Ortner[53] where she follows Levi-Strauss in arguing for a cross-cultural recognition of the supreme importance of the opposition between culture and nature for all humans. In structuralist theory, culture is the predictable, humanly instituted, and exclusive; nature is unpredictable, awesome, beyond human, and inclusive. In other words, culture is part of nature because it is the biological adaptation of humans. The mediator between culture and nature is the concept of Mind, represented both by the physiological brain and by culturally appropriate thoughts.

Allowing for variation among individual cultures, as a general rule Man and right are closer to the pole of culture, especially in its public aspects, while Woman and left are closer to that of nature, since females menstruate with the lunar cycle and are more closely associated with such natural acts as birth, eating, and child socialization.

Left-handed bears would also be closer to the nature pole, allowing for their equally male attributes of ferocity. To understand their role as mediators, we need to recall the observation of Cassirer[54] that many cultures recognize in totemism and other beliefs about animals that there is a solidarity in the society of life, linking all living things together and centering them on the human model. It is in this sense, then, that all of these living species are recognized as various types of people, having ethical, tribal communities and genders like those of humans. Some of these species, however, provide particularly potent symbols for the interrelationships within the overall solidarity. Bears are but one example of such symbolic markers serving as halfway stations, or mediators, along the culture / nature continuum. The most widespread of these markers, based on mythology collections and my own Delaware, Salishan, and Tsimshian fieldwork, are dogs, mice, and bears. Dogs are nearer to culture, mediating between humans and other people as the only fully domesticated animal in North America. Mice are midway along the continuum, mediating between the inside and outside of the house and community, so that a mouse is often a polyglot in myths, translating for several groups involved in an activity. Bears are nearer to nature, mediating between the animal peoples.

It is extremely interesting that the Tsimshian have maintained prayers to an earlier deity called *gfɔl* ("unknown, empty, void") only in rituals following the killing of a bear. Otherwise, they have become thoroughgoing Christians and have rejected most of their older beliefs. Nature has sometimes been characterized as chaos, but this Tsimshian example suggests that there is only the void of space. The cosmos in such cases seems to be viewed as a bubble floating in the emptiness that is nature in its purest form. In this context then, the Tsimshian appear to have preserved the use of the bear in a mediating role as a safeguard against the void, with Christianity serving to maintain the internal structure of the known world.

As with women, it may be the case that natural propensities in bears encourage this association with the left and mediation toward the pole of nature. Biologists have confirmed that

---

[52] Rodney Needham Right and Left: Essays on Dual Symbolic Classification, Chicago: University of Chicago Press 1973.

[53] Sherry Ortner Is Female to Male As Nature Is to Culture?, Women, Culture, and Society, M Rosaldo and L Lamphere, eds, Stanford: Stanford University Press 1974: 67-87.

[54] E Cassirer An Essay on Man, New Haven: Yale University Press 1944.

polar bears really are left-paw dominant,[55] and Fraser River Salish insist that when bears leave hibernation they hug the right side of the cave wall, leaving their left arm free for defense.[56] Yet these observations would only remain biological facts helpful to hunters were they not significant in a wider context, namely the span between nature and culture. As the most humanlike of the Animal People, bears are appropriate representatives for one extreme of mediation. They provide food and coverings to people, but are even better symbols for bridging the genders. As Tanner[57] and Skinner[58] make clear, after it was killed a bear was butchered and prepared so that the upper torso went to men and the lower body to women, all of which reinforces the argument that bears are inclosive mediators.

Similarly, berdaches are regarded by many Amerind cultures as part of the acceptable variation in the society of life. As some individuals are able to switch gender and reverse tasks or identity, so others can seek a compromise position that places them between genders and enables them to tap supernatural reserves of power or energy by virtue of this mediating status. Except where whites have made the subject taboo or embarrassing, berdaches had high status because they functioned like other markers along the culture / nature sequence. Hunting tribes were also astute enough observers during butchering activities to notice that other Animal People had hermaphroditic members, and often equated these with the berdaches, providing a larger status, ambiguous or not, in the society of life.

We began by inquiring into the curious references to "people" of many different species, of berdaches, and of left-handed bears. By now we have hopefully arrived at a recognition of all of these as within the culturally acceptable range of biological variation, differing in terms of their inclosive (mediating), inclusive, and exclusive concentric attributes, but, ultimately, all members in the fellowship of life. In terms of this larger context of mediation, bears and berdaches occupy positions at the extremes of the cuture / nature continuum, as can be expressed in this series:

CULTURE   berdache   dog   mouse   bear NATURE

These mediators provide a three-dimensional framework for the flatter relationships between the inclusive and the exclusive, usually represented by the metaphors of men / right and of women/ left in the overall scheme of cultural life.

---

[55] John May and others Curious Facts, New York: Holt, Rinehart and Winston 1980.

[56] Brent Galloway, personal communication.

[57] Adrian Tanner A Bringing Home Animals, London: C. Hurst and Co 1979.

[58] Alanson Skinner Bear Customs of the Cree and Other Algonkin Indians of Northern Ontario, Ontario Historical Society Papers and Records 12: 203-9 1914.

Masks and Matrilineality Again

In her famous article, Elizabeth Tooker[59] explored "an association between the use of masks in religious ritual and the presence of matrilineal institutions" in Native North America.

She recalled that Fritz Graebner noted an association between secret societies with masks and matrilineal moieties as part of his East Papuan or Matrilineal Two-Class kulturkreis, but when Alfred Kroeber and Catherine Holt tested for such an association, they found no correlation between masks and moieties.

Looking again at the Kroeber and Holt sample, Tooker factored for matrilineal moieties and found that "although masks are frequently found in societies that lack matrilineal moieties, it is of some interest that no society that has matrilineal moieties lacks masks." According to her Table 2, "Masks and Matrilineal Moieties in a Sample of North American Cultures," the five representatives were Haida, Hidatsa, Iroquois, Mandan, Tlingit.

Moreover, looking at masks and general matrilineality, particularly among the Pueblos, she found support "that the more important matrilineal institutions are in the organization of a society, the more important masking will also be in the religious ritual of that society." Her Table 3, "Masks and Matrilineality in a Sample of North American Cultures," listed twelve representatives, the same five (Haida, Hidatsa, Iroquois, Mandan, Tlingit) along with seven others (Crow, Delaware, Hopi, Kutchin, Navaho, Tsimshian, Zuni).

While "no present anthropological theory adequately accounts for" this linkage, she suggested "it seems most likely that there is at least one intermediary variable that can be ascertained only through further study" as neither masking nor matrilineality is mutually causal.

As the source for this variable, she pointed to the role of male authority in matrilineal societies, where "Men do not propitiate the gods; they become the gods by the mere act of putting on the mask" and "men and spirits together work to keep the world in order."

To pursue this line of reasoning, we first need to correct for misinterpretations of some of the previous data. For example, while the Tsimshian have been described as having four clans, this is more a consequence of anthropologists working in resettled communities than of ethnographic reality.[60] In Tsimshian terms, their society consists of moieties, each in turn divided into two semi-moieties. Traditionally, each town functioned with an Owner and an Other moiety which intermarried and performed social obligations for each other, particularly at funerals. Tsimshian society was organized in terms of households, each composed of inhabitants from the classes of nobles, commoners, and slaves. Leaders lived in the well protected rear of the house, commoners along the sides, and slaves near the door, where they were most vulnerable during battles.

Each household had a double pose. During the summer, activities were economic, concerned with the harvesting of inherited resource locations under the direction of moiety leaders. During the winter, religious activities, concerned with the display of wonderous abilities and dramatic incidents, were under the management of the same leaders in their priestly aspect. Thus, summer was a time of moiety loyalties expressed in terms of potlatches hosted by the heraldic crests of the household, while the winter was a time of dramatic wonders displayed during winter ceremonials. Both crests and wonders were associated with hereditary names which were believed to be eternal, passed down through the reincarnating heirs of a household in each generation.

---

[59] Elizabeth Tooker Masking and Matrilineality in North America. American Anthropologist 70 (6): 1170-1177 1968.

[60] Jay Miller and Carol Eastman, eds. The Tsimshian and Their Neighbors of the North Pacific Coast, Seattle: University of Washington Press 1984.

The emblems of moiety-based names were crests, art works of which the most important was a hat worn during rituals. The emblems of the wonder-based names were masks. Pursuing the analogies further reveals that crests were traced through the mother, while wonders were traced to a male, often a supernatural father in the sacred histories of the household. Even within the matrilines, regard was also accorded to the father's side, a source of help, both financial and spiritual. According to John Adams,[61] "there are essential spiritual and physical components of every Gitksan which come from the father as well as from the mother. A child who is living in his father's village will not be harmed because he has some of the look and character of his father's people, some of his spiritual qualities, in the literal sense, which will return to his fathers people eventually." Among the Tsimshian, therefore, there is an equation of moieties and masks, but with the twist that the masks are specifically equated with men.

In contrast to the hundreds of masks used by the Tsimshian until conversion to Christianity, the historic Delaware had only three.[62] Although the Delaware also had three clans, there is no clear association of masks with clans. Two masks were similar, made of braided cornhusk and worn by a pair of men acting as messengers to announce the date of the Green Corn Ceremony in the late Summer. During the dance, these Huskfaces led the line of male dancers. In all, these two masks were ritual specific and associated with men. The single mask was carved of wood and worn by a man costumed in bearskin outfit to embody a being called Masing, the patron of game and crops who lived in mountains floating just above the earth but who was often in the forests. During the fall, a specific rite was dedicated to Masing which lasted one night. As patron of hunters and guardian of children, Masing had associations with the role of father, reinforcing the link between masks and men in matrilineal societies.

Aside from Tooker's surmise about the linkage of masks with men in a context of matrilineality, there have been few theories of masking. Among those most distinctive is that of Laura Makarius,[63] who argues that "masks represent instruments of protection" from the violation of taboos, the most basic of which for her is the shedding of blood. In contexts fraught with ambivalence, masks themselves become sources of danger and, hence, treated with reverence and fear.

While Makarius may help to explain masking connotations, she does not address the intent of mask use in specific societies, particularly matrilineal ones. Fathers, standing outside the vital social fabric, become sources of power, aliens charged with energies from the limits of the known and related. Their connections with the body of the community are superficial since substance came from women, passed on matrilineally. It is just this superficiality that

---

[61] John Adams The Gitksan Potlatch, Population Flux ~ Resource Ownership and Reciprocity, Toronto: Holt, Rinehart, and Wilson 1973.

[62] Jay Miller A Struckon Model of Delaware Culture and the Positioning of Mediators, American Ethnologist 6 (4): 791-802 1979.

[63] N Ross Crumrine, and Marjorie Halpin, eds. The Power of Symbols ~ Masks and Masquerade in the Americas, Vancouver: University of British Columbia Press 1983: 200.

encourages the use of masks, the face of Otherness representing a link based on appearance, on analogy, but not of identity.

The clearest statement in the literature is not from the Americas, but from Papua New Guinea. According to Nancy Munn[64] "Whereas the child's bond to the mother is an intrinsic one of material substance and continuity, the ideal relationship to the father is one of likeness to someone extrinsic to one's own bodily self ... Ideally, a child's face (*magi-*, a term that also denotes appearance) should resemble its father's." That such a statement does apply in the Americas is supported by comments from the Tlingit reported by Ronald Olson and by Sergei Kan[65] with "reference to a resemblance between his or her face and those of his or her classificatory fathers." Olson[66] noted that "A special relationship holds between a person and his [sic] father's clansmen ... This relationship may also be on a joking plane. Thus a person might say to his fathers brother (or anyone he called by that term) ... child of Kagwantan, his face. This is making fun of the face of the person addressed, teasing him. If her resented it he might reply ... from among you, I look the same."

Since Tooker published her article, more has been written about American masking[67] and its various tribal contexts.[68] These studies demonstrate that well-developed masking traditions were rarely simple. Raymond Fogelson[69] observed a distinction, common among Eastern tribes, between carved wooden masks and woven cornhusk or cut gourd masks. The former were associated with the forests and male activities such as hunting, while the latter were associated with clearings and female efforts such as farming. Even so, the husk or gourd masks were worn by men representing both men and women beings. Among Iroquois cultures, genders are reversed from those expected by Anglo-Americans. For Iroquois, female is the unmarked or general category, while male is the marked and specific. It is therefore entirely appropriate for Bushyhead husk masks to represent both men and women beings. Moreover, in keeping with their Otherness, the Bushyheads were believed to be "a people from the other side of the world where the seasons are reversed" who taught humans "the arts of hunting and agriculture".[70] Thus, even when the symbolic equation of the Bushyheads was with women, who were the Iroquois farmers, it was men who expressed the relationship.

Among matrilineal societies, women were substance and men were surface. For a child to admit kinship with a father, he had to rely on external characteristics. In the interest of saving face and claiming affection, masks were used to convey the complexities of such superficial images. In this instance, at least, masks had a profundity which was fully intended to be only skin deep.

---

[64] Nancy Munn The Fame of Gawa ~ A Symbolic Study of Value Transformation in a Massim (Papua New Guinea) Society. Cambridge University Press 1986.

[65] Sergei Kan Symbolic Immortality ~ The Tlingit Potlatch of the Nineteenth Century. Smithsonian Institution Press 1989.

[66] Ronald Olson Social Structure and Social Life of the Tlingit in Alaska. Anthropological Records 26: 1-126 1967.

[67] Crumrine and Halpin, The Power of Symbols 1983.

[68] William N Fenton The False Faces of the Iroquois. Norman: University of Oklahoma Press 1987.

[69] Raymond Fogelson and Amelia Bell Cherokee Booger Mask Tradition, The Power of Symbols, Crumrine and Halpin, 1983: 48-69. p.54.

[70] Fenton The False Faces of the Iroquois 1987: 54.

Indien Personhood

In pulling together these pithy citations from respected Americanist works, sometimes now called Indienology, this commentary attempts a comprehensive overview of notions relating to the person, in both cosmic and personal senses, of Native North America. It uses the European solution for distinguishing those indigenous to India from those of America by the expedient of a single vowel: A or E. Moreover, to clinch the argument, comparable Inuit data are included. This treatment is intended to be balanced, indicating features that both helped and harmed individuals and communities, using citations from scholars who convey statements in a Native voice upholding the interconnectedness of customs, taboos, demeanors, and their likely outcomes.

Though reported as asides or seemingly obscure details for only a single tribe or instance, all these observations can be understood to have continent-wide distribution, providing a coherent worldview that was accepted, rejected, modified, or ignored depending on local conditions of terrain, history, customs, contacts, and inter-group hostilities. Local factors of population densities, social systems, and tending (foraging) or tilling (farming) lifeways are largely ignored here in the interest of tracing more generic patterns. Spatial orientations in worlds and homes are as significant as cultural rules since they provided the basic "staging area" for the active deployment of people and materials for larger tasks and activities.

World

Every community seemingly had its own beliefs about their world. Not all were created in the same way or at the same time since fires, floods, and famines called for successive recreations before the emergence of the present world. For the North American continent, eight different creation epics have been located, though all agree that these universes are pervaded with a mindful flow of power-energy-force that is both diffused everywhere and channeled along rings and rays, like that of a web, with divinity at its center.[71] Over eons, articulations of space, time, and life took form through the applications of this deified power.[72] Earth often emerged from the primordial sea where it was held in suspension until realized by an "earth grasper" intent on global reform.[733]

Best described by the Southern Californian Luiseño, this *ayelkwi* ~ knowledge and power, provided the systematic means of relating all parts and events of existence through four means of access. Either it was commonly available to all, innate by birth within a particular family, residual as thrown around the landscape by their culture hero Wiyot, or formulated by prayers and rituals which enacted their history and laws conveyed in song. As elsewhere, it was engendered as diffuse for women, but particular and specific for men.[74] For the Navajo, the world was transformed from knowledge, organized in manly thought, patterned in language, and realized in womanly speech and other symbolic activities.[75]

After initial thought and speech came lasting memory, since language itself consists of

---

[71] Anna Birgitta Rooth The Creation Myths of the North American Indians 1957.

[72] Jay Miller High-Minded High Gods in North America 1980.

[73] Daniel Brinton The Myths of the New World 1969 [1876]: 209.

[74] Raymond White Luiseno Social Organization, 1963: 137, 139, 140, 145; James Moriarity, Chinigchinx 1969.

[75] Gary Witherspoon Language and Art in the Navajo Universe 1977: 34, 142.

images projected and shared with others who pile up their own details and pictures as conversation goes on.[76] [6]

The inevitable separation of land and water, earth and sky, moon and sun had long range consequences. For the Omaha, night and day became symbols of precision, while the bow came from the moon and the first arrow from a sun ray.[77]

"Primacy is universally revered,"[78] giving precedent to the first born, first kill, first picking, first fruits, first menstruation, and all founders because "all have special merit and powers of freshness" that come from the beginnings of a sequence. Land and sea remain inherently unsteady, except when anchored by mounds, giant snakes, or heavy landmarks.[799] Periodically, shamans, priests, and concerned members must renew, fix, and reinvigorate the universe, often using sexual metaphors and engendered ritual acts. General categories of center, inside, and outside were observed, but each community treated them in its own way. For example, Navajo sand paintings start at the center, but Pueblos ones at the edge.[80]

All species are mutable. In season, beavers transform into geese, "Sturgeon change into bears when the berries ripen, whence the large number of bears at that season," and moose become whales.[81] These changes derive from a belief that all beings are infra-human: they have human hands, faces, and bodies on the inside and an outer covering that can be put on and removed when going or coming home. Though shape-shifting, these immortals at base are shimmering, iridescent humans, sometimes described as rainbow-hued.

Among Inuit, an animal assuming its infra-human form raised its forelimb or wing to push its outer muzzle or beak up and back to reveal its inner humanity.[82] Ojibwa shamans wore bone and wood amulets carved into human faces to protect their souls.[83]

Everywhere powerful local shamans met in caves or other holy homes with the giant immortal boss of a species in order to negotiate the exchange of human and animal souls to sustain the human community. Most often the souls of enemies were given up first, followed by those closer to home, with children and women going before strong hunters.

Overall, this universe is finite. Nothing can exist in or from a void. Everything came from something else. The Achumawi cosmos was made by World Heart, acting through his grandson, Annikadel, "whose underparts are blue and white so no one could see him moving through the sky." At the location of each town, he stuck in feathers that became the first humans, often a separate feather for the chief, for the woman chief, and for the poor.[84]

---

[76] Keith Basso Wisdom Sits in Places 1996: 84.

[77] Francis La Flesche Omaha Bow and Arrow Makers 1926: 493.

[78] Irving Goldman The Mouth of Heaven 1975: 49.

[79] Jay Miller Instilling the Earth: Explaining Mounds.

[80] Ruth Underhill Red Man's Religion 1965 232.

[81] Diamond Jenness The Ojibwa Indians of Parry Island 1935: 80 #2; Frank Speck and John Witthoft Some Notable Life-histories in Zoological Folklore 1947: 345-349.

[82] Jarich Gerlof Oosten The Theoretical Structure of the Religion of the Netsilik and Iglulik 1976.

[83] Jenness Ojibwa Indians: 68.

[84] Istet Woiche *Annikadel: The History of the Universe* 1992: xxi, 87; cf. Malcolm Margolin, ed, *The Way We Lived* 1981.

Settlements

Wherever people build their homes from local materials, the shape and layout of a house is usually the same as that of the cosmos, round with domed housing or square with apartments.

Inside, however, spatial arrangements vary by culture. For example, inside a tipi, Lakota men sat on the right half, and women on the left with their legs modestly drawn up alongside their bodies.[85] Throughout the Great Lakes region, encampments were ethnically obvious since Shawnee suspended a kettle from X-crossed beams, Ottawa from a straight suck, Wyandot between two trees, and Ojibwa from two sticks.[86]

Cleanliness was a concern of both hygienic and religious proportions. When a Mistassini Cree family left its hunting camp, everything was left clean with large bones from its kills decorating a single tree whose trunk was shorn of all but the top branches. This way, when the local spirit-partner of the hunt-leader flew over to make its inspection, it would approve and continue to send good luck.[87] Similarly, other foods were physically encouraged to re-propagate. The Ojibwa, for example, threw back into water a few grains of wild rice wrapped in clay.[88]

Habitat also played a role, with rivers providing the cohesive lifeline for communities linked by its flow. Such "natural" unity has been sadly overlooked by scholars who fail to see that those living upriver have an automatic obligation to those downstream. Dense population and aridity seem to affect this pattern, however, since Henry Dobyns found that rivers were borders among the Florida Timucua, while the Arizona Pai visualize a midstream-dividing backbone along the Colorado River.[89]

Womb

Engendering began in the womb, if not before, with parents making different contributions or infusions to the materials that "cooked" to become a fetus. Actual gender was determined by which parent reached orgasm first or had the stronger will. Oregon Tillamook believed a body template was sent from a land where such beings lived awaiting birth. Patrilineal Kickapoo men reported that women were only a tray to hold the gestating new clansmember.[90] For Quechan (Yuma), successful conception required the conjoining of a father's dreams with a mother's desires. After this birth, a mother did not distinguish between the sex of her children, who all called her "mother," while a father did since his sons and daughters called him by separate terms.[91]

During pregnancy a Delaware father determined the coming gender by hanging a toy bow or wooden mortar off his leggings to keep its spirit nearby. If a bow did not work, then a mortar would.[92] Similarly, when depositing the cord stump in hopes of an abundant future for the

---

[85] Royal Hassrick *The Sioux* 1964: 287.

[86] Charles C Trowbridge Shawnee Traditions 1939: 46.

[87] Adrian Tanner *Bringing Home Animals* 1979: 75, 171.

[88] Jenness Ojibwa Indians: 14.

[89] Henry Dobyns *Their Numbers Become Thinned* 1988: 166, 192 #81.

[90] Felipe and Dolores Latorre *The Mexican Kickapoo* 1976: 157.

[91] C Daryll Forde Ethnography of the Yuma Indians 1931: 83-277, 148, 158.

[92] Jay Miller Delaware Personhood 1991.

infant, Yuchi put a tiny bow and arrow with a son's umbilical, or a mortar and spoons with that of a daughter. Yuchi believed that twins and deformed children were sent to earth as special moral guides.[93][23] Throughout the Northwest, twins were equated with salmon, whose dual aspect was to go away and come back. Lakota make two effigies of a lizard or turtle, both difficult to kill and long-lived; one holds the umbilical cord and the other serves as a decoy.[94]

In a well-described example, a proper Cheyenne was conceived from three sources.[95] Two were the mother and father, who contributed blood and substance, but most critical was the Creator ~ *Ma'heo'o*, who provided two blessings. The first was a life soul, enabling a fetus to grow and move when it became bound into its body, diffused throughout, and indicated by the heart beat, pulse, breath, growth, blinking eyelids, and food digestion. Any loss of body parts, particularly amputations, diminished the effectiveness of this life soul. The second blessing came just after birth when the baby first inhaled *omotome,* or breath, air, speech, articulation, understanding, and power. For these people, a person was conscious of self, the moral order, kinship obligations, careful speech, understanding, virtues of immortal spirits, and a profound sense of being existentially alone, regardless of external appearance or species. Each human had body, breath, memory, and heart, allowing differing degrees of individuality, provided that everyone supported communal tribal identity and purpose.

Regardless of personal genitals, every Cheyenne balanced the genders because the inside of each body is female and the outside is male, with ribs as the divide. Yet because man was the generic, only boys could use sleds made with rib runners.[96] Among Navajos, body substance was considered an outer form (symbolic of woman) and spirit was an inner form (of man).[97]

Birth

Quebec Inuit held that an annoyed or stressed fetus could crack open to change sex at the moment of birth, a process called a *sipiniit*.[98] Biology is not destiny since in everything-is-possible epics men did give birth. Tohono O'Odham (Papago) tell of Handsomeman, who made all women pregnant in one night, then gave birth himself the next day. His baby cried so uncontrolably that the world flooded.

After a child is born, Ojibwa say it was "empty" of any characteristics and identity, so spirits and parents had to fill him or her.[99] Delaware parents bound a newborn to the earth by tying on wristlets and placing the afterbirth someplace where it would beneficially affect the child's career. For example, the afterbirth might be buried in a forest to produce a hunter. The Delaware also dressed newborns in adult clothes and moccasins with holes in them to discourage ghosts from luring them away. As a safeguard against illness, a pet was given to the child to attract any harm to itself.[100] Sauk made a cradle-board from a living tree to transfer its vitality to

---

[93] Frank Speck Ethnology of the Yuchi Indians 1909: 110.

[94] Hassrick *The Sioux*: 270.

[95] Ann Terry Sawyier Strauss Northern Cheyenne Ethnopsychology 1975; Being Human in the Cheyenne Way 1976: 141.

[96] Strauss Being Human: 187.

[97] Witherspoon *Language and Art*: 142.

[98] Bernard Saladin D'Anglure From Foetus to Shaman 1994: 84.

[99] Ruth Landes *The Ojibwa Woman* 1971: 124.

[100] Miller Delaware Personhood: 19.

the child.[10131]

Nicknames and formal names further assured a child's growth. Every Kickapoo baby was given two names, one used during life and the other after death.[102] Among closely related Sauk, the first-born joined the moiety opposite that of the father, while the second-born shared the father's.[10333] If the father was light-color moiety, the oldest was dark, and the second was light. Sometimes, for her comfort and protection, a daughter joined the half of her elder brother.

Men occupied public offices, but Potawatomi women consciously filled in when men defaulted on their duties.[104] Women in the lower Great Lakes had their own strong leaders (see subsection entitled "Leaders" below).

Couvade

Unlike South America, where a new father commonly shared his wife's and baby's postpartum seclusion and taboos, this custom of couvade is rare to the north.

Engendering Childhood

The maturation of a child coincides with marked stages in his or her life. Various communities observed different milestones, such as the Cree "walking out" to cerebrate a baby's first steps, indicating special regard for feet among hunters.[105] After a Navajo infant's first laugh, salt and bread are given away;[10636] an Oto's first haircut followed clan patterns to indicate larger memberships;[10737] a Cheyenne mother's brother fed her child meadowlark meat and eggs to encourage fluency;[10838] a Kootenay couple could resume coitus when their most recent child began to whistle; and Delaware, among many others, offered lost baby teeth with prayers for stronger new ones.

At six, Menominee boys were subjected to icy baths, long runs, and endurance tests.[10939] Time was spent in mediation and labor, building trenches, stone walls, or rock cairns. Ojibwa boys out on a quest remained in "nests" built as platforms in trees to be closer to hovering spirits,[110] though very young Potawatomi fasters slept at home for their parents' peace of mind.[111] In Ojibwa idiom, to "pity" another is to adopt him and care for him like a parent or grandparent. Thus the pitying immortal is bound to the protégé by the firmest loyalties in Ojibwa worldview. Discipline and attitude were hallmarks of those high born, though "Abstinence is considered a negative attitude of insulting indifference; whereas chastity is a positive attitude of desire held in

---

[101] Alanson Skinner Observations on the Ethnology of the Sauk Indians 1925: 137.

[102] Robert Ritzenthaler and Frederick Peterson The Mexican Kickapoo Indians 1956: 58.

[103] Alanson Skinner Observations on the Ethnology of the Sauk Indians I 1923: 12.

[104] Ruth Landes *The Prairie Potawatomi* 1970: 37.

[105] Tanner *Bringing Home Animals*: 90.

[106] Witherspoon *Language and Art*: 185.

[107] William Whitman *The Oto* 1937: 69; cf. Alice C Fletcher and Francis La Flesche *The Omaha Tribe* 1992 [1911].

[108] Strauss Being Human: 207.

[109] Alanson Skinner The Menomini Indians 1915 8: 41.

[110] A Irving Hallowell The Ojibwa of Berens River 1992: 88.

[111] Landes *The Prairie Potawatomi*: 186.

leash."[112]

Being human for Cheyenne was a process of defining conscience on the basis of two antitheses − good or crazy, action or wisdom.[113] Good was anything orderly, controlled, careful, thoughtful, and proper, as taught by Sweet Medicine, the man who learned Cheyenne culture from the spirits inside Bear Butte in South Dakota, and instituted the Council of Forty-Four Chiefs and the worship of the Four Sacred Arrows. Crazy was anything disordered, impulsive, or brutishly animal-like. Humans have both potentials, but should learn self-control to embrace the good and avoid the crazy. Both good and crazy were, in turn, bisected by the axis of action and wisdom. For example, men could choose between two role models, that of the active warrior or that of the sage chief or priest. In the circle of life, associations of these four principals are good ~ spirituality ~ white ~ east, crazy ~ sexuality ~ yellow ~ west, action ~ youth ~ red ~ south, and wisdom ~ elderly ~ black ~ north.

Ideally the young should be active but willing to listen, while the old should be wise and ready to instruct, so that these roles can easily succeed from one to the other. Greater latitude is tolerated in men more than in women, so young men might be crazy and active, but women should always remain good and wise to remain stable, tempered, quiet, and soothing. Some biological males, known as woman-hearted, became transgendered and strictly subscribed to the good of the female role, spending all their time among women (see "Transgenders" below).

The core of every person was the heart, which is why the Cheyenne call themselves "those like-hearted." Over a lifetime, the heart of a person filled with life history, spiritual growth, physical identity, and names; each tribal member did not develop as a distinct individual but as a part of the larger whole.

Associates of any person influence character. If these are crazy − liars, drunks, or thieves − s/he will turn out the same. For this reason, the Keeper of the Sacred Arrows for the Southern Oklahoma Cheyenne or of the Sutaio Sacred Hat for the Northern Cheyenne in Montana must be a superior person so that all Cheyenne will benefit. In ancient times, the Arrow Keeper indicated his willingness to suffer for his people by having four strips of flesh taken from along his arms, shoulders, back, and legs, along with a circle and crescent cut from his chest.

Though underreported, young men often lived by themselves, either roaming around the village to keep it safe by their unpredictable actions or in separate quarters, as was the case with the Gwich'in (Kutchin) boys dorms, which housed those males between the ages of fourteen and twenty-five.[114]

More rare still were Iroquois virgin dorms, *ieouinnon,* where girls were kept busy at minor tasks, helped by very young boys as servants.[115] More commonly, some Ioway and other women took up an amazon-like warrior role after they received a vision from Thunderers.[116]

Girls

The onset of menstruation was marked and celebrated throughout the Americas, largely

---

[112] Landes *The Ojibwa Woman*: 6, 62.

[113] Ann Terry Sawyier Strauss The Meaning of Death in Northern Cheyenne Culture 1978.

[114] Richard Slobodin Kutchin 1981: 524 Fig 7.

[115] Joseph Francois Lafitau *Customs of the American Indians* 1974 [1724]: 129; David Blanchard, "... To the Other Side of the Sky" 1982: 77-102.

[116] Alanson Skinner Ethnology of the Ioway Indians 1926: 104, 106.

because of the arrival of a woman's ability to confer life set her apart from male activities concerned with killing, defending, and boasting.[117] For Kansas Potawatomi, menstrual blood endangered all medicine, youth, "tender" growths of any life form, and masculine life and appurtenances.[118] In one of the few accounts of its origin, lis said that the first menstruation was a punishment upon young girls who mocked an old man with bleeding eyes. "If the girls had not made fun of the old man, men would menstruate [through the eyes] instead of women and would have to sleep outside alone for a certain length of time."[119]

For Dakota, "femaleness, as menstrual and lochial [birthing] bloods, was inimical to men, weapons, and horses. Despite this dogma, a few individual women in each village did drive buffalo on horseback, and did stalk, scalp, and mutilate enemy; often they were young women, of child-bearing age."[120] Formalized Dakota feasts were held as elaborate tests for chastity and provided outlets for honor and malice as a consequence of accepted or failed accusations of undue familiarity.

Among Ioway, fathers with high aspirations had to have their daughters formally tattooed before puberty, "or blood will flow from the wound in the forehead and spoil the mark," while Ioway boys were tattooed all life long in recognition of brave deeds.[121] Among related Siouian Oto, girls of high family were sometimes laced up into a buffalo hide at night,[122] similar to Lakota's use of string chastity belts.[123]

Among Tlingit and other Northwest nations, girls entered puberty with a feast to celebrate the insertion of a labret beneath the lower lip, reminding her to watch her mouth in terms of what she said, ate, and did.[124]

Marriage

All adults should wed. In considering partners, the Kickapoo looked for a wife who was good-humored, honest, clean, fine-cooking, and hardworking, and a husband to be a sober hunter with integrity.[125] New Yurok spouses exchanged the names of their hometowns to strengthen their co-identification.[126] Anyone unwed among Tohono O'Odham was presumed to have a snake for a spouse whose potency left them uninterested in humans.[127]

Among tribes from the Great Lakes, a *Manabus* robe, named for their Great Hare culture hero, was made of deerskin and adorned with tiny metal cones and a strategic hole. The robe was loaned or hired out from its owner to newlyweds to assure strong and healthy births.[128]

Ojibwa and Plains nations might hold a divorce dance to display the fortitude and bravery

---

[117] Thomas Buckley and Alma Gottlieb *Blood Magic* 1988; Mourning Dove 1990.

[118] Landes *The Prairie Potawatomi*: 167.

[119] Thelma Adamson *Folk-Tales of the Coast Salish* 1934: 95.

[120] Ruth Landes *Mystic Lake Sioux* 1968: 40, 48.

[121] Skinner Ioway Indians: 265, 269.

[122] Whitman *The Oto*: 72.

[123] Hassrick The Sioux: 124.

[124] Aldona Jonaitis Women, Marriage, Mouths, Feasting ~ Tlingit Labrets 1988.

[125] Ritzenthaler and Peterson The Mexican Kickapoo: 62.

[126] Lucy Thompson *To the American Indian* 1991 [1916]: 190.

[127] Ruth Underhill The Autobiography of a Papago Woman 1936: 27.

[128] Skinner The Menomini Indians: 30; Observations on the Ethnology of the Sauk: 32.

of "discarding something that is dear."[129] Plains husbands ritually transferred spiritual power through access to younger wives,[130] though shameless wives could and did arrange fatal "accidents" for demanding husbands.[131]

Careers

Men and women had distinct, separate but equal,[132] lives that mutually supported the good of die community and nation. For Delaware, man was container and woman contained. For Mescalero Apache, man is shield and protector; woman is center and protected.[133] For Cheyenne, man is spiritual, woman is material.[134] Since the fishing Sto:lo Salish regard their community as a salmon, men are its nose and women its backbone.[135]

Some activities were biologically determined, as when Coyote decreed for the Karuk that only women would pound acorns because a man's baby maker would get in the way; instead, a man hunted and fished for meat to eat with acorn soup.[136] Pottery was a job for women working in seclusion since it involved a war between Thunderbirds and Watersnakes, as noted by the cracks that could appear to ruin a vessel. Like all else, this skill among Hidatsa derived from the proper ownership of sacred medicine bundles, with potters specifically owning this right through Big Bird, River, or Snake bundles belonging to matrilineal kin.[137]

Parry Island Ojibwa urge hunters not to concentrate entirely on their prey,[138] while Tsimshian[139] insist on total dedication to the game being sought. When planting, Jicarilla "men made holes with digging sticks. The women and children followed, dropping in the seeds and covering them up. It was believed that the crops would grow faster if the children, who were still growing, put the seeds in the ground." Children also kept birds and rodent pests off these fields, each bounded by a turkey feather set in its four corners.[140] Pawnee planted an even number of maize hills in their gardens since corn was a woman and breasts are paired.[141] Delaware kept the sanctity of their corn fields by preventing any misuse by humans or pollution by animals.

A proper Delaware adult displayed responsibility, respect, courtesy, self-discipline, generosity, and social graces. Their lives were a blend of "personal autonomy, respect for others, clan membership, selfless motivations, pleasant attitude, proper upbringing, and diligent training

---

[129] Landes *The Ojibwa Woman*: 89.

[130] Alice Kehoe The Function of Ceremonial Sexual Intercourse among the Northern Plains Indians 1970.

[131] George Bird Grinnell *Blackfoot Lodge Tales* 1962 [1892]: 78.

[132] John Reed Swanton *Social Organization and Social Usages of the Indians of the Creek Confederacy* 1928a: 385.

[133] Claire Farrer *Living Life's Circle* 1991: 149.

[134] Strauss Being Human: 396.

[135] Crisca Bierwert Tracery in the Mistlines 1986: 340. Terms in nearby Salishan languages indicate that women are backbone, men are head, and chiefs are nose.

[136] John P Harrington Tobacco among the Karuk Indians of California 1932: 99.

[137] Alfred W Bowers Hidatsa Social and Ceremonial Organization 1965: 373-374.

[138] Jenness *Ojibwa Indians*: 22.

[139] Jay Miller *Tsimshian Culture* 1997.

[140] Veronica E Velarde Tiller *The Jicarilla Apache Tribe* 1992: 27.

[141] Gene Weltfish *The Lost Universe* 1971: 124.

towards a productive adulthood as a man or woman" to produce children who were "empty" until becoming fulfilled by a "gifted" partnership with an immortal, or *manitu*. Delaware men worked constantly while women labored in spurts, exchanging the products of their separate labors. In old age, elders gained respect and attention for their wise advice, while extremely old women, after a life of dedication, finally had total freedom of expression.[142]

Men would fast, pray, and abstain from sexual relations before a hunt. Plateau women engage in ritual chastity before root digging.[143] These females were strictly forbidden to come within a half-mile of a salmon weir, yet one woman with Salmon power frequently swam around an Okanogan River trap without causing harm.[144]

Women generally had an especially constrained life, since they were under greater public scrutiny and pressure to conform to the roles of wife and mother. Exceptional visions allowed women to break from this mold, but only at the cost of great hardship. Flagrantly promiscuous, lewd, foreign, or adulterous women, particularly if without male protectors, were subject to gang rape,[14575] euphemistically called "running through the meadow."[146] During heated arguments, women occasionally damaged or killed men by yanking out their organ.[147]

As a whole, the Plains culture area recognized at least six gender roles. Aside from "natural, normal" men and women, there were the *berdache,* contrary, or a super warrior who did everything backwards, amazon, and virgin. Among these famous women warriors were Apache Lozen (sister of Victorio), Kootenay Water Sitting Grizzly, Blackfeet Running Eagle, Ojibwa Chief Earth Woman, and Cheyennes Buffalo Calf Road Woman and Yellow-Haired Woman.[148]

Lakota male virtues are bravery, fortitude, generosity, and wisdom; those of a female are bravery, generosity, truthfulness, and fecundity,[149] with patience and wisdom also mentioned.[150] Affinities with nature made elk the "Dakota symbol of masculine beauty, virility, virtue, and charm."[151] Overall for Lakota, "Man is a subset of woman, not only in the empiricality of childbirth but in linguistic terminology which identifies the stages of life."[152]

An Oto man was courageous, gentle, truthful, and generous; an Oto woman was ideally faithful, hardworking, and motherly.[153]

According to the Tohono O'Odham moral code, an adult should be industrious, enduring, skilled, and prepared for battle. In addition, a woman should seclude herself during menstruation, since this blood caused deer to avoid hunters, shaman's crystals to rot, and tobacco

---

[142] Jay Miller The Delaware As Women 1974; Delaware Personhood 1991: 18, 23.

[143] Laura Klein and Lillian Ackerman *Women and Power in Native North Americ*a 1995: 95.

[144] Leslie Spier The Sinkaietk or Southern Okanogan 1938: 160.

[145] James Adair *History of the American Indians* 1930 [1775]: 149 # 55.

[146] John Reed Swanton Source Material for the Social and Ceremonial Life of the Choctaw Indians Office 1931: 111.

[147] Morris Opler *Apache Odyssey* 1969: 239; Colin Galloway, *Crown and Calumet* 1987: 171.

[148] Kimberly Buchanan *Apache Women Warriors* 1986; Carolyn Foreman, *Indian Women Chiefs* 1954.

[149] Hassrick *The Sioux*: 32, 39.

[150] Marla Powers *Oglala Women* 1986; William Powers, *Oglala Religion* 1977: 62.

[151] Powers *Oglala Religion*: 77.

[152] Powers *Oglala Religion*: 198.

[153] Whitman *The Oto*: 63.

plants to shrivel,[154][84] Successful visionaries were called *meeters,* such as Hawk meeter. Coyote meeter, and so forth. Full time professional deer hunters remained in the mountains all year, except for two months, with male kin tending fields for him in return for venison.[155] "To many ... a good field, enough cattle to provide occasional meat and money, a few horses for prestige, and plenty of rain would make an ideal combination."[156]

Ultimately, however, final judgements about a person's life were and are made on the issues of their overall character, contributions, and determination to aid the greater good, along with occasional reports of their fate in the afterworld.

Transgenders

Because Natives lived within a totally engendered universe, special intermediaries functioned to keep it from halving or fragmenting. Often these were shamans, mediating among lonely mortals, sympathetic immortals, inter-species needs, and personal motivations. Certain animals, such as bears or frogs, also played this role across life-forms.[157]

Yet recent attention has focused only on transgendered humans,[158] often called *berdaches* as this term has been redefined and laundered by usage. At base, many may have had biologically androgynous bodies that encouraged them to take a special course in life. Others may have had psychological or societal pressures to assume this role, which was not always as honored and esteemed as some recent authors have projected, though drunk whites were almost killed once by Creeks for undressing a woman suspected to be a hermaphrodite.[159]

Hidatsa *berdaches* had strong religious sanction and hereditary ties to certain mystic bundles. S/He took up this career after a vision of Holy Woman Above, dressed as women but worked much harder, and was the brother or son of a man holding tribal rites in the bundles of Woman Above or Holy Woman. Though hemmed in by especially intricate taboos, they were very nurturing, often rearing orphans, taking center stage in ceremonies, and elaborating craftworks in skins and beads.[160]

But Lakota *berdache,* whose "heart of a woman" was often held in high derision, lived at the edge of a camp with widows, orphans, and social misfits.[161] Yet they also were regarded as *wakan,* or sacred, and gave special names to children. In addition, it seems that warriors visited these Lakota for sexual release before battles and expeditions. In the Southwest, Quechan

---

[154] Ruth Underhill *Social Organization of the Papago Indians* 1939: 80, 163.

[155] Ruth Underhill *Papago Indian Religion* 1946: 17, 86.

[156] Alice Josephy Rosamond Spicer, and Jane Chesky, *The Desert People* 1949: 59.

[157] Jay Miller People, Berdache, and Left-Handed Bears 1982.

[158] Claude Schaeffer The Kutenai Female Berdache 1965; Charles Callender and Lee Kochems The North American Berdache 1983; Charles Callender and Lee Kochems Men and Not-Men: Male Gender-Mixing Statuses and Homosexuality 1986; Sandra Hollimon The Third Gender in Native California: Two-Spirit Undertakers Among the Chumash and their Neighbors 1998; Sue-Ellen Jacobs, Wesley Thomas, and Sabine Lang, eds *Two-Spirit People* 1997; and Will Roscoe *Changing Ones* 1998.

[159] Swanton *Creek Confederacy*: 355.

[160] Bowers *Hidatsa Social and Ceremonial Organization*: 167.

[161] Hassrick *The Sioux*: 121.

parents of transvestites were said to be ashamed.[162]

Ruth Landes provided sensitive characterizations that above all indicate that a *berdache* was regarded as extraordinary, among both Potawatomi and Mystic Lake Sioux.[163] Such a Dakota *berdache* was gently exiled from "his" natal village, as his interests became evident, "by adopting female forms of speech, female fears of water and of bodily exposure ... as always the lurer, the coquette, acting like cousin or sister-in-law of all the village men," commending "himself to women by his industry and helpfulness, and to men by his complete hospitality.... He was accepted by the strange group in a spirit of gingerly tolerance comparable to that covering a truce with enemy visitors; he was treated to the teasing, bitter, flirting conduct of cross-cousins and siblings-in-law."[164]

Leaders

As a general rule, officials on earth took their powers, positions, and authority from identical immortals in the heavens.[165] Differences between leader and led were often imperceptible, yet very real, to the community. In an obvious example, every Ioway chief had two bodyguards who lived with him.[166]

More typically, only the Chemehuevi "high chief could wear turquoise.[167] In northwest California, only Karuk rich families had and have a wide, bare, and cleanly kept plot in front of the house where the wife and children live, apart from the abode of husband and sons in the sweathouse.[16898] Nearby, ancient houses of the Yurok rich were guarded by rattlesnakes while members achieved luck and wealth through self-denial, prayer, fasting.[169]

Among Western Apache, a woman chief was noted for her "industry, even temper, avoidance of gossip and trouble making or other quarrels, wise head, and strong body." The children of such leaders stood out as self confident, wise, unafraid, and unembarrassed. In contrast, other women were associated with a butterfly decoration because "women's minds are as flighty as butterflies and must be attracted by something beautiful, just as a butterfly is." At a Victory Dance, men were lewd, while a few loose women exposed themselves for pay.[170]

In addition to the common joint authority of civil and military leaders for clans, towns, and nations, Ohio Valley tribes, including Shawnee and Miami, recognized similarly paired woman, whose duties of ritual, warfare, and community organization included the disposition of prisoners and the right to force an end to warfare and to community feuds.[171] As mothers,

---

[162] Daryll Forde Ethnography of the Yuma Indians 1931: 157.

[163] Landes *The Prairie Potawatomi*: 182, 195; Mystic Lake Sioux: 31.

[164] Landes *Mystic Lake Sioux*: 112.

[165] Florence Hawley Ellis Foreword, Architecture and Dendrochronology of Chetro Ketl 1983: xxiii-xxxviii.

[166] Skinner Ioway Indians: 205.

[167] Carobeth Laird *Encounter with an Angry God* 1976; *Chemehuevis* 1976; *Mirror and Pattern* 1984.

[168] Harrington Tobacco among the Karuk: 263 #2.

[169] Thompson *To the American Indian*: xxiv, 180,100.

[170] Grenville Goodwin The Social Organization of the Western Apache 1969 [1942]: 167, 183, 306, 566.

[171] Erminie Wheeler-Voegelin Mortuary Customs of the Shawnee 1944: 403.

sisters, and daughters of leading families, they cared for women's matters of planting, cooking, and feasting, when the peace woman cooked white corn and vegetables as the war woman did meats and coarser articles.[172]

Healing

Health and well-being were topics of private and public concern. As a general rule, specific diseases were caused by an animal species in revenge for human malfeasance, and cured using a particular plant intended to remedy it.[173] Allowance was always made for individual expression, provided it was sanctioned by a proper vision and continued success. At its most elaborate, Lushootseed shamans cooperated to retrieve lost or stolen souls.[174]

Though bundles must always be handled with care and respect, one Sauk warrior always smashed his bundle down onto the ground before a battle to make it so enraged that it would take the life of the bravest enemy warrior.[175] Menominee who dreamed of Thunderers began to worship together, but soon their drum was struck by lightning so they quickly disbanded.[176]

Among Mvskogi (Creeks), informal "brush schools" taught special cures so that a few youngsters would hire a fasting doctor to spend four days with them, teaching at noon and early sunset.[177] They could return for advanced training over eight- then twelve-day sessions. Such a novice might be buried in a trench with only a cane mouth tube for breathing as a brushfire of leaves swept over his "grave," teaching the curer to cure by being cured.

More public expressions, in the Great Lakes region, ranged from the shaking tent occupied by a shaman with a host of spirits, to the Midewiwin, also known as Grand Lodge or Shaman's Academy, which was revitalized around 1700 by Ojibwa survivors of epidemics and dislocations. Both rites reversed "normal" time and space to make healing that much more sacred. Shaking tent polarities put the spiritual inside and the physical outside.[178] Inside, these spirits look like sparks or tiny people sitting upon its tier of hoops with Turtle on the bottom rung.[179]

Midé reversals are traced to its bear patron, who is left-handed.[180] Divided into earth and sky halves, each half included about four degrees represented by the pelt of an appropriate animal for earth or bird for sky. Wooden pegs with rounded tops were moved over a sand drawing of the lodge to show new members what to do.[181]

---

[172] Trowbridge Shawnee Traditions: 12.

[173] Raymond Fogelson Change, Persistence, and Accommodation in Cherokee Medico-Religious Beliefs 1961: 216; James Howard, with Willie Lena *Oklahoma Seminoles Medicines, Magic, and Religion* 1984.

[174] Jay Miller, *Shamanic Odyssey* 1988; *Lushootseed Culture and the Shamanic Odyssey* 1999.

[175] Alanson Skinner Ethnology of the Sauk Indians: War Customs 1925: 84.

[176] Skinner The Menomini Indians: 47.

[177] John Reed Swanton Religious Beliefs and Medical Practices of the Creek Indians 1928 # 42: 473-672, 617, 618 1928.

[178] Tanner *Bringing Home Animals*: 218 #8.

[179] A Irving Hallowell The Role of Conjuring in Saulteaux Society 1942: 51.

[180] Alanson Skinner Medicine Ceremony of the Menomini, Iowa, and Wahpeton Dakota, With Notes on the Ceremony among the Ponca, Bungi Ojibwa, and Potawatomi 1920: 157.

[181] Vernon Kinietz *Chippewa Village* 1947: 193; Indians of the Western Great 1940.

An initiate was sponsored by wealthy family members and "shot" by a cowry shell called a *megis* to "die" and be revived by senior adepts. Ioway shot an initiate four times in the right shoulder, left shoulder, right leg, and left leg.[182] Each Omaha member had two *megis,* believed to be a man and woman pair, to breed progeny of tiny shells that grew larger over time to increase their abilities and wealth.[183]

All Native doctors were expected to be wealthy, haughty, and demanding, both for themselves and their spirit partners. Indeed, "Because Jesus healed the sick without payment, he lost his power and perished."[184]

Masking

Throughout the Americas, people could enhance or expand their personae by adopting a mask. Matrilineal societies have a greater propensity to use masks, largely because the face is believed to come from the father.[185] The most complex expressions of masking are the Kachinas of the Pueblo Southwest, where Edmund Ladd, a Zuni and an anthropologist, reported that when Kokko, or Zuni Kachinas, first danced for humans, women became completely allured and followed them back to the lake of the underworld. Since they were not dead, women could not enter the underworld, languishing there until humans were given the right to bring these masks to life as its actual spirit stood in front of the wearer, its movements distinct but visible in the masker. Every detail of dress and dance had significance, intent, and meaning such that, for example, painting was regarded as a "chromatic prayer."[186]

Sorcery

Greed, selfishness, envy, and revenge were causes for sorcery.[187] Most people were wise and cautious enough to take precautions, especially with body waste. All cut hair was burnt, for example, because there "is no way of countering sorcery that used human hairs."[188] In all, about one-tenth of the universe had hostile intent and needed to be restrained or avoided.

Death

Death was not the inevitable end of every short life. Shawnees were promised to live for "200 years," so deaths before that were someone's fault. Those dead who had been especially bad during life were reduced to ashes.[189][119] Just before and after death, stock was taken of a person's life. Often the heir to an office or position only received the final linchpin of vital knowledge as a last gasp to safeguard it for the holder as long as possible.[190] Effective

---

182 Skinner Medicine Ceremony: 165.

183 Reo Fortune *Omaha Secret Societies* 1932: 109.

184 Jenness Ojibwa Indians: 76.

185 Miller *Tsimshian Culture*: 102.

186 Polly Schaafsma *Kachinas in the Pueblo World* 1994: 18, 30, 171.

187 Deward Walker *Systems of North American Witchcraft and Sorcery* 1970.

188 Landes *The Prairie Potawatomi*: 167.

189 Trowbridge Shawnee Traditions: 3, 41.

190 Fortune *Omaha Secret Societies*: 40, where he likens this fatal transmission to a sort of

transitions, therefore, required stable societies, adding another dimension to the destruction of Native lifeways that came from the epidemics rampant in the Americas before Europeans actually settled.

A Menominee soul on the way to the underworld was judged by a dog at a log bridge, either continuing on or plunging into the abyss if it had mistreated pets. The underworld chief had the arriving soul washed in a large wooden bowl, cured of all ailments, and purged of past memories so as to be endowed with heavenly lore to make them less intelligent but more supernatural than humans.[191]

Quileute components include an inner and an outer shade, along with a soul. A week before death, the outer shade went directly to the afterworld, joined a few days later by the inner shade after it had visited favorite places. The recombining of the shades forced the soul to become a ghost, causing death. Each ghost had an elongated human shape, moss covering, long nose, round yellow eyes, crooked gait, and shrill whistle. A spouse could not lie down to sleep for five days, so he or she slept huddled in a large basket. The whole family had to move very slowly and deliberately while mourning, carrying small black stones in their mouths and armpits to limit their speech and movements.[192]

Funeral

A Sauk grave was dug by women using "wooden bowls as spades," with the placement sometimes determined by clan. For example, people of the Turkey Clan were buried sitting up, "in some isolated knoll under a tree suitable for a turkey roost."[193] Females often dug graves because, "a woman has always taken care of a man, all his life."[194]

Navajo gravediggers prepared by removing all clothes, shutting their mouths, closing off the foreskin with a yucca thread tied in a special knot, heating fire and hot water for a bath afterward, using only gestures, and, later, brushing away all tracks to and from the grave.[195]

Delawares had a friend speak to the deceased at the graveside to release its soul. Mourners are expected to linger around the grave, as it was considered disrespectful to rush away. For this reason, many of the grieving lamenters feasted there. Later, at home, all washed in cedar smoke to cleanse any harmful effect. For the next four nights a fire burned at the head of the grave to light the way for the soul along the Milky Way where a dog blocked the way of animal abusers. Unami Delawares hold a feast after these four days, while Munsi waited twelve days. Many families held and still hold annual memorials, where steam coming off fresh cooked food provides its essence to their deceased love ones before the living consumed the rest.[196]

Most families took care to keep very powerful objects out of coffins or graves since these might be used, without deliberate malice, to harm the living. Throughout the Great Lakes region, Midewiwin members were buried with substitute emblems, particularly their cowry shell, ~ *megis*. Thus, instead of an actual gastropod, a stone or button was placed with the body out of

---

   parricide.

[191] Skinner *The Menomini Indians*: 86.

[192] Leo Frachtenberg *Eschatology of the Quileute Indians* 1920.

[193] Skinner *Observations on the Ethnology of the Sauk Indians*: 37.

[194] Wheeler-Voegelin *Mortuary Customs of the Shawnee and Other Eastern Tribes*: 383.

[195] Charlotte Frisbie and David McAllester, eds *Navajo Blessingway Singe* 1978: 197.

[196] Miller *Delaware Personhood*.

concern that a *megis* could restore ~ revive the corpse, sometimes with harmful intent.[197]

Remains were variously treated – some buried intact, while others dismembered tribespeople to dispose of the parts separately, with all or some of the parts cremated, as when the heart of an Achumawi chief or shaman was released into the sky to become a star.[198]

Among the Subarctic Athapaskan, the Carrier, or porteur of French Canadians, were so named because a wife carried the cremated bones of her husband back to the summer salmon-fishing town if he died during the winter. This enabled his death to be noted and his title and consequent ownership rights to be passed on to his heir at a witnessed public feast.[199]

Deading

The fate of the soul was largely the result of the life of the body and its treatment before final disposition. Often the body disassembled into its various components. Consciousness or life-essence was represented variously by breath, clear body fluids – like spit, tears, and sweat, blood, and flesh, in addition to bones, hair, or several intangible souls, shades, shadows, ghosts, or spirits. Cherokee recognized that each of these substances decomposes at different times and they accordingly treated each span as a further release of the life essence.[200]

The loss of breath often began the countdown, followed by clear effluvia. Pawnee regarded a pipestem as "symbolic of the human windpipe and the breath was considered the essence of life itself."[201] The power of a Tohono O'Odham (Papago) shaman resided in quartz crystals primordially formed from the solidified spit of one of their creators.[202] Throughout the Americas, quartz crystals were the most usual insignia of a shaman, suggesting that, regardless of locale or language affiliations, this association of shamans, crystals, and clear fluids was an ancient one. A Kootenay hunter spit on his arrow to make it fly true, implying that his goodwill and respect for the game animal was given in return for its life.[203]

After death, among Jicarilla, if the dead had participated in sexual relations with outsiders their ghosts transmogrified into the animal form of that group, such as a Navajo Cougar, Ute Owl, Pueblo Prairie Dog, Mescalero Wolf, Mexican Burro, or American Mule.[204]

In the Northwest, a Makah ghost repeatedly returned to its corpse so as to remove all its flesh in order to reconstitute that body in the afterlife.[205]

After fleeing British depredations in the Carolinas for haven among Iroquois now in Canada, Tutelos, though long sociopolitically extinct, still hold a spiritual adoption within a year of death "to bring back the soul" for one night before it travels over the sun's rays on the next dawn to its "permanent celestial abode."[206]

Mexican Kickapoo held a memorial adoption ceremony within four years of a death or

---

[197] Kinietz *Chippewa Village*: 144, 208.

[198] Merriam *Annikadel*: 49.

[199] Antonia Mills , *Eagle Down is Our Law* 1994: 40.

[200] Fogelson Change, Persistence, and Accommodation.

[201] Weltfish *Lost Universe*: 475.

[202] Underhill Papago Indian Religion: 271.

[203] Claude Schaeffer Bear Ceremonialism of the Kutenai Indians 1966: 13, 48 #6.

[204] Morris Opier Myth and Practice in Jicarilla Apache Eschatology 1947: 137.

[205] James Swan The Indians of Cape Flattery 1870: 84.

[206] Frank Speck The Tutelo Spirit Adoption Ceremony 1942: 10.

"the spirit turns into a moth and dies of hunger," blaming close relatives.[207] If a Shawnee was buried without rites, he or she was reborn a dwarf.[208]

Conclusions

These ethnographic bits, how-some-ever derived from memory, have the virtues of clear fact stated in proper context in Native voice. Strung together, they speak of integrity and coherence across the continent for notions of personhood as mixings, infusions, and layerings to combine spark, bone, flesh, soul, shadow, immortal partner, and ghost into a living whole that reverses the same series at death. They also speak of flux and flow in ways that many Americans would take for ambiguity and confusion, but this is the incomprehension of outsiders.

Throughout Native North America, an engendered person was and is the predominant outcome of genetics; anatomy; moods and attitudes; outside pressures from parents, peers, self, and role models; community or family needs; training; inheritances; namings; and outcome of vision quest, all accordingly expressed by appearance, gesture, ornament, clothing, and lifestyle.

Gender, for example, is open and fluid, shifting at the moment of birth, over a lifetime, or across generations if *there* is reincarnation.[209] One bewilderingly complex framework for modern sociological gender separates sex as biological, sexuality as erotic practice, sexual identity as type designations, gender identity as personal feelings of patterned subjectivity, gender role as prescriptive and culture-specific expectations of appropriateness, and gender-role identity as personal lived commitment to expected ideals.[210]

Yet "Chromosomes, hormones, sperm production, and egg production, all fail to differentiate all men from all women or to provide a common core within each sex." Instead, genitals and then body type provide primary and secondary attributes for assigning gender, though tertiary ones are usually more significant as culturally defined by posture, movement, dress, adornment, image, sexuality, intonation, speech, and job skills.

Additional influences are gender symbolism of perceived dichotomies, gender structure dividing necessary social activities, and individual gender of socially construed personal identity, which is always "mediated by race, class, ethnicity, and sexual orientation" in lieu of "the numerous privileges of white, heterosexual, middle-class feminists who have the luxury of experiencing only one mode of oppression."

Even more extreme is one attempt to derive transgendered males, subcate-gorized as military, diplomatic, domestic, and religious *berdaches* with specialized functions, from rape and brutalization because "warfare was the incubator of civil institutions,"[211] in blatant disregard of the compelling Native motivations from personal psychology and sacred vision.

For Indiens, everything is connected in a web of energy and thought, uniting each and all together, via sharing across species and beings to hopefully benefit all. Indeed, denying charity can have unpleasant or fatal consequences.[212] The living tree used for a cradle-board has as much to do with raising a healthy child as parents and kin, food, clothing, and shelter.

Danger and harm came from "the devil's tenth," that part of participatory existence that

---

[207] Latorres *The Mexican Kickapoos*: 283.

[208] Wheeler-Voegelin Mortuary Customs: 406.

[209] Mills and Slobodin *Amerindian Rebirth*.

[210] Mary Hawkesworth Confounding Gender 1997 Signs 22 (3): 651, 653, 656, 661, 669.

[211] Richard Trexler *Sex and Conquest* 1995: 64, 82, 102, 141.

[212] Basso *Wisdom Sits in Places*: 24.

was selfish, hurtful, and damaging. While theft, torture, and murder were practiced on enemies, they were sternly repressed at home. Thus, most intra-hostility had to be covert, producing criminals involved in sadism, sorcery, ill will, and abuse. Harm thereby worked by insinuation, though sometimes it became outright and deliberate. In vivid image, it was parasitic like a stylops, a blob that enters through a bee's skin, propagates through a vague brood canal, and, by absorption, transforms its host as colors brighten, behavior changes, and gender switches.[213]

In this heightening, a parasite is a perversion of the keen regard that should be given to the boundaries and passages making life possible, particularly the inter-species requirement to make up for whatever another "lacks." Thus Yup'ik turn driftwood to alleviate its boredom, give fresh water to slain seals, and provide sea oil to land mammals.[214] Thus, a good person constantly fills gaps to keep his, her, and their community whole.

American Indian Culture And Research Journal 24 (1): 121-141 2000

---

[213] Annie Dillard *Pilgrim at Tinker Creek* 1974: 237, 239.
[214] Ann Fienup-Riordan *The Real People and the Children of Thunder* 1991; *Boundaries and Passages* 1994.

Person II

Indien Personhood II:

Baby in the Oven Sparks Being in the World

The process, particularly as a series of sequential timings, of creating an Indien person, according to accepted ("traditional") beliefs, highlights the importance of fire, cooking, infusions, and, ultimately, dissolution.[215] The same pan-human use of fire, distinguishing them from animals, also accounts for the gestation of a baby, suggesting that ontology here recapitulates cosmology.[216] Indeed, the universal equation among the heart of a person, hearth of a house, beacon of a town, and sun of the sky underscores the importance of heat and light for all healthy, communal life.[217] In stark contrast, the "dark" includes disease, harm, danger, and death.

Though underreported, links between sparks, spirits, and life have been confirmed for the Ojibwa Shaking Tent, Delaware curings, Lakota Yuwipi, and, more universally, the flames, or tongues of fire, of Pentecost.[218] Moreover, esoteric beliefs among Pawnee, Delaware, and Lushootseed equate the kindling of fire by friction with coitus.[219]

Each person is an especial instance of "mind" − that primordial vitality, force, movement, energy, and power deified by a high god or creator localized at the center of each tribal universe. According to southern California Luiseño, "All things that manifest or are suspected to possess *ayelkwi* ~ knowledge-power are considered 'persons.'"[220]

In the abstract, each person possesses four aspects that may be characterized as anatomy, attitudes, abilities, and associations.

Anatomy

In Plains Cheyenne belief, a proper person was conceived of blood from the mother, substance (flesh) from the father, and two blessings from the Creator − a life soul indicated by the heartbeat, pulse, blinking eyelids, food digestion, growth, and the like; a consciousness inhaled at birth indicated by breathing, speech, understanding, and access to cosmic power.[221]

---

[215] As in this article's antecedent Indien Personhood 2000, I use the European solution for distinguishing those indigenous to India from those of the United States by the expedient of a single vowel (A or E): Indian for the East Indies and Indien for the West Indies.

[216] Sometimes only mortal humans possess fire, as among Crow *Absoroka* who say their dead go to the Other Side Camp, inhabited by spirits, ghosts, and ancestors who are collectively called Without Fires according to the warrior Peter Nabokov, ed, *Two Leggings* 1967: 156.

[217] Jay Miller The Matter of the (Thoughtful) Heart 1980; High-Minded High Gods in North America 1980.

[218] A Irving Hallowell *The Role of Conjuring in Salteaux Society* 1942: 51; Jay Miller, Delaware Personhood 1991; Yuwipi information from Miller's field notes.

[219] James Murie Ceremonies of the Pawnee 1981: 150; Delaware and Lushootseed statements are from Miller's field notes.

[220] Raymond White Luiseño Social Organization 1963 48 (2): 143.

[221] Anne Terry Sawyier Strauss Northern Cheyenne Ethnopsychology 1975; Being Human in

Person II

In greater detail, Alaskan Tlingit conceptualize the person as a container for holding the "mind" inside at the heart, surrounded by bones, flesh, and skin. As framework, the skeleton consisted of a spine and eight long bones, which hardened over a lifetime, located in the four limbs. Material, mortal components came from the father, while immaterial and immortal aspects derived from the mother, who represented her crest's matriline.[222]

While each child represented a successful conjoining of kin dreams, desires, hopes, and prayers, its external gender was sometimes determined by which parent reached orgasm first or which possessed the stronger or more powerful will; at other times, a child's sex was left to greater cosmic forces. For example, among Quebec Inuit, couples yearning for a daughter set up their tent facing inland and far from shore; for a son, their tent faced the sea at the tideline, "the domain of the hunter and the large marine animals."[223]

In some sense, the pregnant woman provides an oven for the fetus, where water and blood in her womb provide the medium that receives semen from the father to ignite the cooking process of creation. Their heated conjunction congeals into infusions of ever increasing solidity, density, and growth that becomes the baby. In this manner, blood became flesh, semen became bone, and water became clear fluids, lymph, and fibers. The insertion of soul(s) produces a heartbeat, then a pulse, then a breath, most evident as condensed vapor. Similarly, delineation of a face leads to a permanent image that casts a shade ~ shadow which detaches at death and may continue on.

Full-bodied, a baby takes on peculiarities of appearance and attitude derived from its ancestry, both human and cosmic, and from experiences of the parents. Just as her blocking of a doorway will complicate delivery, so his staring at a rabbit will cause a harelip. Thus, both parents must constrain and modulate their actions and thoughts in the best interests of the birth to come. Serious sin or immorality of either parent results in a stillbirth, interfamily accusations of neglect, and, potentially, a divorce.

While life is often set off by a spark, the infant only receives this animating gift at birth, thereby sustaining the body heat its mother had provided until then. Indeed, this link between motherhood and ovens is confirmed by the widespread belief tabooing males away from both a birth and a pit oven while in use.[224]

Attributes

Since Tlingit women provide the immortal and men the mortal aspects of life, a baby's face comes from its father. While each combination is unique, its personality traits derive from inherent links to relatives, as modified by social claims to adoptions, totems, crests, clans, phratries, or moieties. Since many of these are named for animals, certain zoological traits were also expected to be displayed.

For example, in the Abenaki charter epic of the Maritimes, Giant Frog swallowed all the

---

the Cheyenne Way 1976.

[222] Sergei Kan *Symbolic Immortality* 1989: 51, 52.

[223] Bernard Saladin D'Anglure Inuit of Quebec 1984: 496.

[224] For a summary of this pit oven taboo for men among the Salish of North America and Ge of South America, See Claude Levi-Strauss *The Naked Man* 1981: 612-613.

waters, causing a drought, and everyone began to die of thirst. People moaned that they were as dry as some animal − a turtle, beaver, wolf, trout, or haddock, to name a few. Their culture hero killed Frog, then toppled a birch tree onto its body to expel the water. Gushing down the trunk and branches, this flood formed river systems with a pond in place of the leaf at the end of each twig. As water reached the ancestors, some of them plunged in to drink, immediately changing into the animal whose thirst they claimed. Others remained human but took their named animal as the sign, insignia, badge, or totem to their ancestral lands, including camps and hunting territory, along a particular stretch of waterway.

Families were expected to inherit some physical attributes from their animal. For example, among Maine Penobscots, "The members of the Whale family (Stanislaus) are pointed out as large, portly, and dark persons, those of the Rabbit family (Newell) as small, timid, and weak, those of the Bear family (Mitchell 2) as orderly and dignified, and so on."[225]

During a lifetime, moreover, character is strongly influenced by foods, friends, and other associates, both good or bad. Ideally, a person achieved final maturity and full respect as a grandparent, raising a second generation with less demands on earning a living, a parental task.

Styles of hair, clothing, and ornaments reinforce male or female identity. Sometimes, *berdache* wear clothing of both genders to emphasize their intermediate status, but babies with confusing genitalia were dressed as girls simply because boys went nude, as with the Nuu-chah-nulth founder of a famous whaling shrine until he forced the issue by raping two women.[226] Among Lushootseed, where few or loose clothing was worn, obvious anatomy provided primary identity since transgenders are always said to be "acting like" their adopted cross-gender role.[227]

Abilities

Kinship also produced predisposition to particular careers, tasks, and specialties, as in Native California.[228] However, techniques were never enough for success, which relied first and foremost on access to or reserves of power provided by a spirit guide, partner, or guardian met during a quest or vision. In the most dramatic, if extreme, example, an encounter with Thunder, especially as a lightning bolt (a flame writ across the sky), a Lakota visionary became a *heyoka*, a "contrary" warrior doing everything backwards. With the same intensity, for Skidi Pawnee, "Each step in the Creation was achieved through two thunderstorms, one to create the lifeless form, the other to revitalize it; and, as the world was created in tempest, so every spring the [thunder] storms revivified the dormant earth, signalling the beginning of the new year and the renewal of all things.... The male storm fertilized the female earth."[229]

Yet no life runs entirely smoothly. In the event of serious dysfunction or misfortune, a person may default on hopes and expectations. Sometimes, inability to assume proper or expected male or female roles leads to cross-dressing and a transgender identity, sometimes as

---

[225] Frank Speck Abenaki Clans − Never 1934 37: 528-530; Malecite Tales 1917 30: 480-481.

[226] Arnold Pilling Cross-Dressing and Shamanism 1997: 69-99; Aldona Jonaitis, The *Yuquot Whaler's Shrine* 1999: 145.

[227] Jay Miller *Lushootseed Culture and the Shamanic* 1999: 96.

[228] William McKern Functional Families of the Patwin 1922.

[229] Susan Golla Skidi Pawnee Religion 1975: 43-44.

punishment for charges of cowardice and treachery.

Associations

Any and all of these serial infusions and additions is engendered as manly or womanly, so any person can and does combine both male and female attributes ranging from the mind, body, dress, and skills to strong spiritual influences. Overall preponderance of one gender over the other(s), however, determines personal identity, role, and activities. An equal balance between the two, however, seems to result in an honored transgender or *berdache* identity.

Disease, despair, disruption, or harm disable a person through the ill will of powerful others, contact with dangerous substances, puncture by a sharp object magically shot by a hired sorcerer, violation of taboos, or a general lack of self-care. Most can be cured or put right by shamans with powerful immortal allies, but some prove fatal.

Attacks of witchcraft were preconditioned by social anxiety about food, sex, health, success, honor, as well as intensifying frustrations dealing with kin, kith, and competing access to resources.[230]16

Dissolution

At death, or grave illness, the series that began life repeats in the same order to end it, starting with breath and ending with the skull, long bones, and valued possessions such as stone tools. At least one soul became a ghost or other postmortem residues. Another soul went to the afterworld, perhaps to reincarnate in the same family or another species.[231] Other souls in the joints, blood, or pulse points either dissolved or took on independent existences.

Generally, the timed diffusions within this series were marked by rituals, memorials, or post-funerals held by family members or the community for its deceased leaders. After the flesh was gone or removed, the bones could be bundled for secondary burial, sometimes in a communal ossuary, as among the Huron.[232] Skulls and stone tools were left at shrines, while in central California cremated remains were re-cremated at a rite called *Lonewis* a year later.[233] The advantage of these post-mortuary events was that they could be regularly scheduled because the timed series was generally known and guests could be invited with advance notice, unlike the death itself, which was rarely convenient.

Finale

Today, as science and medicine dominate knowledge of the person and the body, the series of infusions making up an individual involves a genetic code – of four nucleotides of DNA and RNA sequencing amino acids and proteins in chromosomes packaged as egg or sperm to produce a fertile zygote conditioned by intermittent hormones and chemicals, affected or not by

---

[230] Deward Walker *Witchcraft and Sorcery of the American Native Peoples* 1989.
[231] Antonia Mills and Richard Slobodin *Amerindian Rebirth* 1994.
[232] Bruce Trigger The Huron 1969: 106-112.
[233] Robert Heizer California # 8 1978: 268, 297, 776.

radiation and other potent exposures – to produce a fetus that then gestates into a baby in timed trimesters until birth, when training begins to struggle with the tensions between nature and nurture.

Instead, for Native America, a timed series of about twenty infusions (counting by ten fingers and ten toes) combines specific genetic and community traits with cross-species bonds and cosmic forces to create one individual who is more a microcosm than a unique being, adding another spark to a world already aglow with complex, gleaming diversity. More than merely lighting one little candle, Indien personhood seeks to enhance multifaceted existences among all beings, throughout time and over space.

American Indian Culture and Research Journal 24 (3): 155-160 2000

Jay Miller holds degrees from the universities of New Mexico, Rutgers, and Princeton and conducts research throughout Native North America. He has taught at universities and tribal colleges in the United States and in western Canada.

Person III

Indien Personhood III: Water Burial

In previous commentaries I discussed the generalized concept of personhood across Native North America.[234] I included funeral rituals in that discussion because of the widespread belief among Native Americans that how a person comes apart can instruct us on how he or she first came together. Well-known methods for disposing of the deceased's physical remains include burial in earthen graves, exposure on scaffolds, and cremation, but burial in the fourth element, water, is virtually ignored. Suggestions that this type of burial was practiced, however, do exist. Tulsa's Gilcrease Museum holds a huge painting that shows bead-and-feather-dressed Natives in Woodland canoes on the verge of sinking a bundled body. Docents are carefully instructed, however, to explain to visitors that the entire scene is the artist's imagining.[235]

Yet the deliberate placement of human remains into water deserves careful consideration. Unfortunately, any review of the past literature usually begins and ends with reports that Alaska Natives unceremoniously threw their deceased slaves into the sea. For our own times the immediate image called to mind is the end result of a Mafia contract that has "Guido wearing cement shoes and sleeping with the fishes." Over and above all of these peculiarities, however, is the common knowledge that "water revives," although, as we will see, this is not always a good thing.

Water is both dangerous and powerful. Blessed as holy water it serves in many rituals and other acts of faith; raging as a tsunami, it destroys. Throughout the Americas, dangerous serpents live in water, perhaps most terrifyingly embodied by mythic anacondas in the rivers of the Amazon Basin. Among the Tsimshian of the Northwest Coast, *spanaxnox*, the abodes of wondrous beings (*naxnox*) were ~ are avoided by all those lacking the spiritual strength to deal with them. Other water beings with great power include Tie Snakes of the Southeast, the serpentine Missouri River itself, the "drawer-unders" of the Delaware, and the Underwater Panther ~ *piasaw* of the Midwest.[236]

Water also transforms, as shown by the amazing change of tadpoles into frogs. Folk beliefs go much beyond this, however, and report such wonders as barnacles becoming geese according to English and Scottish folklore. In the Americas, Pamunkey of Virginia said that frogs turned into birds (shy, webbed-footed sora rails [*Porzana carolina*] who add to the mystery because they migrate at night) after the frost and cold came. Northeastern tribes displaced to Ohio believed that geese changed into beavers to restock dams and that snakes became raccoons for the winter. Micmac of the Canadian Maritimes believed old moose stags went into the sea to change into whales to revitalize their lives.[237] Chitimacha (Shitimushaw) of Louisiana said

---

[234] See Jay Miller Indien Personhood I II III.

[235] The Water Burial, by NC Wyeth (oil on canvas), Thomas Gilcrease Museum, Tulsa, OK, Thanks to Drs Jason Jackson and Dan Swan for drawing my attention to this source.

[236] See Robert Hall *An Archaeology of the Soul* 1997; Ghosts, Water Barriers, Corn, and Sacred Enclosures in the Eastern Woodlands 1976; Jay Miller *Earthmaker* 1992; *Tsimshian Culture*: A Light through the Ages 1997.

[237] Frank Speck and John Witthoft Some Notable life-Histories 1947; Frank Speck Chapters on the Ethnology of the Powhatan Tribes of Virginia 1928: 340.

hailstones provided the spit that turned into clams on tidal beaches.[238]

The most spectacular evidence for the importance of water burial is the archaeological site called Windover, on the central Florida coast.[239] Near the pad for the space launch is a small, dark pond filled with peat Between 7400 and 8500 BP hundreds of bodies were anchored into this shallow muck, held in place by stakes and heavy branches. Half of the pond has been excavated, yielding up 168 burials, evenly divided between males and females and between children (including adolescents) and adults. Of particular note, only females were buried with hollow bone tubes, often decorated with engraved geometric designs. Among the ethnographic Southeast tribes such tubes were symbols of life. In many ways this site points the way to the later development of mounds. Staking the bodies into the peat quagmire, even if it was to keep them submerged during postburial bloating, calls attention to the unstable and unsure world. Grave goods were highly varied, with fabrics especially so. Four types of close twining, one of open twining, one of mat twining, and one of plaiting stand in sharp contrast to the few types of later centuries. Clearly, these Early Archaic peoples had an ideal combination of leisure and skill. Though the bodies were bundled in fabrics and some hides, and some of the stakes stood above the water as (decorated?) markers, these mounded images were not played out on the ground for another millennium or more. Instead, stakes and jellied ooze secured ancestors in this uncertain land, unseen but not forgotten.

The cultural import of water burial best appears in two episodes in mythology. The better-known instance is in the *Popul Vuh*, the sacred text of the Quiche Maya. During their conflict with the Lords of the Underworld ~ *Shibalba*, the hero twins are coerced to jump into a bonfire. Later their bones are ground up and cast into a river, where they revive and reappear with their "same old faces" five days later.[240]

Less well known is the life of *Ya'uk^{w}ekam*, who helped fashion the world of the Kootenay, a language isolate of the Plateau now living in Idaho, Montana, and Canada.[241] ** After *Ya'uk^{w}ekam* provided the world with necessities for creating bows and arrows (wood, feathers, flint, sinews, tools), the people became angry and resentful of him. They killed *Ya'uk^{w}ekam* and threw him into the river, where the fish tried to eat him. When he kicked away the fish, they explained that they were restoring him to life. Then he went ashore and followed his murderers, who had quickly broken camp as soon as they killed him. After careful consideration, he took revenge only on the chief and those who abused his own family.

What is unusual in this story is that there is sufficient biography on *Ya'uk^{w}ekam*'s life to explain why he revived. His mother was Young Doe, the granddaughter of Frog, who seems to be everyone's grandmother and is the steward of fresh water. Once, when Young Doe went to the river for a drink, a man named White Stone pulled her in and married her. *Ya'uk^{w}ekam* is their child, so he partakes of both land and water elements in his very being. Rejected and killed on land, his watery aspect saved him and, in fact, made him even more formidable because after he came back, people were "more afraid" of him. The irony in all this is that his name in Kootenay means "the one from down under," so his affinity with water would have been obvious

---

238 John Swanton Indian Tribes of the Lower Mississippi 1911: 354.
239 Glen Doran *Windover* 2002: 11, 12, 18, 106.
240 See Adrian Recinos *Popul Vu*h 1950: 155; Dennis Tedlock, *Popul Vuh* 1985: 149.
241 See Franz Boas Kutenai Tales 1918: 89, 123.

to these Native speakers if not to those reading about him in translations.

Last, like the Mafia connection, there are indeed unsavory aspects of water, since the element that can revive can also drown. The best reference I know to such use in sorcery is buried in actual field notes, not in publications. In the early 1950s Skagit elder Charlie Anderson explained to graduate student Sally Snyder,[242] in more detail than seems prudent to repeat here, that a shaman could shoot a probe (*liatəd*) into a victim by holding a thin pebble under water in his or her hand until it enlivened and, directed by the shaman's will, shot off and into the other's body. Depending on where it struck, that person became ill or even died outright. In one instance with actual names, the pebble transformed into a bug that did the nasty deed. It was also possible to use a human hair, which was soaked in water and then squeezed until it bled profusely to kill its owner.

Since it was~is quite usual for sorcery to involve human bones, corpse flesh, and so-called ghost powder from human remains in order to kill victims, the availability or even the possibility of waterlogged burials anchored in shallow ponds begins to boggle the imagination. Surely, the regular visitation and continued use of a place like Windover was also, to a degree, a security measure to protect the living of the community.

Because a body is itself almost all water, it is remarkable that the watery grave evoked for sailors and others at sea was not much more common, at least in remote areas where such burials would not pollute a water source. Moreover, a fetus develops in amniotic fluid within the womb, water sustains all life, and after death liquidity is a major feature of decomposition.

Water burial is a way to return a body to its key primal element. It revives and transforms both the soul and the person. Sometimes water burial leads to a new life floating in a womb. Sometimes it disperses to provide a moist and nutrient-rich medium for a vast variety of other lives, making a contribution to the much larger whole.

8/24/5 9:38:56 PM

American Indian Culture and Research Journal 29 (3):   2005

Jay Miller, PhD, is the coordinator of American Indien Studies at The Ohio State University, where his research spans the breadth of the Americas and the enigma of earthen mounds. He has degrees from the Universities of New Mexico and New Jersey and has taught at colleges throughout the United States and western Canada to classes of all Native or mixed students.

---

[242] Sally Snyder Skagit River field notes [1952-54], University of Washington Allen Library, Archives Division, Oct 21, 195?: 53.

Ashes Ethereal:
Cremation in the Americas

The ultimate inevitability for most Americans is death, but for the Native peoples of both these continents, death is not a single event but a prolonged process with stages between the living now and the deading after.

On December 12, 1997, I was standing in the chill of the Northwest, freezing from the toes up while waiting to help as needed with an annual "burning for the dead" in preparation for an evening candlelight service in the local smokehouse (Native church) at which everyone in attendance could light a candle in the name of a deceased relative, friend, or loved one. Regardless of religion – Catholic, Pentecostal, Indian Shaker, or traditional – participation was community-wide.

This sacrificial burning required a rectangle about five-by-fifteen feet composed of crushed papers, kindling, and logs. Upon this table, or pyre, plates of varied food were to be placed individually as the name of the person for whom it was intended was loudly called out. In addition to familiar groceries purchased from any store, plates also held Native foods and personal favorites. Inevitably, after an early afternoon of preparations spaced among long waits, the arrival of the officiating ritualists from Canada called for a renewed flurry of activity. All cedar logs had to be replaced with split alder brought from their home across the border. From the moment of their arrival, these ritualists took charge of the situation by organizing us into an effective work force to do their bidding.

Using special words (*dicta* ~ enchantments) inherited only in certain families, both ritualists prepared the blank table before it received thirty plates set in rows. Then more enchantments were recited to fix all the settings before flames were lit. The paper plates burned smoothly and efficiently across the table, which was taken as a good omen. Near the end, certain people were called forward and quietly instructed by the ritualists about specific issues they felt had been expressed by the diners, and everyone was reminded that, via such burnings, those beyond are still with us and able to "discipline" now as they did in the past. Later that night at the candlelight, these female ritualists repeated the same message to the whole gathering.

As I helped pour drinks into cups to go with the plates, I keenly anticipated the fire that would soon be lit, knowing that its heat would come as a welcome relief from the chill of the day. If it had been raining, conditions would have been warmer, but instead it was clear and cold. In either instance, the fire would provide warmth and shelter.

That December day I was well prepared to muse on the meaning of fire, heat, and the dead, leading directly, of course, to a consideration of cremation.

Weeks before this burning, I finished teaching linguistics to Tsimshian speakers in northern Canada, and sporadically received commentary on my book-length study published that July.[243] In keeping with their nobility and dignity, my Tsimshian students, friends, and family have not yet found damning fault with the book, but rather quietly comment on what details were left out, clearly reminding me that they will always know more about their own culture, wherein light, as in fire, is a key metaphor.

Among my greatest oversights, we all agree, is a failure to emphasize that to this day, after a funeral and burial, Tsimshian burn clothing and food on behalf of the deceased. Before the arrival of William Duncan as successful missionary for low church Anglicanism, moreover,

---

[243] Jay Miller *Tsimshian Culture* 1997.

Tsimshians cremated their high-ranking dead in a process that might involve removing and burying the heart and filling the chest cavity with cedar bark to aid combustion.[244]

Recently, prehistorians looking at the five-thousand-year continuum in Prince Rupert Harbor have been denying any archaeological evidence for cremation, regarding it as only an ethnographic tradition, probably introduced from Athabaskans. Unless the ashes were kept together or placed in some kind of urn, there is unlikely to be any permanent evidence, especially since historic cremations took place in a locale away from town. Sometimes ashes were redeposited inside cedar poles or boxes, themselves subject to decay in that damp climate. Indeed, the only lingering evidence for cremation might be stone monuments or memorials, though much less elaborate than the tombs built for cremated Hittite kings.[245]

Instead, modern Tsimshian provide indirect evidence for the lingering importance of cremation because such incineration of offerings bridges the past and the present, calling for an examination of wider contexts. Was this burning a memento, a survival, a holdover from ancestral cremation? Probably. Yet, more importantly, we must ask, Why cremate in the first place? What are its correlations? What are some cultural explanations? As Richard Huntington and Peter Metcalf have documented, Robert Hertz expostulated that "the fate of the body is a model for the fate of the soul. As the corpse is formless and repulsive during the intermediary period, so the soul of the dead person is homeless and the object of dread."[246] Unfortunately, only a few justifications of cremation have been published, phrased within tribal literature, particularly the epics of genesis, creation, reform, or finishing off, near the modern Arizona-California border among the Cahuilla and Maricopa, both considered in this article.

Certainly, cremation is ancient in the Americas, particularly in present Washington State, where, before Kennewick Man, there was Marmes Man from the Palus, a cover term for at least nine ancient humans, including five from a cremation pit in the range of 10,000 years old.[247] Further, about 7,000 years ago (8500-6000BP), an Eden-Scottsbluff cremation marks the Renier Site in northeastern Wisconsin.[248] At the archaic mound site of Poverty Point, only cremation is suggested,[249] while it is well represented elsewhere during the Archaic Period and after.[250]

Cremation

In her survey of death customs, Effie Bendann[251] found eight "motives" linking fire and death and six involving cremation, which can be combined into eight examples to prevent the

---

[244] Miller *Tsimshian Culture* 1997: 44.

[245] JG Macqueen *The Hittites and Their Contemporaries* 1975: 136.

[246] Richard Huntington and Peter Metcalf *Celebrations of Death* 1979: 14.

[247] Ruth Kirk *The Oldest Man in America* 1970: 93.

[248] Ronald Mason and Carol Irwin An Eden-Scottsbluff Burial in Northeastern Wisconsin 1960.

[249] James A Ford and Clarence Webb *Poverty Point* 1 956: 35.

[250] Jane Buikstra and Lynne Goldstein The Perrins Ledge 1973; Dena Ferran Dincauze Cremation Cemeteries in Eastern Massachusetts 1968; Richard Gould Aboriginal California Burial and Cremation Practices 1968; Robert Neuman *An Introduction to Louisiana Archaeology* 1984; John O'Shea Social Configurations and the Archaeological Study of Mortuary Practices 1981: 39-52; Maurice Robbins *Wapanucket* 1980; John Walthall *Prehistoric Indians of the Southeast* 1980.

[251] Effie Bendann *Death Customs* 1969.

return of the dead, purify the pollution caused by death, protect the body from wild beasts, prevent sorcery, secure warmth and comfort in the future world, produce an ethereal body, hasten dissolution, and light the way to the afterworld.

In addition, my own review of the ethnography indicates that burning also provides a finality to tainted, dangerous, or explosive events, much as the local villagers assemble with torches to attack Frankenstein's castle in an all-too-familiar movie scene.

In a classic case, regarded by all as most bizarre because it was so totally out of character, fire closed an incident among the Western Apache. A married young man raped a divorced woman of his father's clan and killed her when she would not let go. As word spread, his mother announced that gifts would be collected to pay the mourning clan and the girl's family. Everyone, even boys, gave clothes, weapons, baskets, blankets, and horses. Lastly, his mother took off and added her own clothes to the pile, proclaiming that all these goods were to save all her other children and family members. The murderer, however, she gave up to his fate if anyone could find him. Then the girl's survivors set fire to this huge pile, taking away only the four horses. Shortly after, one of her relatives shot the murderer in the back of the head while he was eating in another camp.[252]

In an interesting twist, Kashaya Pomo[253] cremated not only to protect the body from wild animals but also to prevent the body from becoming a wild animal itself because "if the dead are not burned they will become grizzly bears.... Hence cremation is an act of religion, of redemption, of salvation, which it were a heinous impiety to the dead to pretermit."[254]

Today, in the Hispanic Southwest, Catholic mestizos recognize a certain appeal of cremation. For example, near the end of *Bless Me, Ultima*, the New Mexican classic, during a mock cremation exorcism, this ancient woman curer agrees that burning is a good way to return to the earth, avoiding the confines of a damp casket as "the spirit soars immediately into the wind of the llano and the ashes blend quickly into the earth."[255]

Deading

Within the overall context of Native American death ceremonies, moreover, it is vital to recall that a series of intricate processes and rites marked the progressive stages of disassociation for the corpse and its physical and spiritual components.

Among the Delaware, rituals functioned as time-releasers to mark stages in the deconstruction of a body "into increasingly more resistant parts: starting with the loss of breath; proceeding to clear fluids, blood, flesh, hair, and nails; and finishing with the skeleton" from cartilage to the long bones and the skull.[256] Each stage also released spiritual components, such as a soul localized in the breath, blood, or bone. To ease messy biological realities, the body

---

[252] Grenville Goodwin Social Organization of the Western Apache 1969.

[253] The identification of Power's E-ri-o can be traced through Alfred Kroeber Handbook of the Indians of California, Bureau of American Ethnology Bulletin 78: 234 1925, as the Pomo near Fort Ross, and Sally McLendon and Wendell Oswalt, in Robert Heizer Smithsonian Handbook of North American Indians: California #8, Washington, DC: Smithsonian Institution Press 1978: 278, as Kashaya Pomo, derived from the Spanish *el rio*.

[254] Stephen Powers *Tribes of California* 1976: 194.

[255] Rudolfo Anaya *Bless Me, Ultima* 1994: 233.

[256] Jay Miller Delaware Personhood 1991; *Shamanic Odyssey* 1988: 32, 141.

itself was equated with the chrysalis (cocoon), or more recently with a mere suitcase, from which a beautiful butterfly emerges.

The Tillamook of coastal Oregon believed in a Babyland on the other side. The template for each eventual human lived there in fetus form with others, including spouses, until he or she was reborn to human parents. In the womb, the other attributes and aspects of such a life were brought together and combined until the last of them, probably breath, was provided at birth.

In standard Native American belief, the mother provided the flesh and blood, the father the bone, and the creator the spark of life. In contrast, Northern Cheyenne say the father provides the blood, the mother the substance, and the creator the blessing spark of life-giving breath, which a newborn uses to inhale consciousness at birth, along with the potential to speak and a tragic self-awareness of personal loneliness.[257] Over the next twelve years, a child lost spirituality in favor of biology, learning to balance four internal tensions, two humane and good with two bestial and bad. Successful integration led to effective parenting and careers. Later, as a grandparent, life began to unravel, with spirituality increasing as an elder moved ever closer to the Milky Way, the path to the beautiful after-world of the Creator. At death, the fetal blessing from the Creator, previously diffused through the body, concentrated in the bones until these disintegrated and the vitality finally reunited with the Creator. At the death, however, any Cheyenne guilty of murder, suicide, incest, or promiscuity was cremated and its ghost sent along the short fork of the Milky Way also to vanish into oblivion.

In the Northeast, if a Huron drowned or froze to death, that body was taken to the town cemetery and placed between a fire and trench so it could be cut up. The flesh and entrails were cremated, but the bones were buried to appease angry spirits of the sky or water.[258] Here, cremation was a partial solution, also used for violent deaths and executed witches, to keep disruptive ghosts out of the common ossuary formed every decade at a Feast for the Dead called the Kettle.

Throughout the Southeast, tribes hastened the deconstruction process of disincarnation by dismemberment, with long-finger-nailed specialists called Buzzards picking the bones clean before they were reburied in specially made and measured baskets.[259] These procedures occurred along the length of the Mississippi River, although at Aztalan in Wisconsin such Mississippian mortuary processing was mistaken for cannibalism.

Maricopa

Among Yuman-speaking tribes of the Southwest, Maricopa[260] required cremation for all who entered their afterworld; otherwise he or she smelled bad.[261] Should a Maricopa happen to be buried, his or her ghost stayed only on the north side of a "deadline," wandering around carrying their coffin box on their head, sometimes putting it down to sit on. Twins and the

---

[257] Anne Terry Straus Northern Cheyenne Ethnopsychology 1975; The Meaning of Death in Northern Cheyenne Culture 1978. See also Miller, *Shamanic Odyssey* 1988: 131-132.

[258] Bruce Trigger The Huron 1969: 104.

[259] John Swanton Source Materials for the Social and Ceremonial Life of the Choctaw Indians 1931.

[260] Leslie Spier Yuman Tribes 1933: 296, 299, 302, 308.

[261] To further offset this concern, the pyre used aromatic mesquite, extolled as "the ultimate in fragrant fuels" by Aldo Leopold *A Sand County Almanac* 1978: 153.

deformed, who had a separate town, were reborn to visit the living for a time. An adult could be reborn up to four times, ending the last existence as a bit of charcoal lying in the desert.

Maricopa recognized that for each person four spiritual aspects transformed at death into a soul that goes to the afterworld, a ghost that becomes a whirlwind, a heart that becomes a horned owl, and a pulse that becomes a screech owl. The crucial importance of the heart is indicated by a belief that it is the last part of a body to burn.

The pyre was strongly made by first setting a big post into the ground until it stood a yard tall. Four logs were laid down to abut it to the west, with a smaller post set on the outside to hold these four in place. Logs were then piled up to a height of three feet, even with the top of the big post. Dry arrowweed was stuffed as kindling between the layers.

The corpse was removed from the house with four halts, the last resting on the ground beside the south side of the pyre. During each pause, a speaker orated. Finally, a man climbed onto the north side of the pyre, the corpse was handed up, and he briefly placed it prone with head to the east, before turning it onto its right side to face north. Its feet were unwrapped from the shroud and wedged between logs, left one to the north and right to the south, to anchor the body before it was covered by gifts of clothing and blankets. While the fire burned, an old man with a long pole kept the body hidden under burning wood. Everyone present fasted, hearing orations at the half way and end of the cremation. If a dead man had been a musician, his favorite songs were sung throughout his burning.

Afterward, four holes, two on the north and two on the south, were dug and the ashes divided among them. The fire tender first divided the remains from south to north, then west to east. While the ethnography is otherwise silent, these four deposits probably relate to the four souls.

The deceased's home and all possessions were burned or buried. After mourning for four days, family and officials returned to routine tasks. If the deceased were exceptional, a mourning ceremony (Cry) was held a few days later. Unlike neighboring tribes, it was not annual and did not involve effigies, only reenactments of great moments (battles, songs, orations) from that life.

California

The best regional overview of ethnographic cremation practices remains Alfred Kroeber's 1925 monumental Handbook of the Indians of California, still preferable to the quick-fix 1978 California Handbook,[262] though the California Handbook does provide the most current tribal ethnonyms and its index includes a useful entry for "recreation" under death practices of Lake Miwok and Pomo.[263]

Throughout California, the usual reason for cremation or partial cremation was ease in transporting back home someone who had died away because "All California Indians have strong sentiments on this point; old people will express satisfaction at the prospect of being buried adjacent to the house in which they were born."[264] Tohono O'Odham ~ Papago of southern Arizona add that cremating a body killed in battle prevented its use in sorcery by enemies.[265]

In northeastern California, Modoc cremated all their dead at spots associated with a

---

[262] Heizer California.
[263] Heizer California: 268, 776, 297.
[264] Kroeber Handbook: 499.
[265] Ruth Underhill Social Organization of the Papago Indians 1939: 190.

patriline,[266]24 with everyone but shamans attending. Possessions and beads were placed on the pyre, but these goods, along with any slaves intended for immolation, could be appropriated by anyone present with due compensation.[267] Mourners and others sat during the burning, apparently to avoid interfering with the rising smoke. Later, the house was burned if the deceased was a child or a spouse to residents because of a "desire to eliminate any reminder of the dead person, and thus to ease mourning."[268]

Pomo

In central California, "The Pomo were opposed to burial because they believed that the ghost of the dead person would continue to haunt the spot,"[269] so they cremated – along with beads, robes, and baskets – on a pyre set in a trench, with the body face down, head to the south, allowing the spirit to more easily lift itself to journey to the afterworld.[270] For Pomo, the essence of a person – variously called breath ~ soul ~ knowledge – was contained in the heart (*kam*).[271] During the burning, mourners were so distraught in grief that family friends kept a tally of all gifts and offerings, such as beads, so these kin could later give proper thanks.[272] The close male relative who used a long pole to expose the body to maximum flames became polluted for a few years afterward and was forbidden meat, hunting, and gambling to emphasize this too-close association with human meat and the seriousness of the duty.[273] The next day, a father or other close male gathered up the remains, put them in a basket, buried it nearby, and then obliterated any further evidence of the pyre.[274] All possessions were burned so as not to attract the ghost with the potential of harming the living, even inadvertently.[275] Mourning continued for a year, with women visiting the deceased's favorite haunts to sing and sprinkle acorn meal (*pinole*).

A year later at a rite called *Lonewis*, the remains were dug up and reburned along with donated gifts, a version of the famous Californian Cry shared with the Maidu.[276] Even after the Pomo began burying, they still burned offerings on the grave for the dead a year or so later.[277]

Maidu

While other Maidu buried their dead, the hill (Konkow) and southern (Nisinan) provinces cremated. The Hill Maidu mourning anniversary was the northernmost example of the Cry celebrated throughout the lower half of Native California in the fall to resupply the distinguished

---

266 Verne Ray Primitive Pragmatists 1963: 113.

267 Ray Primitive Pragmatists: 116.

268 Ray Primitive Pragmatists: 119.

269 Edwin Loeb Pomo Folkways 1926: 290.

270 Loeb Pomo Folkways: 287.

271 Loeb Pomo Folkways: 290, 296.

272 Loeb Pomo Folkways: 286.

273 Loeb Pomo Folkways: 292.

274 Loeb Pomo Folkways: 289.

275 Loeb Pomo Folkways: 291.

276 Loeb Pomo Folkways: 288.

277 Loeb Pomo Folkways: 294.

dead.[278]

For each Cry, a round brush fence was set up on the community's burning ground, open to the west and sometimes also the east. A director led the whole rite, but the functional sponsors were bereaved families who had given payment to the director in return for a special necklace to mark their own mourning. The patterned sequence of beads, by colors and counts, in this loop was specific to that ground. After use in five Crys, a necklace was redeemed by return payment from the director, who then cremated it. Interestingly, a poor family could participate in this ceremony by receiving payment instead of giving it, highlighting the prestige that came from generosity across the Americas.

When a ground was ready for an observance, its director sent out to guests strings of knots, one untied each day so all visitors arrived on the same day. The first night, family mourners came to the old enclosure around sundown to keen and sprinkle acorn meal. The second day, the enclosure was repaired and poles up to twenty feet long prepared to hold offerings that had been amassed for a year or more.[279] A widow had probably spent the past year making many baskets to be burned. By evening, each mourning family had a dozen poles filled from top to bottom to set up as pairs across the fire at the north and south. Bulky items were placed around their bases.

For the noteworthy deceased, effigies were made of stuffed and decorated wildcat skins arranged to look like standing humans, staked near the entrance, and "fed" during the night. Each such effigy was literally called a "spirit within" because the ghost of that person actually resided in it during the Cry.

As an old man lit the central fire, bargaining began to rescue offerings in return for an exchange, barter, or purchase. Such claims should be understood as the same as gifts given to guests at a memorial potlatch, where it is clear that, for hosts, others are both their guests and their dead, each substituting for the other but with the living bodies the more obvious.

When negotiations quieted, the director spoke about the intent, purpose, and procedure of the Cry, as Kroeber said,[280] "carefully instructing the people in what they perfectly well know how to do" in upholding high moral standards. During the night, in distinct groupings composed of mourning families, everyone wailed, keened, and sang. Their speakers periodically expressed pity and concern for these ancestral dead and placed bits of food into the fire to "feed" them.

At dawn, the tall poles were stripped and everything piled on the fire while the elders mournfully keened for their loved ones. Effigies were "walked" to the fire to enter the blaze. Mourners continuously exhaled forceful breaths, presumably to blow away harm. At first light, emotional intensity peaked and old women had to be retrained from throwing themselves onto the pyre. Everyone was totally exhausted with grief, prostrated from their lamentations.

In the morning, after the fire faded, the director urged all to eat, gamble, and have fun for a day or more to end their gathering on a happy note. Throughout Southern California, this Cry overlapped with the *toloache datura* cult, and in the Sierra Nevadas with Kuksu.

Luiseño

Among the so-called Mission Indians, the Luiseño of San Juan Capistrano had hereditary

---

[278] Kroeber Handbook: 429-432, 859-861.
[279] Heizer California: 383, fig 10.
[280] Kroeber Handbook: 860.

officials in charge of all cremations. Like other Luiseños, the Juaneño shared a Polynesian-like epic of creation from the primordial union of sky and earth, culminating in the appearance of Wiyot, whose fearful powers led to his being poisoned and then cremated to protect his body from desecration. All this to no avail, however, since Coyote rushed into the flaming pyre, grabbed a bit of his flesh, and ate it.[281]

To this day, the consumption of a bit of cooked flesh by a loved one remains an aspect of Southern California cremations,[282] recalling customs the breadth of the Americas − from South America, where cremated remains are turned into a drink because it is "better to be inside a warm friend than inside the cold earth," to the Northwest where the *Hamatsa* of the Kwakwaka'wakw and the *Xgyet* of the Tsimshian are metaphors for chiefly consumption of the possessions of their followers to enhance the prestige of their noble house by giving generously to others, both living and deading. Incidentally, the name of the patron of this consumption (consumer) cult among the Kwakiutlans has finally been carefully translated to indicate an increasing perfection into the human state because "you are what you eat."[283]

Similarly, in Southern California, at a later time, in consequence to Coyote's cannibal act, Chungishnish, the founder of the *datura* jimsonweed *toloache* cult, appeared to finish the world by changing the first people into present species, spirits, or sacra before making modern humans from earth and giving them cultures, laws, and the ceremonial enclosure (*wankech*).

Kamia

Kamia of the Imperial Valley trace their culture to a hermaphrodite with two sons who moved south along the Colorado River into this valley, where most Kamia ancestors fled from them in terror because of their frightful appearance. One brave woman, however, stayed and married one son, producing twins who provided corn and bean seeds, bows, arrows, war clubs passed out by patrilineages, and death ceremonies.[284]

As death approached, a person's soul could be seen leaving his or her body, going south of Black Butte (*Wiespa*) in lower California, where it glided on the wind waiting to rejoin with a twin spirit, which arose from the body at the moment of death, but lingered nearby for four days, visiting everywhere that person lived.

As the body cremated, this spirit returned to gather the burnt clothes, rub charcoal on its eyes to enhance them, and go south, where it was escorted by deceased relatives and rejoined the soul to reconstitute that person, who lived, died, and was cremated four times. After each death the shape of the "body" changed until after the fourth death it became a black beetle or other insect that returned to the Kamia country. "If heart did not burn, it was buried in the pit with the ashes, to enliven and emerge as a young owl that later grew up."[285]

Yokuts

In a declaration that resonates with Native understanding of this and all cremation,

---

[281] Kroeber Handbook: 637.

[282] Kroeber Handbook: 740, plate 69.

[283] Susanne Hilton and John Rath Objections to Franz Boas's 1983.

[284] Edward Gifford The Kamia of Imperial Valley 1931: 79.

[285] Same: 71, 72.

Yoimut, a woman who was the last of the Chunut Yokuts who lived on the northeastern shore of Lake Tulare remembered that her mother

> ... saved her money for a year and had bought a good suit of clothes at Mr Sweet's store in Visalia. She paid sixteen dollars for it. She had a good hat, shoes, socks, and underwear.
>
> Mother stuffed the clothes with tules and fastened them together so they looked like a man. She painted the face. Then she got out the fine baskets she had made to burn, and all father's things she had saved. Then she was ready for the *Lonewis*.
>
> By daylight everything was burned up and only a few people were singing and crying around their own fires. They kept that up all day.
>
> My mother worked hard to get the money to buy the clothes to burn in the fire for my father. She washed for the Blankenships and for Mrs "Fish" Rice. But you white people do the same thing. You save money and dress dead people in good clothes. You spend lots of money for coffin.
>
> Then you bury your father, mother, maybe your wife. You put everything in ground and all decay. We bum good clothes and they *do not* decay. They go to *Tih-pik-nits' Pahn* [great bird in charge in the hereafter + land] so our dead person always had good clothes to wear.[286]

Łingits ~ Tlingits

Such insight and background now allows us to return to the Northwest, particularly the matrilineal north of the Tsimshian, Haida, and Łingit who once cremated virtually all their honored dead.

Among Łingits, a person is believed to be composed of layers outward from a vitalizing "mind" located in the heart at the center of the body, then to bones, flesh, and outer skin, along with spirits or souls. The most ideal of persons was said to be dry, hard, and heavy − a humane and moral member of the nobility who dispensed cultural expertise in return for labor and help from others.

The great (if tragic) irony of a successful Łlingit life, however, was that a noble reached his or her apex just after death, particularly after cremation when they fully attained ideal attributes by being transmogrified into "heat, light, smoke, charcoal, and ashes"[287]45 as fire consumed one life in order to rekindle another.[288]

When a Łlingit body reclined on the pyre, the soul spirit more easily arose to travel in stages from the cemetery,[289] into the forest, and up a mountainside where it entered the second land of the dead to take up residence in its ancestral house. According to an explicit statement, those who were cremated had the virtue of staying near the fire,[290] warmed and ready to receive offerings sent by the living through mortal fires.[291] "In the house of the spirits the essences of

---

[286] Frank E Latta, Handbook of Yakuts Indians 1977: 667, 675, 682.

[287] Sergei Kan *Symbolic Immortality* 1989: 114.

[288] Miller *Tsimshian Culture*: 44.

[289] Kan Symbolic Immortality: 127.

[290] Kan *Symbolic Immortality*: 112.

[291] This custom was reported in the first detailed, balanced, and coherent Americanist ethnography by Reverend Ivan Veniaminov *Notes on the Islands of the Unalaska District*

the food, clothing, and other objects burned by the living descended through the smokehole upon the spirits sitting around this ancestral fireplace."[292]   Indeed, the Łlingit root *gaan* gets compounded into words meaning burn, cremate, and shine.[293]   "Located in the center of the house, which itself was the center of the human-occupied space, the fire was firmly associated with humanity and social life and was opposed to the peripheral domains of the rain-soaked forest and the sea."[294]

The bodies of shamans and battle-slain warriors were not cremated. Shamans instead were encased and left on some lonely rocky point to become the object of questing for shamanic power, especially by a nephew (sister's son). Warriors killed in battle went into the sky to join the Northern Lights, where their life was spartan but well attended by slaves and slain enemies.[295]

A year later, with the awkward body replaced by a monumental pole or other great artwork, a mortuary potlatch was held to install a successor to the name, persona, and position of the deceased, confirming the continuity of society and its eternal character as yet another person was given to a name so that, as Gitksan say, only the skin changes. Yet such transfer also involves an element of personal will since one Gitksan grandmother who felt neglected by her family threatened to be reincarnated outside of her matriline and, when really piqued, into some undeserving Anglo baby.[296]

Conclusions

All told, cremation cannot be understood apart from the reverence for fire throughout the Americas and the world. Whether or not a society cremates, all recognize fire as a portal between dimensions and existences. William Beynon, Tsimshian Wolf chief, collected a marvelous account of two friendly shamans, one on the coast and the other upriver, who sent each other gifts from a home fire through the other's smokehole. Thus, shellfish put in the fire on the coast fell from the interior smokehole, as chokecherries did in reverse.[297] As Mohave and Pomo noted, fire also improves smell, with cooking preferred to putrefation.

Via this fire portal, the dead are supplied with their possessions, houses, foods, and warmth at the time of the funeral and periodically thereafter. The late Wick Miller once told me how startled he was at a Gosiute funeral, which promised to be done the old way, when the deceased's house trailer suddenly burst into flames to mark his passing, presumably updating residence styles in their afterworld.

As Native California makes clear, cremation can be an expedient for transporting human remains back home when that is a priority, as Homer explained in the Iliad:

after Achilles's stand-in (Patroclus) was killed by Hector, his shade came to Achilles

---

1984: 398. This work was published in 1840 to describe and compare Aleuts and Indians (Kolosh), particularly Łingits.

[292] Kan *Symbolic Immortality*: 113.

[293] Kan *Symbolic Immortality*: 112.

[294] Kan *Symbolic Immortality*: 112.

[295] Kan *Symbolic Immortality*: 120-121.

[296] John Adams *The Gitksan Potlatch* 1973: 32.

[297] Miller *Tsimshian Culture*: 277 #44.

in a dream to plead for cremation since hordes of battle dead kept him from crossing the river Styx into Hades.... explaining that burning would quickly send him through the Gates of Hades, he predicted Achilles' own death, asked that their ashes be buried together within the same gold urn, and then vanished in a wisp of smoke.[298]

Thus, when deciding upon cremation, convenience is not as important a reason as protection of the body, relief of the bereaved, or quick release (clean break) of the innermost essence of a person. One explanation for Viking ship cremation is that the soul is a ray of the sun that must be returned at death to its source, with both fire and ships speeding the process.[299] Sometimes cremation has prestige, as among Tsimshian, Hittites, and ancient Germans, according to Tacitus, where famous men were cremated using special woods in the pyre.

Throughout northern Europe, burial followed a long period of cremation, as the sky god replaced the earth goddess.[300] "Cremation, appearing in the north as early as the Stone Age, two thousand years before Christ, becoming supreme in the Early Bronze Age and running through the Celtic Iron Age, is bound up with the belief that the soul is freed from the body with the help of fire, and flies to a distant land of the dead, where it is re-born."[301] At one Danish mound, wings of jackdaws and crows were added to the pyre to assist this flight.

In addition to this predominant means of burial, Celtic religion made three modes of offerings to their trinity of Teutates by bloodletting, of Esus by hanging from trees, and of Taranis by burning.[302] Therefore, final disposal of a loved one must be distinguished from sacrifice to a deity.

Among California Mission tribes, burning the body protected it by removing a temptation to use it for bad intentions such as cannibalism or sorcery, although some violations of this taboo have led to compensations like the arrival of Chungishnish.

Among Pomo, removing the body, possessions, and house of the deceased served to take away reminders of this loss for the living, and, more importantly, keep any ghosts from being lured back to retrieve a favored item or person.

In a few cases, cremation was a way of making sure someone dangerous or repellant was really dead, but even that was not always certain. For example, in the 1840s Crees killed a Blackfoot warrior named Low Horn by driving an elk antler into his ear, since his powers turned away all bullets. Then, to be sure he was dead, they burned his body, but an ember exploded to produce a grizzly bear that attacked the Crees, who fled as lightning bolts killed several others. Low Horn later reincarnated into a boy who became a famous shaman who died in 1899.

Ultimately, however, cremation was a shortcut to transmogrification into another reality, freeing up intangibles like spirits, names, and honors to be reclaimed by heirs, as among the Łlingit and Tsimshian. This quick release explains the concern with easing the passage, with consideration given to the placement of the body, on the side for Maricopa, face down for Pomo, or reclining for Tlingit, so that souls can more easily arise and go forth. Such a quickening, the

---

[298] Homer *The Iliad* 1950: 414.

[299] Robert Hall In Search of the Ideology of the Adena-Hopewell Climax 1979: 169, quoting Francis Huxley, The Way of the Sacred, New York: Dell 1976: 262; Robert Hall *An Archaeology of the Soul* 1997.

[300] PV Glob *The Bog People* 1969: 144-192.

[301] Glob The Bog People: 145.

[302] Gerhard Herm *The Celts* 1993: 157.

quick of the dead, also hastened their re-creation in the beyond in some form.[303] In instances of a Babyland, the outer form seems to reconstitute as a fetal template, ready to recombine with other elements to become a newborn. The soul, shade, shadow, ghost resides in a land of the dead, sometimes a series of them, until, in the ultimate tragedy for Native peoples, it no longer has anyone among the living who remember it at all and thus it passes into oblivion or perhaps fuses with the Creator as a greater cosmic awareness. Throughout the Americas, memory is the ultimate binder holding together the past, present, future, and eternal.

As expressed in phrases like "flame of life" and "spark of intelligence," fire enlightens, binds, and renews. "Like the burning of fields in preparation for planting, or to encourage the return of game and other edible plants, burning corpses and their possessions emphasized the regenerative power of fire."[304]

Crow of Montana explicitly say that the all pervasive power in the universe, which they call *maxpe*, appears as a white, wispy vapor, seen as clouds, smoke, cold breath, foggy mists, frosty earth, and more. Indeed, when set ablaze, tobacco, like a cremated corpse, changed into its essential soul-power form, as did words and prayers on chilly mornings.[305]

Thus death, funeral, burial, cremation, reburial, recreation, and timed memorials all serve to mark these passages in deading in the same way that namings, marriages, birthdays, and anniversaries mark such stages in living.

I want to end with some speculations about gaps in the ethnography, both distributional and emotional. First, since cremation shortcuts an elaborate series of ongoing deconstructions by cooking down the body, someone somewhere sometime should have a belief, probably esoteric, that the flames of the pyre provided the means to a higher existence, a new form of "enlightenment." Certainly among Pueblos, membership in various communal cults and priesthoods is still phrased in terms of metaphors of cooking so that non-initiates are "raw" while initiates are "cooked" and officials are "well done, ripe, ready, and finished." Throughout the Americas, standard belief held that spirits owned the land, the dead held it as permanent residents, and the living used it. Thus, graves and cremation pits served as deeds of claim.

Second, looking at distributions of mortuary practices shows them to be obviously discontinuous. In the prehistoric Southwest, for example, neighboring traditions used alternate procedures. Thus, Hohokam of southern Arizona cremated but the Anasazi {Early Pueblo} to their north interred. Then the situation became more complicated when, after about 1200AD, Hohokam instead buried, suggesting to me that cremation traditions of present southern Arizona and California gave way to intercultural hostilities such that Yumans centered on the lower Colorado River kept cremation as they moved eastward, while Pimans dug in along the Gila and Sonoran desert by shifting to inhumation. Yet for the earlier Hohokam, Emil Haury astutely mused,

> Unexplained are the meanings of caches and the mass destruction of cultural goods, in both of which fire played an obvious part. These customs appear to be connected in some way to cremation as such. But I strongly suspect that the relationships of many activities derive from fire as a revered and sacred agent, essential in death, in making sacrifices, and in ritual."[306]

---

[303] Robert Hertz *Death and the Right Hand* 1960.
[304] Kathleen Bragdon *Native People of Southern New England* 1996: 235.
[305] Fred Voget and Mary Mee *They Call Me Agnes* 1995: 6.
[306] Emil Haury *The Hohokam* 1976:166.

Similarly, throughout Native California, adjacent nations used alternate means with their dead. This patterning suggests that despite all its internal consistency as strong cultural beliefs, cremation or burial also provided a primary means of national identity. Therefore, any and all such practices need to be put into a regional context with the understanding that people will often adhere to something just because their neighbors do not.

Third, all sources imply that ashes have a unity of their own, with the integrity of each individual indicated by the separate treatment of his~her ashes, though the Mohave divided them fourfold. Yet the care that was taken to conceal these ashes suggests that there was a concern to protect them from use in sorcery against the family. This potential for divisive use seems to be the closest Native America came to the commodification of cremated remains so prevalent in modern America, where divorced parents divide up the ashes of their dead child, or, in Seattle, old Hoofers have packets of their ashes taken to many favorite scenic spots.

Cremation initially stuck me as both an anonymous and amorphous way of dealing with the dead, but my review has proven to me otherwise. By taking a loved one from flesh to ashes, mourners make the greatest manifestation of their regard. Natives who attend Anglo burials are often shocked when the family walks away from the grave with the coffin still resting above it. All Native funerals I have ever attended end with the family lowering the coffin and filling in the grave, often with separate lines of men or of women tossing handfuls into the grave to soften the later impact of loaded shovelfuls.

Cremation is definitive and quick. When a British Columbia trapper cut off his thumb axing through a tree knot, he saved both until he could invite friends to their combined burning as "Any bastardly chunk that can trick me out of a thumb has got a cremation coming to it."[307]

With cremation, the passage from intact body to manageable ashes takes several hours of constant attention, but the results are both comparatively quick and lasting. Always, personal articulations by those involved stress not the convenient outcome but the ongoing careful concern with freshness evidenced by these mourners toward their lost relative.[308]

In Japan, where cremation is the rule, friends assure me that their final act of picking out the remains of a parent at a crematorium was among the most intimate and psychologically satisfying releases in their entire grieving process. In contrast to the mechanized cremation of Japan, Hindu India continues a practice both ancient and full, integrated within a closed universe wherein "nothing new can be produced except by destroying, or transforming something else."[309] Benares has two *ghats* (cremation grounds) because this city is sacred to Shiva, who promised final liberating salvation to all who die there. The oldest *ghat* marks the place where Lord Vishnu sat for 50,000 years "performing the austerities (*tapas*) by which he created the world" and where the corpse of the cosmos itself will ignite at the end of time. "By entering the pyre here the deceased – as it were – refuels the fires of creation at the very spot where creation began."[310]69 Death is counted not from the loss of breath, but from the moment a kinsman cracks the skull to allow its combustion within the pyre. Then the corpse rises as smoke from

---

[307] Roderick Haig-Brown, *Measure of the Year* 1990: 183.

[308] Portability, however, remains a concern. Families that fled to America from the Baltic states quickly adopted cremation in the expressed hope that they would eventually be able to take remains of their loved ones back home, as many have indeed begun to do lately (Astida Blukis Onat, PhD, pc 31 October 2000).

[309] Jonathan Perry Sacrificial Death and the Necrophagous Ascetic 1982: 72.

[310] Perry Sacrificial Death: 77.

pyre turns into clouds, rain, and vegetables to be eaten and transformed into semen to repeat the process. Only small children, lepers, violent or sudden death casualties, and smallpox victims were not cremated, but instead immersed in the Ganges River, though an effigy of each was later burned. Only ascetics have no contacts with cremation at all. For Hindus, "Cremation is cosmogony; and an individual death is assimilated to the process of cosmic regeneration."[311]

Thus, from situated local knowledge within Native America, we move globally toward the human condition, where anthropology still has the most to say in terms of cultural integrity, ethnic diversity, and cross-cultural understanding, especially when it gives full heed to the Native voice in its cultural context.

American Indian Culture and Research Journal 25 (1): 121-137 2001

---

[311] Perry Sacrificial Death: 76.

The Bluejay Dance

by Harry Turney-High

THE Dance of the Bluejay is probably the principal expression of the hopes and woes of the Montana Salish. It is performed but once a year, near Arlee, generally about one week after the New Year, though sometimes as late as the first of February. As the time approaches, the Salish assemble, and with great care and devotion scrape away the snow and remove all debris from the place where the Medicine Lodge is to be erected. After the ground is seen to be clean, the lodge is set up by joining many tipis so that they form a long hall with a common roof. It is doubtful if in ancient times the tipi was used for this purpose, as it is apparently intrusive from the Plains at a relatively recent date and at first used only when on the hunt or during the season of bitter-root and camas gathering. Within the lodge many poles are set upright and other lodge-poles are fastened upon them in the manner of rafters. The use of this frame is discussed later.

Three days before the ceremony is to begin, the shamans, who are called *quasquays* in Salishan, assemble and begin their purification rites. For these three days they sit in the sweat-house, an important trait of this culture, stewing in their own perspiration, praying to their personal "medicine", called in Salishan *sumesh*, and rigidly abstaining from all food and drink. This *sumesh* is usually in the form of an animal who became the guardian of the man at the time he developed into a *quasquay*.

When the time for the ceremonial has arrived, all members of the tribe who have some ailment to be cured, some ambition to be fulfilled, as well as those who are merely interested, assemble in the *sumesh* lodge. Within its walls no one may wear shoes or moccasins or bring in any article of clothing or otherwise which was made by the white man. The dancing then begins, led by the *quasquays*. The shamans themselves have no elaborate costume or paraphernalia. They are dressed only in breech-clouts, their faces entirely blacked with charcoal. No other paint is used, nor is any other part of the body smeared.

The dance itself consists of regular hops in the same rhythm as the music. Aside from rattles made by stringing deer hoofs on thongs, the music is entirely vocal. No drums or flutes are used. This dance is very tiring to the Indians, and as it is kept up until dawn, many become exhausted. But no one may leave the lodge to rest or sleep without the permission of the *quasquays*, else the success of the affair is endangered and ill fortune will follow the refractory. There is apparently no difference in the dance as performed by the *quasquays* and the people. The folk form two long lines down the sides of the lodge, and they do their utmost to increase the hysteria of the shamans, who dance up and down the rows.

No food may be taken by anyone during the night, nor by the *quasquays* at any time. The first night is spent in singing and dancing in the above fashion.

When the sun has gone down, and the dance of the second night begins, the sick lie down before the *quasquays*. These shamans are specialists in certain kinds of disease and illness, and do not profess to cure any outside their specialties. Furthermore, they do not attempt to cure the lame or defective. Sickness cannot be acquired through natural causes. It is invariably the work of a hostile *quasquay* who has "thrown" his sumesh into the afflicted. *Quasquays* may do this for hire, should a person wish to be avenged on any enemy, and the fee must be good. But the *quasquay* professes considerable hesitation at this, as the practitioner may die of his own medicine. Should, for instance, the sumesh of the *quasquay* be the Blue-jay, he will throw a feather into the vital organs of an enemy. Unless this is removed by another medicine man, the victim will surely die. If, however, another medicine man successfully removes it, the perpetrator will die unless he can persuade his sumesh to accept his client as a victim. Once the malevolent force is released, someone must suffer. And since in primitive life disease generally meant death, this fiction was not hard to maintain.

Even in sport, however, there is great rivalry among the *quasquays* of the tribe. Wherever there is an assembly of Indians one of the principal sights is the contest of shamans. Each tries to out-sumesh his rival, throwing his medicine into him, and by craft avoiding that of the other. The *quasquay* who has successfully repelled the sumesh of the others, and who has visibly affected his rivals, gains great prestige. In the annual encampments on the flats at the head of the Bitterroot valley near Missoula, the *quasquays* of one camp continually try to bewitch the other camps, sometimes a merely for amusement, at other times to keep them from finding the highly prized bitter-root, the staple delicacy of these people.

By this time in the dance, the Bluejay sumesh has begun to possess the *quasquays*, and they undoubtedly perform cures of an hysterical nature, as do the faith-healers of the whites.
By this time also the people have become somewhat hysterical and the *quasquays* entirely so. The old men of the assembly decide that it is time to allow the *quasquays* to "go wild," and suddenly dash out the various fires built down the length of the lodge, leaving all in complete darkness. At this the *quasquays* are entirely possessed by the Bluejay, in fact become bluejays, and begin to "speak in tongues," talking backwards, in gibberish, and making bluejay sounds. They profess to have no knowledge of what they say, and persons are delegated to remember all their words and noises, so that they may use them for prophecy and prediction when they have recovered from the influence. Wildly they run about the lodge, everyone avoiding their touch, as the person touched by a *quasquay* in this Saturnalia will faint on the spot. Chirping and cawing they ascend the lodge-poles and run about the rafters with remarkable agility, perching and twittering in bird fashion.

About this time the "Bluejays" are seized with a desire to escape, and make every apparent effort to run out of the lodge. Effort is made to restrain them without touching them. Almost always some do escape, however, in which case they are carefully followed. The "Bluejays" run very rapidly, sometimes as far as two miles from the lodge. Usually they climb some tree much closer and perch in the branches until dawn, when they are coaxed down and back into the lodge. Should a *quasquay* succeed in escaping permanently with the Bluejay still upon him, he will run and hide in the Mission range, where he will die of starvation and sumesh. I have not discovered a recent case of this, and no doubt the care is not all on the side of the congregation.

All during this time the dancers are not permitted to talk, although the laity may do so during the day while outside the lodge. Care is also taken not to think, as during the fury the *quasquays* are capable of reading the thoughts of the dancers, and might blurt them right out regardless of their embarrassing nature.

The "Bluejays" are permitted to "go wild" until the beginning of the third night. Then the old men take those who are yet in the lodge and collecting those who are perching in the trees round about, smoke the spell out of them. A certain species of sweetgrass has been gathered beforetime for this purpose. This incense is slowly burned and the *quasquays* are held over the smoke until they regain their senses.

After this is done they are given a drink of sumesh water. Before the ceremony had commenced, the shamans picked certain youths of the tribe and gave them minute directions as to where to find the proper water. Just which stream was specified, and from which part of the stream the water must be taken, and they were instructed in every detail as to the route to take and the behavior to be followed both to and from the stream. Infraction of these instructions would bring great harm to the *quasquay*, who in turn would avenge himself upon the heedless youth.

When the *quasquays* become somewhat normal again they once more doctor the sick. Most people prefer to be treated at this time rather than at the first clinic, as the *quasquays* could be expected to be more powerful after being seized with the Bluejay. This ends the third night.

As the dancing resumes for the fourth and last night, certain young men are detailed to go cut the sumesh tree. This is an evergreen of small size. When they return they set it up. in the middle of the lodge after the fashion of a Christmas tree. The same monotonous dance is performed before the tree and prayers to the *sumesh*es are offered. As the night advances each person who has a wish prays and hangs a gift on the tree as an offering. These wishes run the gamut of human desires; success in the hunt, in gathering bitter-root and camas, success in love and hate. When everyone has hung his gifts on the tree, the shamans ask if everyone has completed his wish. If so, they give signal to a chosen man, who wraps the tree in a blanket as tightly as possible. This done, two youths seize the tree and, rushing down the two lines of dancers, flee with it to the wilderness, where they hide it. No one is supposed to find the tree. But if it should accidentally be found, the finder must not touch it or remove any of the offerings or terrific misfortune would overtake him. In the present civilized state of the Indians great disbelief in *sumesh* is voiced, especially by the young. But few of them will touch any of these offerings or do anything to enrage a *quasquay*.

The tree being removed, there is some sporadic dancing, then all depart.

Attempt has been made to ascertain if there is connection between this gift to the sumesh and the potlatch festivals of the North Pacific Coast. While the writer is personally convinced that there is some diffusion from the coast, it is very weak indeed. No one seems to acquire any prestige in the community by making expensive gifts, nor, on the other hand, does lavishness seem to gain any particular favor from the *sumesh*. However, there is a general feeling that big wishes demand big gifts, and that it is a wise act of supererogation to deck the tree as expensively as is convenient.

Though most of the very young Salish have had their ideas rather thoroughly "civilized" by Haskell, Rapid City, and the fathers and sisters of the St. Ignatius mission, belief in the potency of *sumesh* is far from dead. Persons of middle life may profess to disbelieve, but their actions belie them, and one suspects that they believe much more than their shame before the white man permits them to admit.

An amusing incident occurred in this region some years ago. An unusually severe winter had all but wasted the land. Cattle were dying in droves, as the snow was so deep that they could not paw down to the grass. Blizzard, starvation, and coyotes took their toll. The Indians saw that unless the mild Chinook wind came from the Pacific coast and melted the snow, all would be lost. So the *quasquays* whose *sumesh* was the Chinook were told that the one who would produce the mild wind would be made a present of a good steer. Those whose *sumesh* was the blizzard were urged to restraint for patriotic reasons. Great was the rattling and dancing, the weather becoming even colder, until one by one the *quasquays* lost prestige. This pleased the fathers of the mission who proposed to the Indians that if they would make them the same present of meat, they would produce the Chinook. The offer was taken, and the fathers, wishing to destroy the influence of the *quasquays* once and for all, prayed mightily and performed their civilized ceremonial. Unfortunately, their results were no better than those of the shamans, and they, too, lost caste.

Now when everyone had made up his mind to starve, an elderly Indian around Hamilton offered to bring the Chinook. Dubiously the Indians took up his offer. But, indeed, after he had done a bit of desultory dancing, the Chinook did come and the saving grass appeared. The grateful people showered him with gifts, much to the chagrin of the *quasquays* and padres, and he became The most noted shaman of the region. Upon interrogation by a professor of the State University, the old man confessed that he was not a *quasquay* and had no *sumesh* at all. But he reasoned that the cold weather could not possibly last much longer and that he was bound to win. He enjoyed great reputation, however, until he died a few years later.

UNIVERSITY OF MONTANA
MISSOULA

American Anthropologist n.s, 35: 103-7 1933

The Contrary Behavior Pattern in American Indian Ceremonialism Verne F Ray
Southwestern Journal Of Anthropology Vol. 1 (1): 75-113,1945

The Bluejay Character in the Plateau Spirit Dance
by Verne F Ray

PERHAPS nowhere in America did the guardian spirit play so great a role in the lives of a people as among the Salishan groups of the Plateau. Long ago James Teit made this discovery in his work with the Salish of interior British Columbia, and his descriptions practices[312] furnished both the type picture[313] and a documentary material for Dr Benedict's subsequent for North America generally. More recent studies have demonstrated a similar intensity of the concept among the Salish of interior Washington.[314]

Not only was the guardian spirit idea highly developed religious complex in which very nearly every man participation was no passive acquiescence to cultural rather an intense identification highly charged with emotional content. This emotional intensity reached its peak during the winter period of spirit dances in which all those possessing guardians participated. But this winter period was not a time when otherwise absentee spirits returned or were recalled for sake of the ceremony, as, for example, in nearby Puget Sound. For here spirits were ever present. A man and his tutelary led parallel existences; the one had only to reach out, so to speak, and draw the other to him when the occasion made unitary action or cooperation desirable. The power inherent in the possession of a guardian spirit was not, in other words, a talent once conferred and thereafter effective, or a vague store of energy to be drawn upon when needed; but rather a highly specific relationship with a powerful ally available for personal action in any exigency. Over-formalization in ethnographic accounts has obscured this fact.

In everyday life this intimacy of relationship was reflected in countless references to one's own or another's tutelary, and in the invariable explanation of all unusual, impressive, or significant occurrences in terms spirit power. Reference to one's own spirit was never specific,

---

[312] James Teit The Lillooet Indians (Publications, Jesup North Pacific Expedition, Vol 2, pp. 193-300, 1906); The Shuswap (same series, Vol. 2, pp. 443-789, 1909); The Thompson Indians of British Columbia (same series, Vol. 1, pp. 163-392, 1900); The Salishan Tribes of the Western Plateaus, Franz Boas, ed. (Report, Bureau of American Ethnology, Vol 45: 23-396 1930).

[313] "The type picture of the North American guardian-spirit practices corresponds most nearly to the customs of the Plateau area, let us say the Thompson River Indians (Teit: Thompson Indians). There was here the isolation in the mountains at puberty, the long ceremonial purification, the intentness upon supernatural communication, and the acquisition of the name and power and song of the guardian spirit in a vision. For months or even years the youths carried out strict dietary regulations with frequent rigid fasts; purged themselves with medicine and induced vomiting by pliant sticks; purified themselves by sweat bathing, followed by a plunge into the cold stream. There were no limitations of rank or ownership upon the experience or the tutelary spirits; the quest was open to and incumbent upon all the young men of the tribe" (Ruth Benedict The Concept of the Guardian Spirit in North America, Memoir, American Anthropological Association, No. 29 1923: 10.)

[314] Verne F Ray The Sanpoil and Nespelem: Salishan Peoples of Northeastern Washington (University of Washington Publications in Anthropology, Vol. 5 1932: 169-211; Walter B. Cline, et al, The Sinkaietk or Southern Okanogan of Washington (General Series in Anthropology, No. 6, in press. 1938)

however, always couched in vague or generic terms: "my power," "my helper," or, in colloquial English, "my partner." This last expression, heard constantly among these peoples even today, reflects most accurately the native attitude toward spirit power.[315]

Another key to the depth of the personal relationship is the spirit-ghost concept. When a man died his tutelary did not return to its genius, disappear, or merely become non-existent. It was inconceivable that an entity so intimately associated with the deceased should not undergo a major transformation likewise. Consequently, the spirit "died" also, becoming thereby transformed to a spirit-ghost, one of a class of supernatural beings closely resembling in form the ghost of the soul. The identifying characteristics of the spirit were no longer retained, the new form being vaguely anthropomorphic.[316] The full distribution of the spirit-ghost concept is not yet determined, but it is known for the Southern Okanogan,[317] Sanpoil, Nespelem, Kalispel, Wenatchi, and Kittitas. It apparently is present in modified form among the Lakes (Senijextee), but is definitely absent for the Klikitat.

The winter dance was mentioned above as the period when spirit consciousness reached the point of saturation. Impersonation of guardian spirits was a well recognized feature of the ceremony. Another aspect, far more instructive for a fundamental understanding of the complex, was identification – as opposed to mere impersonation – with the spirit. Identification involved radical and thorough transformation from the normal human state to a condition in which all social relationships were abjured, and activities duplicated, as closely as physical limitations permitted, those of the spirit.

Such identification may seem to do violence to the strongly developed duality principle. To resolve this apparent difficulty it is necessary to recall the native theory of genesis for the guardian spirit. During mythological times there were no human beings; neither were there guardian spirits. But the beings of that time possessed attributes of both. Their physical and psychological differentiae were those of animals, but for the most part they appeared in the superficial guise of men. The animal form as such was taken only when an emergency demanded. They sought no spirit power since they possessed it inherently. "When people came on earth," it is explained, "these beings became the spirits." But in the new era the dominant form became that of the animal; the man-like form was taken only when in communion with men. Human beings appeared at the same time, inheriting as their guise the prevalent form of the previous beings. But men did not receive the power to reciprocate with their spirits and appear in animal form. This was possible, in modification, only in ceremonial identification. This identification was not an amalgamation or a substitution, but a reversion to the conceptualized form of the mythological being.

Such transformation was peculiarly the prerogative of persons with Bluejay[318] power; thus the term "Bluejay character" may conveniently be used for purposes of designation. Despite the dramatic nature and theoretical implications of this aspect of the dance it has been largely overlooked.[319]

---

[315] * Cf. Ray loc. cit. The description holds for the Salish of interior Washington generally.

[316] Cf. Ray *op. cit*, pp. 73-76.

[317] Cline *op. cit.*

[318] The terms bluejay and owl are here capitalized when the guardian spirit character is intended; uncapitalized, the reference is to the bird as such.

[319] In 1932 I {VFR}described the Sanpoil form (*op. cit*, pp. 191 f); in 1933 Dr Harry Turney-High provided a description for the Flathead (The Bluejay Dance, American Vol. 35 1933:

A short summary of the Sanpoil form will serve as a basis for discussion. Subject to the transformation were those with either Bluejay or Owl as tutelary. With the approach of the winter period given over to guardian spirit dances (December, January) these individuals removed all clothing except the breechcloth, and blackened the face, hands, and feet. For the two months of the dances they donned no clothing despite the rigors of the weather. They shunned "human beings" and avoided conversation, even among themselves. Further, they ate apart, becoming scavengers or refuse from meals and stale food (in keeping with the habits of bluejay and owl). During the dances they acted as sentries, patrolling the grounds outside the dance house or perching on the rafter supports inside the building. From the latter vantage point they observed intently the actions of those below to detect any breach of the formal rules of conduct. If one were seen eating during the dance, for example, the sentry "flew down and recovered the food from the person's throat." In like manner other rules were enforced. The sentries themselves never danced or mingled with the dancers. Sometimes they disappeared from the dance for a time to perform duties in other parts of the village; restrictions of conduct during a dance applied to the village as a whole. The sentries were capable of detecting violations, no matter where they occurred. Similarly, they perceived the approach of visitors long before the dance house was reached; this information was conveyed to the dancers by symbolic actions. When the dance season ended it became necessary to capture the sentries in order to return them to their former state. Though the original metamorphoses had been achieved by the characters themselves, they were powerless to effect the retransformation. In fact they violently opposed it. They were caught by being waylaid by friends, whereupon they "died." Through being held over a smudge they were revivified as normal human beings. Had they been allowed to go their way, "they would have gone wild and run themselves to death."[320]

The Colville are adjacent to the Sanpoil on the north. From Walter Cline we have the following description which is quoted in full:

> Among the Colville, power derived from the bluejay differed from any recorded for the [Southern] Okanagon, for it especially enabled its possessor to find lost articles and people, and sometimes impelled him to flee human society and lead an insane life in the woods. Bluejay shamans[321] used black face-paint. A man with this power once disappeared from a settlement near Marcus just after the winter dance and was not found till the next autumn. His brother dreamed that he might be discovered with a group of wild horses at noon on the day following the dream. Enlisting the aid of a few good ropers, the brother went out to capture him. They found him as foretold in the dream, leaping from one horse's back to another. The horses escaped, but the maniac was bound, fumigated with *xacxac*[322] root, and restored to normal life. David, the narrator, knew of no other instance of this kind, but Johnnie's account of the behavior of Colville bluejay shamans when they went out to find lost things, and the repeated

---

103-107); an account for Colville is contained in Cline (*op. cit*). I am aware of no others.

[320] Ray loc. cit.

[321] Apparently the word shaman here is intended to convey a meaning analagous to my term character. Cline in general uses the word shaman in a very broad sense. It is certain from my own acquaintance with the Colville that there could be no confusion between the Bluejay character and the true shaman.

[322] This is a small plant, found in the mountains, which was valued for the fragrant odor characteristic of the root. The Sanpoil used it both as a perfume and a medicine.

statement that they "turned into bluejays," indicate a much more violent form of spirit possession than occurred among the Okanagon. Johnnie recounted that those with this power turned into bluejays at a dance, which no one was allowed to leave. They would fly through a crack in the door. They would stay naked in the mountains for months, living only on pitch. One such named *inyăs* (Aeneas, Ignace ?) could jump up a tree and dance with one foot on its tip. People "spoke backward" to him. If a man was lost in the mountains or drowned, or if horses were lost, he was asked to find them. He hopped out on one foot; reporting on his return, "I did not find him," meaning the reverse. Another named *q!aī´ïya* would hop out and find a coin secreted in the snow. In all given, the shamans had possessed their bluejay power for some time; we obtained no account of their conduct soon after getting the power.[323]

These data place the Southern Okanogan definitely outside the area of the Bluejay character. For the Colville, it introduces two new or modified features: the ability to find lost objects or persons; and the "talking backward" as contrasted to the careful avoidance of conversation among the Sanpoil. Also, Owl has disappeared as a participant, and, to anticipate, will not reappear.

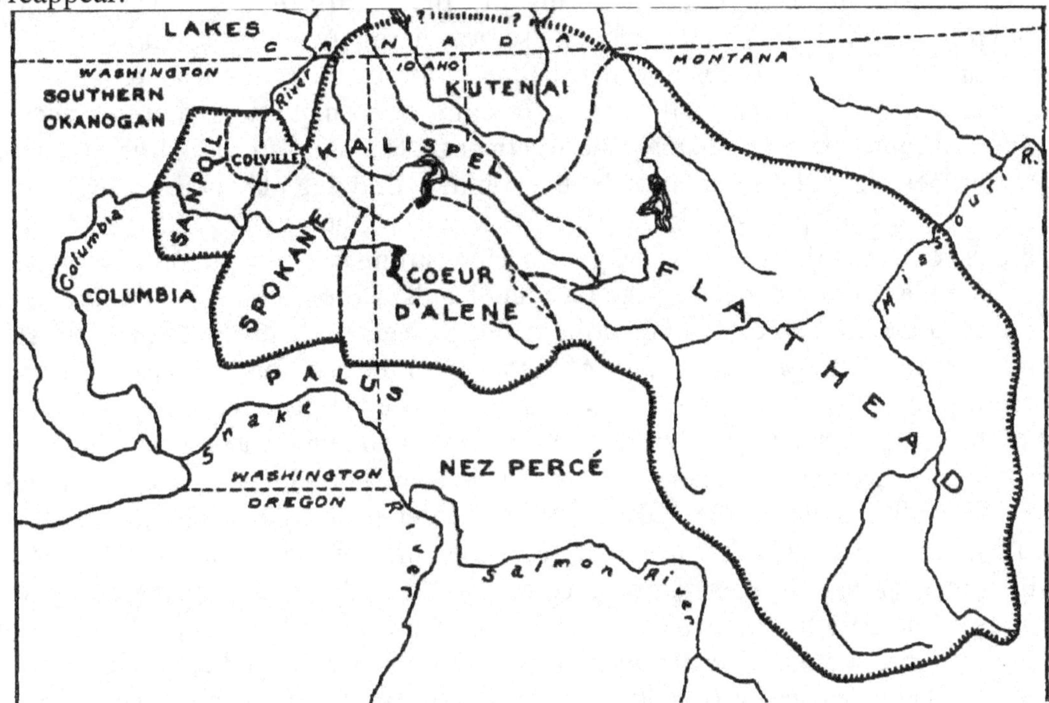

FIG. 1. Probable distribution of the Bluejay character

Among the Spokane, adjoining the Sanpoil on the east, a new element appears in the participation of the Bluejay character in the dance as a pseudo-shaman. Treatment was limited, however, to cases where the peculiar attributes of the bluejay indicated aptitude. Thus, just as among the Sanpoil the sentry retrieved food from a person's throat, among the Spokane he withdrew from a patient's stomach foreign matter which inadvertently had been swallowed.

The Kalispel, immediately north of the Spokane and east of the Colville, extended this curing power to include one of the typical shamanistic procedures, that of sucking. Bluejay

---

[323] Cline *op. cit.*

characters were paid by ailing dancers to treat those illnesses for which sucking was deemed proper. They were privileged to use the other shamanistic modes of treatment, namely blowing and drawing out with the hands.[324] The Bluejays were definitely set apart from true shamans and contrasted to them. Informants emphasized distinction by pointing out that true shamans never were paid.[325] The talent for ferreting out the missing is encountered here also. The phrasing is closely parallel to that of the Colville, especially in the interest expressed over objects recovered from under the snow. Thus one informant told how his father had regained a knife by enlisting the services of a Bluejay during his father had regained a knife by enlisting the services of a Bluejay during a winter dance. The knife had been lost the previous summer; it was found at some distance under three feet of snow. It was explained that this power of the Bluejay was limited to such objects as contained material derived from animal life. If this provision were met, success was certain regardless of distance or elapsed time. The knife in question had had a handle of buckhorn; had it been of wood the Bluejay would have been powerless.

The Kalispel characters observed a "complete" fast of water as well food for as long as eight days, the duration of the dance. Clothing was shunned as uniformly as among the Sanpoil, this being largely an individual matter. Likewise, some blackened their faces and hands, some did not. The transformations occurred during the first hours of the dance, not prior to it. Bluejays often left the vicinity of the dance house, remaining away for several hours or a whole night. But contrary to Sanpoil custom, the nature of these escapades was kept strictly secret, even from one another.[326] The revivification and return to normal was sometimes accomplished by smudging but more often by shamanistic treatment. The shaman in charge of the dance, or another practitioner, allayed the condition by the common drawing out and blowing procedure.

South of the Kalispel and east of the Spokane lay the Coeur d'Alene. Here familiar elements are encountered together with new ones and a strong emphasis upon Bluejay as a seer is discerned. Like the Sanpoil blackened the face and hands, wore nothing but the breechcloth, sat among the roof poles, and strictly avoided the dancers. Sentry duties were likewise similar but somewhat more formalized in that a badge of authority in the [599] form of a diminutive bow and arrows were carried. The Coeur d'Alene sentry was not exempt from the food tabus but was restricted to the same degree as the dancers. As a seer the Bluejay was not only able to find lost or hidden objects or persons but made a point of using this knowledge to the embarrassment of the dancers, by calling down to the audience from his perch in the rafters and disclosing secret activities, tabu violations, and other irregular actions on the part of members. The foretelling of events with great specificity was likewise characteristic. Speech with the dancers was not restricted. In keeping with the character of the bird, the Bluejay was said to travel with great speed, ignoring impediments. The characters travelled from one dance to another throughout the dance period. No pseudo-shamanistic attributes were possessed. Here even more than elsewhere the Bluejay resisted being returned to the human state. Informants tell of pursuits over many miles of snow covered ground before the capture of one or another Bluejay could be effected. Once caught, the retransformation was accomplished by holding live coals covered with aromatic roots under the subject's nose. Smudging the whole body was never practiced.

Among the Flathead, east of the Coeur d'Alene and Kalispel, the complex appears, at first

---

[324] Cf. Ray *op. cit*, pp. 205f.

[325] But they might receive presents. This distinction may seem artificial, but to the Kalispel it is very real and strongly defended.

[326] This explains the "eight day complete fast."

glance, to have been considerably altered in character. Turney-High writes:

> The Dance of the Bluejay is probably the principal expression of the hopes and woes of the Montana Salish.... [327]
>
> Three days before the ceremony is to begin, the shamans, who are called *quasquays* in Salishan, assemble.... Their personal "medicine," called in Salishan *sumesh* ... is usually in the form of an animal who became the guardian of the man at the time he developed into a *quasquay*.
>
> When ... the dance of the second night begins, the sick lie down before the *quasquays*.... Should, for example, the *sumesh* of the *quasquay* be the Bluejay, he will throw a feather into the vital organs of an enemy [to cause illness or to demonstrate power in the dance contests].
>
> By this time in the dance [second night], the Bluejay *sumesh* has begun to possess the *quasquays*.... The old men of the assembly decide that it is time to allow the *quasquays* to "go wild." ... At this the *quasquays* are entirely possessed by the Bluejay, in fact become bluejays, and begin to "speak in tongues." ... Chirping and cawing they ascend the lodgepoles and run about the rafters with remarkable agility....
>
> The "Bluejays" are permitted to "go wild" until the beginning of the third night. Then the old men ... smoke the spell out of them. [328]

Translations of the native terms used above are required before this data can be interpreted. [329] Turney-High's word "*sumesh*" is simply the familiar Salishan term for guardian spirit (Sanpoil: Okanogan: *sumi'x*; Lakes: *su'mi'x*^{u}), while "*quasquay*" is the common term for bluejay (Sanpoil: *qwa'skei*; Coeur d'Alene: *qwa sqwl*; Klallam: *kwa'ckwac*[330]). But if the native terms in the quotations confusion still prevails. [331] It is obvious that Turney-High, after incorrectly equating the terms shaman and "*quasquay*," proceeds to use them interchangeably. This at once accounts for the apparent transformation of all shamans into Bluejay characters, regardless of their tutelaries; resolves the contradiction in the statement that the guardian spirit is the animal that becomes the patron of the Bluejay; and renders meaningful the tautological statements.

---

[327] Turney-High uses the term Salish for the group more commonly called Flathead. The name Salish is ambiguous since it is more widely used to designate the extensive linguistic stock to which Flathead speech belongs.

[328] Turney-High *op. cit*, pp. 103-105.

[329] Without such translation it would appear from the first remarks that the actors dance were true shamans and that all such participated. This would imply that all possessed Bluejay as guardian, or that participation in the "Bluejay Dance" was not to those with this power. But this will not hold in view of the statements, "Should, example, the sumesh of the quasquay be the Bluejay," and, "the Bluejay sumesh to possess the quasquays." This implies that shamans possessing guardians other jay nevertheless "become bluejays."

[330] Herman Haeberlin Types of Reduplication in the Salishan Dialects (International Journal of American Linguistics, Vol. 1, pp. 154-74, 1918: 167).

[331] We then read: "the shamans, who are called bluejays in Salishan;" "their 'medicine,' called ... guardian spirit ... is usually in the form of an animal who guardian of the man at the time he developed into a bluejay;" "the sick lie down bluejays;" "Should, for example, the guardian spirit of the bluejay be the Bluejay;" Bluejay guardian spirit has begun to possess the bluejays;" and, "At this the bluejays entirely possessed by the Bluejay, in fact become bluejays."

The identification of the shaman with the Bluejay might be accepted at face value were it asserted for Flathead ("Salish" cf #16) culture. A step in this direction was found among the neighboring Kalispel. But Turney-direction was found among the neighboring Kalispel. But Turney-High presents the identity as a feature of the Salishan language ("called in Salishan") which has been shown to be false.

The "Bluejay Dance" of the Flathead was merely the familiar winter guardian spirit dance of the Plateau, telescoped to comprise but four days of activity. Bluejay characters played a somewhat greater role than among groups to the west, but on the first and fourth days, half the duration ceremony, there were no distinctive features of the Bluejay complex. In the quotations above appear direct parallels with the spirit dance elsewhere (power contests, shamanistic curing). Other analogues include purification rites, ritual preparation of the dancing ground, guardian spirit dancing, similar formal rules of conduct, ritual quenching of the fires, a ritual expedition to bring in the center pole, branches allowed to remain on pole, giving of gifts, and dancing for weather control.

The Bluejay feature itself exhibits numerous parallels with groups discussed above. Transformation occurred after the opening of the dance, as with the Kalispel. The old men (presumably the shamans) decided to let those with Bluejay power "go wild," that is, become transformed. Metamorphosis was complete; the characters perched among the rafters; retransformation was accomplished through smudging. Further perusal of Turney-High's text reveals many other parallels, including: lack of clothing, blackening of the face, duty as sentries, fasting, curing, specialization in curing, no conversation with human beings, and inability to retransform themselves.[332]

The expanded curing role of the Flathead Bluejay character deserves emphasis. But the questions, "Were the Bluejays true shamans; did they practice curing apart from the dance?" can be answered in the negative with reasonable safety. On the whole, the Bluejay complex of the Flathead fits well into the general pattern.

The distribution of the Bluejay character now apparently is exhausted, with the possible exception of the Kutenai. I was unable to visit this group, but the southern Kutenai, at least, may very well have shared the trait. Lakes (Senijextee) and Columbia informants declared the complex unknown to their groups. It was absent, as we have seen, for the Southern Okanogan. Spinden does not mention it for the Nez Percé.[333] For peoples to the east of the Flathead the complex is not mentioned, to my knowledge, in the existing literature. The accompanying map shows the boundaries of the Bluejay complex.[334]

UNIVERSITY OF WASHINGTON
SEATTLE, WASHINGTON

Verne Ray Bluejay Character in Plateau Spirit Dance
American Anthropologist n.s, 39: 593-601 1937

---

[332] Turney-High op. cit, passim.

[333] Herbert J. Spinden The Nez Perce Indians (Memoirs, American Anthropological Association, Vol. 2, Pt. 3, 1908).

[334] The name Sanpoil as used in this paper and on the map should be understood to include the Nespelem who were culturally identical. Likewise, the term Spokane is used broadly to include the three divisions, the Lower, Middle, and Upper Spokane. (See Verne F Ray Native Villages and Groupings of the Columbia Basin, Pacific Northwest Quarterly, Vol. 27, pp. 99-152 1936.)

The Contrary Behavior Pattern in
American Indian Ceremonialism

Verne F Ray

Introduction

DISTORTED or unnatural behavior is extensively exploited as a ritual device by the Indians of North America.[335] Available information points to the Southwest and the Plains as the two areas of richest development. In the former area the behavior distortion is epitomized in the ceremonial clown. In the Plains the emphasis is quite different. Anti-natural behavior is the point of focus as contrasted to the merely unnatural. The exact opposite of normal human behavior is the ideal sought. The ideal is reached in speech inversion but a compromise is necessary in behavior categories where true inversion is impossible. Humorous performances sometimes result; one trend led to the development of a near-typical clown. But clowning is not the objective; indeed, hardly more than incidental. In many instances the activities are profoundly serious. The terms of designation indicate the character of the cults; "contrary" or "crazy" are the most common descriptive terms. Accordingly, the phrase "contrary behavior" is here adopted to characterize the phenomena.[336]

In view of these facts it will be seen that the title of this paper limits present consideration to the Plains-type phenomena. The phenomena, however, are not limited to the Plains cultural or geographical area. Discovery of the Bluejay Character of the Plateau winter dance extended the distribution over a considerable portion of that inter-mountain area.[337] Great Basin parallels carry the survey southward. And related rituals among the central Algonkin and Iroquoian peoples project the study eastward into the Woodlands.[338]

A mere recital of the elements common to the contrary behavior rituals of these areas

---

[335] The historical present tense is used in the descriptive sections of this paper. Some of the rituals described are still performed in attenuated form but most are retained in memory only.

[336] The term "crazy" has implications in English which are not present, e.g, in Algonkin; consequently the word is undesirable in a name. Neither "contrary dance" nor "contrary society" would be satisfactory since some are not dances, some not societies. "Anti-natural" or "'contra-natural" would be acceptable. Both arc used occasionally in this paper to avoid repetition.

[337] Verne F Ray The Bluejay Character.

[338] Even so, the boundaries drawn for this study are somewhat arbitrary, especially the elimination of the Southwest and California. However, the latter areas, and all remaining areas of North America, have been studied with reference to clowning and related ritualism, by Julian H Steward and the present author. This joint effort will be presented in the near future.

Steward began his studies of American Indian clowning many years ago; his paper, The Ceremonial Buffoon, appeared in 1930. He most generously placed at my disposal his notes on the Plains area, which have proved highly useful. I wish to acknowledge my indebtedness and express my deep appreciation for his kindness.

would demonstrate the existence of extensive and significant cultural contacts. But my hope is to show to some extent the nature of those contacts; to distinguish the unidirectional from the reciprocal in cultural transfer; to ascertain whether organized systems of thought and behavior were transmitted, or elements only; and to follow the lines of growth, where the evidence permits. Thus one object of this study is historical: to contribute modestly to our knowledge of the growth of ceremonialism in North America with data which may also be used for illumination of larger historical matters, such as the cultural contacts, direct and indirect, between the Woodlands and the Plateau. A second objective is to determine the character of these psychologically significant rituals in which normal behavior is inverted: to distinguish the basic from the superficial, to analyze the factors in development, and to study the interactions of variants in contact.

The manifestations of contrary behavior are so numerous and varied that some kind of classification is a prerequisite to intelligible discussion. The system here employed is a compromise between an arbitrary expedient for temporary use and a logical classification emerging from analysis. Certain rituals exhibit unifying characteristics which are relatively easily ascertained. The most obvious linkage is that of a common name. Such a clue suggests structural unity among tribal variants, but is inadequate as proof. Rituals lacking the name may nevertheless belong in the category. Furthermore, certain connections are demonstrable despite variation in the traditional names.

We may first catalog those rituals which exhibit conceptual integration as opposed to merely formal unity. The criteria applied are three: source of membership or the basis of individual participation; the character and form of the ritual; and the individual and social function of the ritual. The varieties and distributions thus isolated are the following: the Bluejay Character, of the east central Plateau (native name); the *Heyoka* of the Dakota and the Ponca (Sioux name); and the Buffoons of the Plains Cree and Ojibwa and the Assiniboin (arbitrary name). These are described below at which time the individual criteria of classification are given. It will be seen that these cults are mere aggregations of individuals, not societies in the formal sense. Another common feature is that the criterion of membership is usually a supernatural experience.

In the second category the distinguishing traits are quite the opposite. Formal unity is characteristic, the specific formalism being that of the graded society. Conceptual integration is lacking. Supernatural sponsorship is also lacking. The most common naming pattern involves a "Dog" designation. Examples are found among the Mandan, Hidatsa, Blackfoot, Arapaho, and Aa'ni (Atsina, Gros Ventre) ; that is, in all tribes with graded societies.

The third group is that in which fire ritualism is the dominant feature. The Hot Dances of the Hidatsa, Arikara, and Iowa are examples; also the Pawnee *Iruska*.

Brief descriptions of type examples and comparisons of variants are presented below. These are followed by analysis of the history of each as far as it can be traced without more than incidental involvement of other types. Finally, the interactions of the various types are discussed and over-all problems analyzed.

The Bluejay Character

Description. The Bluejay Character is found as a ritual personage in the winter guardian spirit dances of the following southeastern Plateau tribes which occupy a compact area: Flathead, Coeur d'Alene, Spokane, Kalispel, Colville, and Sanpoil. The name is derived from the guardian spirit common to these ritualists and is the designation used by all.[339] Interpretation of the ritual is relatively uniform from tribe to tribe; all variants are recognized as belonging to the same pattern.

The criterion of participation is the possession of Bluejay as guardian spirit.[340] Dramatic epitomization of the mythological era is the function of the participants; some serve also as seers and pseudo-shamans and others act as sentries or sergeants-at-arms during the spirit dances. The ritual consists of assumed identification with the Bluejay character of mythological times and extreme demonstrations of this supernatural state.

The Spokane variant will serve as a type example. (I present a description in full since this is the first time it has been reported.[341]) At the time of the winter dances all persons with Bluejay "power" undergo a transformation which strips them completely of human characteristics; substituted are all the traits of the mythological being. Since the usual guise of the mythological character was similar to that of the human being today, complete identification is possible.

Clothing is discarded but a breech cloth of willow bark, from which hang twigs of fir, is worn. The face is painted black, also the hands, and the legs below the knees. During the two month period of the dances the Bluejay divides his time between performances at the dance lodges and wandering about the hills. Home contacts are completely severed; normal human associations abjured; and no food is eaten except pitch. The Bluejay's hair and ears are always full of pitch; likewise the spaces between his fingers and toes. At the dances he may be seen from time to time removing bits of this pitch and eating it. Usually he perches among the rafters at the dance lodge. He may dance with the others upon occasion but with unnatural and irregular steps. He is easily frightened; his defence is to clamber into the framework of the roof and hide. The dancers attract him to the floor again by making miniatures of various objects such as bows and arrows. These have an irresistible attraction for him; the dancers offer these objects as compensation for the services of the Bluejay in the recovery of lost objects. His clairvoyant powers toward this end are very great; it is especially easy for him to find objects which lie buried under the snow. Upon undertaking such a task he sights through a ring made of a twig. Then he leaves the dance house but returns after only a moment's absence. The brief period suffices for even the most lengthy journey he is reputed to undertake. Upon his entry the recovered object is seen fastened to a small staff which he always carries.

The Bluejay may also be employed in a pseudo-shamanistic capacity. He is capable of removing from the stomach any foreign matter unintentionally swallowed. This ability is an analogue of the (bird) bluejay's grasping power. In his brief conversations with the dancers, in connection with events such as the above, the Bluejay always says the opposite of what is meant.

Sometimes the Bluejay is absent from the dance for several days at a time. Occasionally he is seen sleeping in the branches of a tree. Even though he falls from his perch to the frozen ground he is never injured. He will "fly" back to the limbs of the tree, jump from one tree to another, and finally settle down once more.

At the end of the dance period the Bluejays must be captured and returned to the human state, else they would remain in character permanently. They resist capture until physically

---

[339] Sanpoil: *qwa'skei*; Coeur d'Alene: *qwa'sqwel*.

[340] Or Owl, among the Sanpoil.

[341] The original field data presented in this paper were obtained in the course of work sponsored by the Department of Anthropology of the University of Washington.

overcome by the dancers, who sometimes pursue them for great distances. Then the pitch is carefully removed from their bodies, and the paint likewise. Re transformation is accomplished by smudging with sweet grass or throwing wetted ginseng root upon the body.

Among the Sanpoil, Colville, and Coeur d'Alene, the pseudo-shamanism is absent. The Kalispel and Flathead, however, emphasize curing procedures even more than the Spokane. The power for such cures is inherent in the Bluejay as a mythological being; as a human being he possesses no such talent.

Emphasis upon the Bluejay as a seer is strongest among the Coeur d'Alene. His ability to find lost articles is recognized also by the Colville, Kalispel, and Spokane.

The speech inversion of the Spokane is shared by the Colville and the Flathead. Among the latter it is little used; animal sounds and gibberish are more common forms of vocalization. The Sanpoil Bluejay foregoes all speech.

Food tabus are found in all examples. The Colville Bluejay eats pitch only; the Sanpoil, dirty or contaminated food; the Kalispel, "nothing at all"; the Coeur d'Alene and Flathead observe the food tabus common to all participants in the spirit dance.

Black body paint is used by all; the perch in the rafters is another common feature. Immunity to cold weather despite lack of clothing is a universal anti-natural trait.

The Sanpoil and Coeur d'Alene Bluejays serve as sentries at the midwinter guardian spirit dances and are charged with enforcement of the formal rules of the dance procedure. This is probably true for the Spokane also, at least in former times, and perhaps for all others.

Revivification or retransformation by smudging or shamanistic treatment is practiced by all tribes.[342]

In addition to the traits mentioned above for the Flathead — traits shared with others — certain additional features characteristic of that tribe must be enumerated. With reference to the Plateau alone these aspects are unique or markedly variant, but parallels will be found in other areas.

[On the evening of the fifth day of the Flathead spirit dance] the leader returns to the center pole and shouts, "Now we shall call the Bluejays." A series of four songs is sung; during the last one the dancers utter animal cries and stamp out the fires. A great deal of noise and whistling ensues. Within two or three minutes the leader orders the fires rebuilt.... Several dancers are seen to be absent. The leader addresses the audience ... "Our Bluejays will soon be coming; don't laugh at them when they appear."

The Bluejay characters appear with faces, hands, and clothing blackened.... The characters carry miniature bows and arrows, crudely fabricated during the few moments of absence. They jump and run about erratically, climb onto the rafters of the lodge, and utter shrill, bird-like cries.... They sing a song of their own which conflicts in tempo with the dance song, and dance wildly about with no respect for order or time.

As the characters dance about they pick up small articles, such as feathers, strings, and twigs, that are found on the ground. These are secreted in the clothing. Later ... a dancer approaches the character, saying, "Friend, let me care for your property." The

---

[342] Colville references above are taken from Cline Southern Okanagon, pp. 152-153. All other data were collected by the present author. Except for the Spokane, fuller descriptions may be found in Ray The Bluejay Character, and Ray Cultural Relations, pp. 114-116; 121-122. See also Ray Culture Element Distributions, pp. 251-352.

Bluejay protests, but after repeated entreaties he gives up, one by one, the articles retrieved from the floor. As his "possessions" are diminished he circles about, faster and faster, shouting, "I'm rich; I'm rich," but meaning "I'm poor; I'm destitute." Finally, when nothing else is left, he gives up his bow and arrows. [Soon the Bluejay "dies"; he is revivified by smudging.] The black paint is washed off and he once more takes his place among the dancers. He becomes the center of attention as he tells of his "wanderings" while a Bluejay.[343]

History. The preceding descriptions show an impressive uniformity in ideology among all the variants. The Bluejay is always an adjunct of the great midwinter spirit ceremony; his character and actions epitomize the basic object of the dance, that is, contact with the supernatural world. The mythological identification is a non-volitional process to which all persons with Bluejay as guardian spirit are subject. In this role social relationships are abjured and all behavior is contrary to the nature of man.

The Flathead interpretation conforms in all respects to these ideological principles. We must look to the formal aspects of the ceremony to account for the apparent distinctiveness. Among other tribes the Bluejay is a lone performer and he initiates his own ritual activities. There may be several of these characters at one dance but each acts independently. But among the Flathead the initiative comes from the audience, the normal dancers; and the Bluejays perform as a group. The sequence of activities conforms to a stable pattern. In no other tribe can the specific performances of the Blue-jays be predicted prior to the dance. All the activities of the Flathead performer takes place in or near the dance lodge; the peregrinations of others carry them far afield. But the Flathead Bluejay nevertheless "tells of his wanderings" after he has been returned to normal. This suggests that the formal pattern of performance has been imposed upon or has grown out of a less rigid procedure, such as that of tribes characterized by actual wanderings.

The Flathead version not only differs in ritual character but also in numerous details, for example, the retrieval of small objects from the dance floor. There are no parallels for these traits in other ceremonies of the Plateau. But since the Flathead is the easternmost of Plateau tribes we may anticipate the appearance of analogues to the east. Also the ceremonial rigidity proves to be a reflection of the Plains pattern.

Among other Plateau tribes, ritual variables which appear to be of significance are the curing role, the use of reverse speech, and the clairvoyant powers.

The Bluejay is never a shaman. In the three tribes, Flathead, Kalispel, and Spokane, where he practices curing, his pseudo-shamanistic abilities are limited to the period of the dance, that is, the period of his identification with the mythological being. His techniques are restricted in like manner. Techniques and emphases differ in the three tribes; all have neighbors who do not delegate curing power to the Bluejay. Only local differences of interpretation seem to be involved.

Are any historical clues to be found in the distribution of the use of inverted speech and the emphasis placed thereon? The Colville, Spokane, and Flathead share this trait. The Flathead use it least although they are nearest the Plains where the practice is common. However, this lack of emphasis may merely be the result of greater play given to the use of animal sounds. Human speech is used but rarely. At the opposite extreme, geographically, are the Sanpoil whose Bluejay characters do not; speak at all. This speech silence is thought to be in keeping with the ritual character. We may conclude that a choice must be made between simulation of

---

[343] Ray Cultural Relations, pp. 121-122.

the non-human mythological being by inversion of normal speech or by silence, gibberish, or animal cries. All tribes were acquainted with all techniques; each chose selectively.

The recovery of lost objects by means of clairvoyant powers (Colville, Coeur d'Alene, Kalispel) appears to be a borrowing from the widespread conjuring ritual which was shared by the Kutenai, Lakes, and Colville of the Plateau. Such recovery is often the primary object of the conjuring seance. Only the Colville share the two ceremonies; in their hands the typical conjuring talent was added to the Bluejay complex. The adjacent Spokane accepted this enrichment of the old ceremony; in turn it was borrowed by the Coeur d'Alene. The Kalispel adopted the innovation in limited and rationalized form. Only those articles consisting of animal organic matter can be found; for example, a fur robe, not a tule mat. The new trait did not reach the Flathead; it was rejected by the Sanpoil. Since it has been demonstrated that the conjuring ceremony reached the Plateau at a late date, it follows that the recovery talent is a recent addition to the Bluejay complex.[344]

The possibility that the Bluejay ritual itself is a recent innovation must be considered. The boundaries of the distribution are sharply defined. This might be explained on the east in terms of the basic Plateau-Plains boundary. But on the west the Southern Okanogan do not practice the ritual although they are a typical Plateau people. Nor do the Lakes, north of the Colville. These breaks could be understood if the ceremony had diffused westward at a recent time and hence failed to reach these outlying tribes. But there is no evidence within the Plateau of a westward diffusion. The easternmost tribe, the Flathead, exhibits the least typical ceremony. Furthermore, we know that both the Southern Okanogan and the Lakes are familiar with all the details of the Bluejay complex; in fact they often observe the ritual when visiting their neighbors, the Colville and Sanpoil, and are able to describe the ceremonies in detail.[345] They insist that the rituals are of immemorial age. They explain that they have not adopted the practices because they do not care for rituals of such extreme character.

Such evidence does not prove great age but does dispose of the suggestion of recent westward diffusion. Since there is no internal evidence of foreign origin we may ask whether a local point of origin is suggested. The answer is negative. It must be remembered that the area concerned is relatively small, the cultures homogeneous, and the people well acquainted with the practices of their neighbors. All share the mythological background which furnishes the ideological basis for the Bluejay concept.[346] Under such circumstances it is probably presumptuous to look for a locale of origin; it seems obvious that all tribes would have participated in the building of the complex. Our distributional analyses support this view.

It will be noted that the tribes of the Canadian Plateau did not accept the Bluejay ritual. This is one more example of the general subareal distinction between the northern and southern Plateau.[347] This may also account for the absence among the Southern Okanogan. Their connections with the Canadian Plateau are stronger than those of any other tribe of the southern area.

The Buffoon

Description. As indicated earlier, contrary behavior often results in humorous performances. We saw that the Flathead must caution their dance audiences not to laugh at the

---

[344] See Ray Historic Backgrounds of the Conjuring Complex.
[345] Cf. Cline Southern Okanagon, p. 152.
[346] Cf. Ray Bluejay Character, pp. 593-595.
[347] Cf. Ray Cultural Relations, pp. 147-148.

Bluejay. In the complex we are now to examine no such prohibition exists. Although the performers receive their powers through religious channels, and serve as shamans, their ludicrous anti-natural behavior is occasion for merriment. Through exploitation of this phase, the complex differs from all others in the contrary behavior sphere. A psychological affinity with the clown of the Southwest is apparent, but historical linkage is doubtful.

The Buffoon role is taken by the contra-natural characters of the Plains Ojibwa, Plains Cree, Assiniboin, Crow, Oglala, and possibly Blackfoot and Canadian Dakota — all northern Plains tribes. The first three use variants of the same term for designation; the Crow name is unrelated; the others are unknown.[348]

The criteria for this grouping are: participation by those experiencing a dream or vision of a specific supernatural being, usually "Skeleton" or "Cannibal"; the function is to provide amusement by performing in anti-natural and ludicrous manner; the ritual is a masked dance in which the performer is absurdly anti-natural both in costuming and in his actions.

As a type example we may select the Plains Ojibwa cult. Those who dream of the Skeleton Being gain the right (and perhaps the duty) of performing as buffoons. Their activities include masquerading in absurd costumes and the healing of the sick by exorcism. The costume consists of ragged shirt, leggings, and moccasins together with a cloth mask, sometimes conical, provided with an elongated nose and narrow eye slits. Crude staffs are carried, from which hang pieces of cloth, owl feathers, and deer dew hoofs. A bone whistle is used. Upon occasions the buffoon gathers followers, for whom he prepares costumes, and all live together in a special tent. During such times food is obtained by canvassing the camp for offerings which others hang outside their tipis.

The offerings are stalked in ludicrous fashion. The clown crawls until at very close range, then crouches, draws his bow and shoots at the gift. If the arrow misses its mark the party moves on without claiming the food. However, the arrow may be retrieved and broken. But if it strikes the meat the performers rush frantically to the food, smell the point of the arrow and gesticulate wildly. Upon reaching their own lodge the food is thrown through the smoke hole, never carried through the door. No attempt is made to recover food which misses the smoke hole.

These buffoons are called to treat illness diagnosed as spirit intrusion. The whole troop participates; the treatment involves dancing", shaking of rattles, singing, and whistling. Their grotesque and fantastic actions are presumed to frighten away the offending spirits.

Throughout all of their activities these clowns use inverted speech.[349]

The Plains Cree buffoons correspond closely to those of the Ojibwa. Warfare is included in the activities of both groups. These ventures, which are of brief duration, are conducted on a pattern resembling the dance. Bison hunting is similarly pursued by the Cree. Formalized caricature includes dancing up to the enemy, and dancing fearfully around the fallen buffalo. The Cree leader drafts followers by surreptitiously entering- a lodge and pointing his staff at any man present. Costumes include one which produces the effect of a great hump on the back.[350]

The Assiniboin buffoons are hardly to be distinguished from those of the two preceding

---

[348] Plains Ojibwa: *windigokan* (Skinner, Political Organization, p. 500); Plains Cree: *wetigokan* (Skinner *op. cit*, p. 528), *wihlikokan*, "cannibal-like," (Mandelbaum The Plains Cree, p. 274); Assiniboin: *wi"tgogax* (Lowie The Assiniboine, p. 62); Crow: *akbi'arusacarica*, "woman-impersonator" (Lowie Military Societies, p. 207).

[349] Skinner, Political Organization, pp. 500-505.

[350] Skinner *op. cit*, pp. 528-529; Mandelbaum The Plains Cree, pp. 274-375.

tribes. Followers are drafted as among the Cree. Only one variation of critical significance appears: the Assiniboin clowns apparently lack curing functions of any kind.[351]

Among the Crow, details vary somewhat and organization differs. Supernatural sponsorship is apparently unnecessary. Curing practices are unknown. Ludicrous antics on horseback and absurd dances form the core of the procedures. Food is not stalked but bows of willow are used to shoot harmless arrows to "frighten" spectators. A clown masquerading as a pregnant woman plays an important role, and sex play is emphasized. Reverse speech is not used.[352]

Scanty information from the Blackfoot indicates the presence of a clownish character who dresses in a long black robe and black paint, if not a mask. Like the Crow clown, he rides a horse but the nature of his performance is not known.[353]

The Oglala recognize a kind of cult known as the Dogs. Members possess spiritual power but act foolishly and perform to make observers laugh. They wear absurd clothing, peculiar ornaments, and body paint.[354]

The Canadian Dakota, formerly of the Wahpeton division, consider the clown to be the most powerful of shamans. He derives his ability from the guardian spirit "Clown" but is also associated with Thunder. His role is predestined before birth.[355]

History. Plains Ojibwa, Plains Cree, and Assiniboin variants exhibit an impressive degree of identity. All three conform to all criteria for this group but the Ojibwa and Cree versions are the more complex. They function more significantly in the total cultures since an important curing role is involved as well as clowning. Since the Assiniboin not only lack the curing function but also lack the Siouan name, using instead a corruption of the Algonkin term, we may assume that they borrowed the complex from their northern or eastern neighbors. The stalking of a slaughtered bison and the method of drafting followers are common to the Assiniboin and Cree but do not extend to the Ojibwa. This suggests that the Siouans borrowed directly from the Cree.

Although the Assiniboin lack the curing rule, participation does depend upon the possession of spiritual dream power. The specific interpretation of the Algonkins, Skeleton, or Cannibal power, gives way to the more Plains-like concept of Owl or Crow sponsorship. One step farther west, among the Crow, the supernatural feature is absent or at least unreported. To this extent the Crow practices fail to conform to the type criteria. Only if historical linkage can be demonstrated are we justified in including them. Similarities are numerous: ragged costumes including a cloth mask are worn; the leader enlists his followers; foolish and clumsy antics characterize the dancers; a circuit of the camp is made; bows and arrows are used in an unnatural manner to furnish amusement for the audience. The performance is a closer approach to pure clowning than that of any other Plains tribe. As such it is distinctly non-Plains like in character. None of the immediate Plains neighbors of the Crow share the practice.[356] Hence this clown ritual is either an innovation by the Crow or a remnant of the Algonkin buffoon complex. The latter alternative seems

---

[351] Lowie The Assiniboine, pp. 62-66.

[352] Lowie Military Societies, pp. 207-211.

[353] McClintock The Old North Trail, pp. 291-292.

[354] Wissler Societies and Ceremonial Organizations, p. 99.

[355] Wallis Sun Dance of the Canadian Dakota, pp. 324-325.

[356] With the possible exception of the Blackfoot, whose clown-like performer is too meagerly described to justify comparative interpretations. See above.

more probable in the light of the parallels and the distribution. The Crow adopted only the clowning phase of the foreign ritual; they received this, apparently, via the Assiniboin.[357]

The place of the Oglala in this picture is uncertain because of insufficient data. Apparently the quality of the ritual is about the equal of the Assiniboin, which might be anticipated if the ceremony were received directly from the Plains Ojibwa. We know that spiritual power is a prerequisite. The Oglala consider the ritual a very ancient one; without further evidence this belief is suggestive only.

In the fragmentary data on the Canadian Dakota appears the significant statement that the buffoon is a powerful shaman. This is a specific linkage with the Algonkin tribes.

The Heyoka

Description. All the Dakota divisions practice an anti-natural ritual known as the *Heyoka*. The adjacent Ponca also have a version of the ceremony which is known by the same name. In this complex the emphasis is placed upon the contrary behavior of the participants rather than upon the derived clowning. Indeed, the name itself means "anti-natural".[358]

Those experiencing a supernatural vision involving Thunder or Lightning participate in the ritual; the performance of feats of supernatural and anti-natural character, together with buffoonery incidental thereto, is the function of the participants; the ritual focus is the withdrawing of pieces of meat from pots of boiling water with the bare hands.

Among the Eastern Dakota, participation follows an unsought dream of Thunder or Lightning, lest calamity befall the dreamer. The common dream experience is the only group tie; no society is recognized. The *Heyoka* ceremony includes much that is contrary to nature or custom but the most spectacular is that of plunging the arms into a container of boiling water and removing pieces of meat which have been cooked therein. At the same time the dancer splashes the hot water over his bare back, all the while complaining that it is cold. In preparation for these feats the arms are rubbed with a certain grass or covered with a root which is chewed and blown upon the skin. At other times the *Heyoka* parade through the camp performing in a clownish manner, or enter other dances and act in typical fashion. The costume exhibits numerous variations, including: near-nakedness, with strange body painting; ragged raiment together with a black cloth masking the face; tall conical hats; bark hats; simulated baldness with a bladder and white powder covering the head. Crooked sticks are used as bows; straw serves for arrows. Contrary speech is not used except among the Wahpeton.

---

[357] Lowie is of the opinion that the Assiniboin, generally, were not to any extent originators or disseminators (Plains Indian Age-Societies, p. 912). Perhaps that is why the ritual reached the Crow in abbreviated form. In any event the assumption of westward diffusion is strengthened. Cf. Lowie, loc. cit.

[358] J.R Walker slates that "the term heyoka applies to any being who acts anti-natural." Mrs Eastman speaks of "haoka, the anti-natural god." (Both statements quoted by Wissler Societies and Ceremonial Associations, p. 84.) Referring to the Dakota generally, Lowie writes that "everywhere the idea seems to be uppermost that the performers imitate some supernatural being or beings acting in a way contrary to [88] nature and custom, so that possibly heyoka should he construed as a generic term covering all who indulge in such activity.... Backward speech was called *heyoka eyapi* ..." (Dance Associations, pp. 113-114).

The mythological associations of *Heyoka* are complex. Apparently four or more personifications are recognized: a two-faced man with a bow streaked with red lightning and a deer hoof rattle; a man with enormous ears and a yellow bow; a man with a flute; a whirlwind. These are sometimes visualized as giants, sometimes as dwarfs.

The *Heyoka* possess great supernatural power and it appears that their activities are essentially serious and are accepted as such.[359]

Oglala practices vary but slightly. The supernatural association with Thunder and the ability to withstand the heat of boiling water are similar. Mythological interpretation differs somewhat. Power is conveyed by a vision of the Winged God or any of several spirits which may come from that god. This god, whose symbol is a zig-zag red line, is endowed with an exceptional degree of supernatural power. Even so, the role of *Heyoka* is a dreaded one; the position brings little esteem but many inconveniences.[360]

An obscure sentence in an account given by an Oglala *Heyoka* may be of critical importance; "There are two kinds of *heyoka*, one kind is crazy or foolish.".[361] This suggests that the clowning activities are appurtenances, not basic to the concept. The presence or absence of the trait is doubtless determined by the character of the dream. The variation in dress is apparently the consequence of differences in dream experiences also. since the individual patterns his costume on that of the supernatural donor.

The Ponca *Heyoka* are meagerly described but the pattern is familiar. The source of power is a dream, meat is removed from boiling water, the water is poured on the body and backward speech is used.[362]

History. Our information on the *Heyoka* offers no obvious clues with reference to local origins, except that there seems no reason to doubt that the Ponca borrowed the ceremony from the Dakota. The Ponca version is apparently the simpler and plays a lesser role in ceremonial structure than the Dakota counterpart. Skinner suggests that the Teton were the specific donors.[36329]

The Ponca and Wahpeton use reverse speech; other groups do not. The latter fact may appear strange in view of the marked anti-natural character of the *Heyoka*. But other forms of vocal expression of a contrary character are present. Each Oglala ritualist has a special song but this is sung in company with others, resulting in a confusion of voices and consequent unintelligibility. Also, the Oglala performer is expected to make witty remarks when participating. This is hardly consistent with reversal of speech. We do not know the type of wit which is expected but may surmise that it is specialized in character — akin perhaps to that found in the mythology — in keeping with the supernatural role of the performer.

In making comparisons and reconstructions it must be remembered that a wide range is permitted the *Heyoka* in actions and dress. The individual derives his pattern from his personal spiritual experience. These experiences all conform to the cultural criteria (Thunder symbolism; power and compulsion to perform unnatural acts, including the boiling water performance) but vary widely in details. This latitude is so definitely organic to the complex that any step toward greater formalization gives the impression of recency and superficiality. Thus even reverse

---

[359] Lowie Dance Associations, pp. 113-117; Dorsey, Study of Siouan Cults, pp. 468-471; Neill, Dakota Land, p. 268.

[360] Wissler Societies and Ceremonial Associations, pp. 82-85; Dorsey, loc. cit.

[361] Wissler *op. cit*, p. 83.

[362] Skinner Ponca Societies, p. 789.

[363] Ibid.

speech, since it is a restrictive formalism, may be a late innovation. Likewise, the role of ceremonial clown is surely artificial and recent. Some reports of ceremonies make no mention of clowning, but rather present pictures of profoundly serious ritualism.[364] Even in the narrative of an Oglala informant who classes himself as a "crazy or foolish" type, the only mention of buffoonery is "joking with each other." Walker, on the other hand, states that the *Heyoka* "act the buffoon in all their helping, doing the opposite of what should be done, jesting, or doing anything which may be comical," and they are "expected to act the clown all the time"; further, "this feast is a hilarious occasion for all the people who attend it." But in the same account it is explained that if one experiences a *Heyoka* vision he must conform to the instructions or he will experience misfortune and perhaps even death. The *Heyoka* "is more or less shunned and is apt to become morose and melancholy and spend much of his time alone." He "may even be advised to kill a man, woman or child, in which case he must obey.... "[365] Recalling the statement that there are two types of *Heyoka*, one of which is foolish, we may conclude that the buffoonery is characteristic of the complex only when derived from the spirit experience and expressed individually. It is not a criterion of identity nor a part of the basic ritualism.

It is true that the boiling water and meat performance is itself a rigid formalization of contrary behavior; that here there is no latitude since all must perform this act. This is, indeed, the one ritualistic device unifying the variants of the *Heyoka*. The trick is not exclusive to the *Heyoka*, as we shall see later. But only in the *Heyoka* is it found uniformly associated with the types of participation and function reviewed above. Wissler suggests that whatever group first made the meat withdrawing trick the core of the contrary behavior ritualism was, by virtue of that fact, the originator of the *Heyoka*. But evidence on this point is lacking if we limit ourselves to the present ceremony and its distribution. The two adequately known versions, Oglala and Eastern Dakota, are equivalents in this respect. Wissler introduces broader distributional data before reaching his conclusion, which is that the Eastern Dakota were the originators.[366] We shall return to this question later.

The *Heyoka* is certainly not a shamanistic or curing cult. But Pond refers to "inflicting and healing diseases, especially those resulting from the gratification of their libidinous passions".[367] Although ambiguous, this statement indicates that these pseudo-shamanistic powers are limited in scope. This is apparently an individual or local variant. The Canadian Dakota, however, class their *Heyoka* as powerful shamans. Furthermore, the spiritual power is derived from "Clown." These highly atypical features indicate marked revision of the concept at this outlying point, doubtless through influence of the Buffoon complex which flourishes in that area.

Graded Societies

The contrary behavior rituals so far considered are not societies in the sense in which the term is commonly used with reference to Plains Indian ceremonialism. The fixed organization of the association type, with initiations, officers, membership structure and the like, is not found in any of the above. However, contrary behavior is present in the true societies, both the age

---

[364] e.g, Mrs Eastman's account (quoted in Lowie Dance Associations, pp. 115-116), and the various accounts, original and quoted, in Dorsey, *op. cit.*

[365] Wissler *op. cit*; pp. 83-85.

[366] Wissler General Discussion, p. 861.

[367] Quoted in Dorsey Siouan Cults, p. 469.

graded and the ungraded. The graded type is present among the Mandan, Hidatsa, Arapaho, Aa'ni Atsina, and Blackfoot. All utilize anti-natural behavior as a ritual characteristic of one or another society grade.

Mandan. In this tribe the Crazy Dog society exhibits anti-natural behavior by treading on fire and removing meat from boiling water. In recent times the society has been fourth in the graded series; earlier it may have been first (lowest).[368] Maximilian states that the dance was purchased from the Arikara by the Hidatsa and shared by the Mandan.

> A large fire is kindled on the occasion, and a quantity of live coals is scattered on the ground, about which the young men dance, quite naked and barefooted. The hands, and the lower parts of the arms, and the feet and ankles, are painted red. A kettle, with meat cut in small pieces, is hung over the fire; and when the meat is done they plunge their hands into the boiling water, take out the meat, and eat it, at the risk of scalding themselves.[369]

Hidatsa. The description above was attributed by Maximilian to the Hidatsa as well as the Mandan. The informants of Maximilian and Lowie disagree as to whether the Hidatsa version falls in the graded or ungraded categories. The information furnished by Lowie's informant pertains to the independent society and will be presented later.[370]

The Hidatsa Crazy Dog society is wholly distinct from the above. Members exhibit no contrary behavior.[371]

The Real Dogs practice contrary behavior in some but not all phases of their ceremonies. Inverted speech is used and others are expected to address them in like manner. Inverted action is practiced as a derivative of the speech pattern. Thus if one inadvertently speaks in normal fashion to a Real Dog he will nevertheless do the opposite of what is requested. Another form of unnatural behavior is the ceremonial practice of embracing women at random regardless of closeness of kinship. The Real Dogs also perform the meat and boiling water ritual. At least one member is known to have traveled naked during the winter "to prove that he was a Real Dog." Sacred objects are shown no respect and proprieties are disregarded. The howling of dogs is imitated, especially before singing. The characteristic body paint is red.[372]

Arapaho. The third dance of the Arapaho graded series involves contrary actions of various types, but only during the latter half of a six day ceremony. The transformation to the anti-human state is attribute to the owl feather head bands of the dancers; when these are not worn actions are normal. The circlets have a small bit of root, probably the wild parsnip, attached. Likewise an arrow which is carried has this root fastened near the point. Paralysis may be inflicted by the touch of this arrow, it is believed; the affliction may be cured by rubbing the patient with the headband.

The elaborate ceremonialism includes shooting arrows at a bison chip and shouting and

---

[368] Maximilian's data place the society first in the series; Lowie's, fourth (Maximilian Travels, vol. 23, p. 296; Lowie Societies of the Hidatsa, pp. 306-309).
[369] Maximilian loc. cit.
[370] Lowie *op. cit*; p. 252.
[371] *Idem* pp. 280-282.
[372] *Idem* pp. 284-290.

jumping toward it. A fire dance concludes the activities of the third day; the participants trample on the fire with bare feet until it is extinguished. During the three following days the dancers act in a most foolish and extravagant fashion; they are permitted to engage in all manner of mischief. Contrary actions and contrary speech are characteristic. Animal and bird antics are imitated. A dancer climbs a lodge pole and sits bird-like on top of the tent. Other dancers shoot at him, aiming their arrows backward over their shoulders, whereupon the performer falls down, rolls over, and lies as dead.

The dancers wear red robes and on the final day of the ceremony cover their bodies with soot. One performer of higher rank and distinctive dress is recognized. This is the "white fool," so named because his cape and body are painted white.[373]

Thunder symbolism is encountered in the Arapaho second dance, where it is associated with the fierce temperament of the dancer of the highest degree.[374]

Aa'ni Atsina. The *Aa'ni* contrary dance conforms closely to the Arapaho pattern, but ranks second in the graded series- The fire dance is similar. Dancers show contrary traits only during the second half of the ceremonial period but it is not certain that their owl feather headbands are the effective agents. Paralysis is caused and cured; the root is identified as wild parsnip. Arrows are shot in the air so that they will fall within the crowd; supposedly they hit no one. Ceremonial seizure of moccasins is practiced. Inverted speech is used.[375]

Blackfoot. Anti-natural behavior plays a very slight role in Blackfoot ceremonies. The Piegan Mosquito imitates his namesake at one point in the dance by scratching others. In this activity instructions are interpreted in reverse but apparently the dancers do not themselves speak inversely. The Blood Mosquitoes, in addition, use tipi covers turned inside out in the construction of their transfer ceremony lodge.[376]

The Blackfoot Braves cast away moccasins, use inverted speech, and pretend to shoot arrows into the crowd, but the many other features of the ceremony lack contrary significance.[377]

Discussion. The Mandan and Hidatsa Crazy Dog societies are not only alike in name but are equated with respect to form and content by Lowie. Yet one, the Mandan, practices the boiling water and meat trick in typical form while in the other it is absent altogether. On the other hand, the Hidatsa do know and utilize the performance, in fact in two separate rituals. One is the graded Dog society where one or more officers. Real Dogs, are the actors; the other is the Hot Dance, which is probably ungraded. In the former the trick is a ritual incidental; in the latter it plays a central role.

The Mandan almost certainly borrowed the idea from the Hidatsa. Maximilian states that this is so and the Mandan distribution is restricted to one village. Furthermore, it seems reasonable to assume that if the Mandan Crazy Dog society had been the source of borrowing by the Hidatsa, the latter would have introduced the trick into their own Crazy Dog ritual, which lacks it.

The fact that the boiling water trick is geographically limited among the Mandan supports the above view and at the same time indicates a late reception. Likewise, the failure of the

---

[373] Kroeber The Arapaho, pp. 188-196.
[374] *Idem* pp. 168-169.
[375] Kroeber Ethnology of the Gros Ventre {*Aa'ni*}, pp. 241-250.
[376] Wissler Societies and Dance Associations, pp. 376-377, 409; cf. p. 120.
[377] *Idem* pp. 377-382; McClintock The Old North Trail, pp. 462-464.

Mandan Crazy Dog innovation to react on the homologous Hidatsa ritual indicates a brief history.

The Arapaho and Aa'ni Atsina parallels are extensive, as is to be expected in view of the former unity of the tribes. Even so, the societies occupy different grade levels and differ considerably in ceremonial organization apart from the contrary behavior phase, which occupies only half the ceremonial period. During that half, however, the contrary concept dominates all behavior, numerous specific traits are identical, and ritual interpretations are similar.

The Blackfoot graded societies exhibit mere isolated Fragments of contrary behavior. The Blackfoot Mosquito society is said to have been derived from the Sarsi society of the same name but contrary action is not mentioned for the latter.[378] The particular interpretation of Mosquito contrariness, reverse compliance with instructions, is found among the Hidatsa Real Dogs, from whence the suggestion may have come.

The only feature common to all expressions of contrary behavior among the graded societies is the type of organization involved. The particular societies differ and the ritual utilization of anti-natural devices varies. Only one pair of rituals can be said to be unified in both content and structure, the Arapaho and Aa'ni Atsina. In all other cases the diffusion of the societies has proceeded quite independently of the diffusion of the contrary concept. For example, it was demonstrated above that the meat trick of the Mandan Crazy Dogs was borrowed from the Hidatsa. But the society itself was originated by the Mandan and transmitted to the Hidatsa, as Lowie has shown.[379]

We may therefore discard the hypothesis that the graded society has served as a unit of diffusion of the contrary behavior pattern.

Fire Rituals

The Hot Dance. Among several tribes the ceremony which utilizes the meat and boiling water trick is known as the Hot Dance. Manipulation of other heated objects and handling of fire are also involved, but no other form of contrary behavior is practiced.

The Hot Dancers of the Hidatsa perform the hot water and meat trick after protecting their arms and hands with a plant substance which is mascerated by chewing and then applied. Dancers pretend to strike the kettle as they approach it. When the hot meat is withdrawn it is thrown upon a piece of hide prepared for the purpose. Sometimes a piece is placed on another member's back "by way of joking." A dance upon live coals is also performed. Other ceremonial procedures include the lighting of pipes with hot embers carried in the mouth, and the presentation of the pipe to the four quarters when dancing and singing. Various kinds of body painting are used, including red lightning lines on legs, arms, and chest. The origin myth attributes the dance to Raven.[380]

In the dance of the Arikara the withdrawing of meat from the pot is conceived as analogous to meeting and defeating the enemy, albeit at the cost of injuries. The dancers approach the fire, retreat, then rush back and remove the meat. It is said that they are imitating animals. The medicine is applied after the burns are suffered. It is probably the same plant as that used by others since it is chewed before use. Hot water is splashed on one another by the

---

[378] Goddard Dancing Societies, p. 467.
[379] Lowie Plains Indian Age-Societies, pp. 942-944.
[380] Lowie Societies of the Hidatsa and Mandan, pp. 253-253.

dancers as they remove the meat, which is carried on the shoulders and given to the ceremonial "fathers".[381]

In the Iowa version the society members prepare for the ritual by sweating and singing. The songs refer to the supernatural donors of the fraternity's powers. The dancers then proceed from lodge to lodge, in each of which a pot of boiling meat awaits them. When withdrawn the meat is given to the spectators. No reference is made to the use of a protective herb. The nickname of the society, "coal grabbers," suggests that performances with fire are observed also.[382]

The meat withdrawing trick is mentioned in the origin myth of the Oglala Omaha or Grass dance.[383] It is also found in the *Wabano* of the Ojibwa. The significance of these occurrences will be discussed later. We must now examine the elaborate Pawnee society.

The Pawnee Iruska. This society is a powerful organization which "originally" consisted of leaders of the various animal medicine societies. Apparently no concern with fire was involved until a certain member, through lonely vigils, achieved an elaborate supernatural experience. The following excerpts from the story of his vision and subsequent activities present only the most pertinent data:

The leader [of the supernatural beings which Crow-feather, the Pawnee, met in his vision] said to him, "Brother, you have been wandering over the hills for some time. We heard your cries and were sad and agreed to pity you and give you a new dance. You will call this dance *iruska* (fire inside of all things)....

A bucket of water rested on the fire. The men now began to sing while four of them rose and danced, holding corn husks in their right hands. They danced around the fire toward the bucket of water. They pretended to be attacking an enemy. Finally, they dipped the corn husks in the boiling water and swung them against Crow-feather, scalding him. When the people noticed that he paid no attention to his burns, they shouted, trying to frighten him that way. This too was of no avail. They seized him and held him over the fire. He screamed but they held him and rolled him in the hot coals. After a time he ceased his clamor for he no longer felt the pain. Finally they took him back to his place.

Another song was sung and all the men around the fire attacked it, now charging it and now retreating. During the third charge. Crow-feather noticed that the screaming and grunting was as of birds and animals. At the fourth charge, he saw that the dancers were imitating animals and birds. As they moved hastily toward the fire he saw each one drop something into it. They turned quickly: some flew away in the shape of eagles, turkeys, and crows, and others ran away as deer, wolves, and dogs.

[Later a stranger appeared to Crow-feather.] "Now I will show you the herbs and roots you must rub on your body when you dance; also the kind of wood you are to use in your fire.... Before the root is rubbed on the body, it should be put in a wooden bowl filled with water in which four live coals have been placed. Dip some of this up with a small buffalo horn spoon and put it in a wooden bowl and it is ready for use. If an enemy should attack your village do not mix the medicine in a bowl, chew some of the root, take it in your hands, and rub them on a kettle that is covered with soot and then

---

[381] Lowie Societies of the Arikara, pp. 668-669.
[382] Skinner Societies of the Iowa, pp. 702-703.
[383] Wissler Societies and Ceremonial Associations, p. 49.

rub the soot on your joints. You will have no tear of the enemy's fire. If anyone is burned by fire or scalded, chew some of the root and place it upon the affected part and the cure will be immediate. ..."

Crow-feather went home. Several days later he determined to see whether the medicinemen understood the fire. He built a sweat lodge.... In the center he built a fireplace. He put the stones on the fire. When the stones were red hot he sent a messenger to invite eight medicinemen....

"Brothers, I invited you into this sweat lodge for I have heard of your wonderful doings in the medicine lodge. I brought the timber which now stands over you; I gathered up your grandfathers who were seated upon mother earth and now they are ready to blow their hot breath upon us. The water is before us. We are seated in a dark place. Each one of you prepare yourselves, for no one must leave because of the heat. We are now imitating animals and birds. ..."

The people began to hold medicine ceremonies during which sleight-of-hand tricks were performed. One night the crow imitators performed. They built a fire and put a large stone on it. When it was red hot they put it on the ground and each man stood on the stone....

[Several months later Crow-feather prepared his tipi for a great ceremony. All those who wished to be initiated came at the appointed time.] Then the candidates were received one by one. The first one who came was told to bathe in the preparation made ready by Crow-feather. When he was ready, he was taken to the fireplace and forcibly placed on the fire....

[On the next day the ceremony was continued.] Crow-feather said, "Now we will begin our dance; the assistants may make a big fire, cut the dried meat and have the brass kettle ready." When everything was prepared he put a new knife in the bottom of the kettle, added water and then the meat....

Finally Crow-feather danced up to the kettle which was full of boiling soup and took a piece of meat out with his bare hands. He gave it to one of the spectators who burned his hands with it. The rest of the members also did this....

This was the first ceremony of this kind.[384]

Historical Relations

The *Iruska* account to my mind provides conclusive evidence for the solution of several fundamental problems, which may be considered as the first step in a general discussion of larger historical relationships. Those relating to the anti-natural treading on fire and the meat and hot water trick may be considered here.

The meat withdrawing performance is shown to be a minor and nonessential feature of the Pawnee ceremony. It is not mentioned in that portion of the narrative which recounts the numerous manifestations of the fire handling power as exhibited by the supernatural beings. It is described in the historical sequel as an innovation of the Pawnee, Crow-feather. It is quite possible that the postscript was added, not several months later as in the recorded versions, but at an indefinitely later time determined by the actual invention or reception of the specific trait. I am assuming that the body of the narrative represents a roughly correct picture of the more

---

[384] Murie Pawnee Indian Societies, pp. 608-616.

ancient practices involving the handling of fire. This does not mean that the Pawnee invented these procedures. Fire handling of the types described is far more widespread than the whole of the contrary concept. But it is highly probable that the Pawnee were the most effective organizers of these practices in the area under survey and that the ritual complex was more or less widely distributed in the region before the particular trick with meat was invented; furthermore, that the elaborate and well integrated ceremony of the Pawnee exerted considerable influence in the area. Most of the regional fire dances which show a logical complex of features may be safely assumed to have been derived from the Pawnee. For example, the Arikara dance involves identification of the performance with meeting the enemy, mimicry of animals, and the application of the medicine as a curative agent. The Hidatsa carry hot embers in the mouth, pretend to strike the kettle, and dance on glowing embers. The Iowa ritual includes sweating, songs of the supernatural donors, and probably the handling of live coals. None of these exhibits any other type of contrary behavior; in fact the performance itself is not considered contrary in nature. There is no complaining that the water is cold, no reverse talk, and no buffoonery.

All of the tribes just mentioned practice the meat withdrawal trick but this fact has not been utilized in the analysis because of the suggested recency of the trait and the certainty that it has diffused, at least in part, independently of the *Iruska* complex. Its presence in the Hidatsa Real Dogs' ritual is an example. More impressive is the occurrence in the Wabano ceremonies of the Ojibwa and Cree. Skinner attributes the Wabano to the Menomini, Sauk, Potawatomi, Ottawa, Ojibwa, and Cree. According to the Menomini the name means "men of the dawn" or designates the god Morningstar. "Just at dawn he stands master of the day. He has an enormous mouth, and when the world is in danger he opens it and takes in the whole earth with all its inhabitants to guard it." Men who dream of this god become shamans of great clairvoyant powers. Among the Parry Island Ojibwa (Georgian Bay, Lake Huron), the *wabano* are specialists in plant medicines, the most talented and powerful of three classes of herbalists. The powers possessed are associated with "the twilight that precedes the dawn," but must be acquired by fasting, supernatural experiences, and apprenticeship to old doctors. The supernatural talents and botanical knowledge thus gained enable the *wabano* to cure the sick and to perform marvelous feats.

> At intervals it is customary [for the Menomini shamans] to give a public performance and exhibition of their power. At such times the *wabano* provides a feast of deer or bear meat for his guests, and, after the proper ceremony and songs, he chews up certain medicines and sprays them on his hands and arms. He then has the ability to handle fire, or plunge his naked arms into boiling water or maple syrup. He will hold up one finger, and, as he dances in a circle it will appear to blaze. He is also said to be able to eat fire and to blow it from his mouth. Sometimes a wabano will spray his whole body with medicine and then apparently setting himself on fire, dance about blazing; yet he is never burnt. Often a wabano will hold a glowing brand in each hand, and never be scorched.[385]

It will be noted that there is no mention in Skinner's account of the specific meat withdrawing trick.

Likewise, in Hoffman's Menomini descriptions the wabano applies chewed root to the

---

[385] Skinner Associations and Ceremonies, pp. 191-192.

skin and handles fire but does not remove meat from the pot.

This feast is given at night; singing and dancing are boisterously indulged in, and the wabeno, to sustain his reputation, entertains his visitors with a further exhibition of his skill. Through the use of plants he is alleged to be enabled to take up and handle with impunity red-hot stones and burning brands, and without evincing the slightest discomfort it is said that he will bathe his hands in boiling water, or even in boiling sirup. On account of such performances, the general impression prevails among the Indians that the wabeno is a "dealer in fire," or a "fire handler." Such exhibitions always terminate at the approach of day.

The wabeno is believed to appear at times in the guise of various animals.... [386]

The Parry Island Ojibwa definitely include meat removal in their procedure.

At intervals in the dances one of the medicine-men might drum and dance alone around the fire, then, stooping, pick up from the embers a hot stone; or he might dip his fingers into a boiling cauldron, extract a piece of meat, and swallow it without evidence of pain. Some Indians say that he derives these powers from the medicines he rubbed on his hands.... [387]

These Algonkin observances constitute a distinctive fire ritual complex with significant historical implications. Before pursuing these implications, however, it is essential that we ascertain the specific role that the meat withdrawing trick has played in its various contexts.

Skinner implies that all the central Algonkins practice the trick.

The Sauk,[388] the Parry Islanders far to the east of the Menomini, and the Dakota to the west, make use of the device. John Tanner mentions it for the Ojibwa.[389] We may conclude that the Menomini and other central Algonkins do know and occasionally use this particular trick. But for them it is not a distinct element of the fire ritualism. It is merely one of the variable interpretations of fire handling, a device which may be used at the option of the ritualist. He may handle hot rocks or hot coals; he may set fire to his finger or his body; he may plunge his arm into water or syrup — in the case of water he may remove meat if it be there, and if it occurs to him to do so. The significant fact is that this act is not a separately formalized element, to say nothing of being the core of the ritual.

In the *Heyoka* it is of course just that: the center of the ritual and, indeed, very nearly the whole of it. Now it is certain that all instances of the formalized meat withdrawing trick are historically connected. There can be no doubt of this because of the arbitrary character of the performance. It is reasonable to expect fire handling to be associated, occasionally and independently, with hot water performances. But nowhere in the *Heyoka*, for example, is the arm merely immersed in hot water, or the body bathed in hot water, or hot water swallowed; nor is hot roasted meat handled, or eaten or thrown at the spectators. Instead the ritual is simple, rigid, and arbitrary.

Only among the Pawnee and the central Algonkins do we find the variability,

---

[386] Hoffman The Menomini Indians, p. 151; Cf. Hoffman, The Mide'wiwin, pp. 156-157.
[387] Jenness The Ojibwa Indians, p. 63. Cf. Jones, The Central Algonkin, p. 145.
[388] Skinner Observations, p. 55.
[389] Tanner Narrative, p. 135.

experimentation, and elaboration which suggest a point of origin. Furthermore, among both of these the protective plant substance is used in connection with the many types of fire handling, not just meat withdrawing. The Pawnee data indicate that this plant was used before the meat trick appeared. Indeed, it seems clear that these spectacular fire rituals could only have been developed with the aid of such a medicine.[390]

The evidence favors the claim of the central Algonkins over the Pawnee as originators. The *Iruska* is a reinterpretation of an earlier animal society, hence at least relatively late; whereas the fire rituals of the Algonkins are deeply rooted in the regional shamanistic complex. The latter involves animal identifications as well. Knowledge of the plant medicine is an isolated bit of esoteric lore to the Pawnee ritualist. But the wabano is a doctor who not only prescribes medicines but experiments with them. Surely he is the more likely inventor of the two. Indirect evidence of the relative recency of the Pawnee ritual is the fact that the Mandan, who doubtless received their fire dance via the Pawnee, did not get the performance until Maximilian's time. Yet in the early 1800's Tanner found the Ojibwa use of the trick traditional. Wissler believes that the Pawnee borrowed from the Dakota, rather than the reverse. In turn the Dakota could only have received the meat trick from the Algonkin, perhaps directly from the Ojibwa.

Apparently this was not the first diffusion of fire ritualism from the central Algonkin source. The larger picture may be conceived as follows. At the earliest level the Pawnee and central Algonkins, together with many other American tribes, shared shamanistic organizations which involved animal identifications. Each organization became elaborated in its own way. The Algonkin shaman, an herbalist, discovered a plant substance which permitted impressive amplification of fire ritualism. The knowledge and practice spread to the Pawnee, probably via the Iowa. At this time the three groups were in closer contact; the westward expansion into the true Plains had not yet occurred. The Arapaho, and possibly others who later moved westward, obtained their fire dances at this time.[391]

Somewhat later the Arikara broke away from the Pawnee. Their present fire ritual exhibits the old Pawnee method of applying the medicine after the burn. The Arapaho migrated to the western Plains and the Dakota began their expansion. There followed a period of great ceremonial elaboration. The Dakota seized upon a spectacular unit of the Wabano ceremony, the meat withdrawal, together with the protective medicine, and made it the ritual core of a cult which doubtless already existed. The members of this cult were individuals who feared or revered thunder and lightning because of dreams or visions of supernatural character in which these phenomena were symbolic. The further association of this cult with grotesque mythological beings or semi-deities, giants, and dwarfs is indicative of complex cultural depth. Anatomical distortion is seen in both *Heyoka* (e.g, large flapping ears) and *Wabano* (Morning-star's enormous mouth). *Heyoka* dress is another example of grotesquesness and variation.

---

[390] Grinnell identifies the plant used by the Cheyenne as *Dasiphora* [*Potentilla*] *fructicosa* (The Cheyenne Indians, vol. 2, p. 205). Some plants of this genus produce medicines which are powerful astringents and are used to allay pain. The plant is widespread over North America, hence this source provides no evidence of place of origin of Indian utilization. For the same reason the distribution of fire ritualism is not governed by the flora, as Wissler guessed (General Discussion, p. 872).

[391] For the history of migrations and tribal movements in the area see: Strong, The Plains Culture; Kroeber Cultural and Natural Areas, pp. 76-91; Wissler Population Changes, pp. 18-19.

These beings are not only supernatural but anti-natural. The only ritualistic character possessed by the cult prior to the introduction of the meat trick was apparently a mild sort of anti-naturalism. The Heyoka flourished with the expansion of the Dakota and the stimulus of the spectacular trick. The contrary pattern grew apace, but never became highly formalized; it continued to be a serious affair. Formalism came, however, at the hands of the Hidatsa who borrowed the skeleton of the Heyoka as the distinctive ritualism of the officers of one of their graded societies, the Dogs.

The Pawnee accepted the formalized meat trick as an adjunct to the *Iruska* and added an explanatory passage to the myth of origin of the society. In time the impact of the contrary behavior pattern of the *Heyoka* led the Pawnee to develop a new society, the Children of the *Iruska*, which reflects the spirit of the *Heyoka*. The anti-natural complex was too foreign in character to be amalgamated with the *Iruska* itself. This fraternity was apparently quite a late innovation. It borrowed from other contemporary societies as well as the *Heyoka*. Its role is a minor one; its members are few.[392]

The Arikara were likewise influenced by the growing emphasis upon specifically anti-natural behavior. The result is their "Foolish People" cult; again the membership is small. The contrary behavior is associated with an apparently intoxicating beverage which is drunk at initiation. The concern with strange snakes is a linkage with the Pawnee.[393]

Meanwhile the meat withdrawing trick had diffused to the Ankara, Hidatsa, and Mandan. The specific sequence of events is uncertain. The Arikara added the trick to their fire dance but whether they got it from the Pawnee or directly from the Dakota is not clear. The Hidatsa Hot Dance must have come from the Arikara but we saw above that the use of the trick by the Hidatsa Real Dogs was in all probability adopted directly from the *Heyoka* of the Dakota. The Mandan dance and trick, of the Crazy Dog society, was taken from the Hidatsa Hot dance very recently.

The Cheyenne reached their western home at about the same time. During their migrations they had been in fairly prolonged contact with the Assiniboin, whose Buffoon was well developed, and with the Dakota, and their *Heyoka* cult. Later they became the neighbors of the Pawnee and the Arapaho. Receptive and energetic as they were, it is little wonder that they developed the most elaborate interpretations of the contrary behavior concept of any tribe. Even so, the basic patterns as indicated above are visible and indebtedness consequently ascertainable. The descriptions of their two ceremonies have been reserved for presentation here where they may be most meaningful.

[Members of the Cheyenne Contrary Society] — people who greatly fear lightning and thunder, most o£ them old men and old women — take part in a ceremony which is held at irregular and infrequent intervals. In this society by their actions and words members attempt to reverse things, to do the opposite of what they are supposed to do; they back into and out of the lodge; and sit on the ground upside down, that is to say, with head and body on the ground and legs in the air. They are fun-makers, and their absurd actions are enjoyed and applauded by the people.

It is believed that the Contraries can do much for the sick. If one of them touches a sick person, or jumps over him, it is a great help to him. Sometimes on the occasion of these ceremonies they lift up the sick and then put them down, or sometimes lift them up and hold them head downward....

---

[392] Murie Pawnee Indian Societies, pp. 580-581.
[393] Lowie Societies of the Arikara, pp. 673-675.

When the time for the ceremony has been determined on, some old woman, who has taken part on a previous occasion, is sent to call those who have pledged themselves. She backs into the lodge where one of these resides, and says, "I have not come for you." The person addressed knows that the ceremony is about to be performed and that he must attend. When the one who is to make this sacrifice takes the pipe to the priest in charge of the ceremony and asks for instruction, the pipe is reversed; that is, the stem is fixed in the bowl of the pipe and the hole which commonly receives the stem is filled with the smoking material.[394]

The ritual revolves about the meat withdrawing trick, which is performed in typical manner. Attendant dancing and other activities are all of an eccentric character intended to amuse the spectators. Some of the performers wear scanty costumes of rags.[395]

In addition the Cheyenne have a cult called by the same name, "Contraries," which is a small aggregation of individuals — not a society — likewise fearful of thunder and characterized by contrary behavior of a highly serious nature. Such a person is not permitted to associate equally and familiarly with others in his camp, nor is he allowed to join in any of the gay activities around him. Indeed, even marriage is prohibited. Reckless abandon must be shown in warfare.[396]

The Cheyenne elaboration is the consequence of possession of all three contrary behavior themes, each of which they intensified or reinterpreted. The Buffoon is seen in the costume, the absurd actions, and the specialized curing techniques of the Contrary society. Even the meat trick is made a humorous performance. In the Heyoka such levity is unthinkable. But the trick and the thunder symbolism were surely taken from the Dakota ceremony.

The cult, the Contraries, is reminiscent of the Children of the *Iruska*, in the small membership, the prohibition of marriage, the sober and lonesome life, and recklessness in warfare. We may assume that it developed only after the Cheyenne came in contact with the Pawnee.

Contra-naturalism is carried very near its logical conclusion by the Cheyenne. They apply the principle to all aspects of behavior within reasonable physical limitations; others select certain activities only for ritualization in anti-natural terms. The Cheyenne were essentially borrowers in the larger view, but the intensity of their pattern exerted considerable influence on their neighbors. The consummation of the contrary behavior pattern is to be credited to them.

Certain antecedents of the Buffoon complex remain to be examined. We found that the pattern diffused westward from the region of the Plains Ojibwa. But the latter moved to the Plains from a former Woodland home and we may look to that area for possible connections. Indeed, Skinner long ago pointed out striking parallels with the Iroquoian False Face society.[397] These include dreams of the supernatural as a prerequisite for participation, the exorcism of disease spirits, the appropriation of food, the ragged costume, the carrying of staffs, and the wearing of masks. Skinner notes, however, that the masks of the Iroquois are carved of "wood, that the dancers do not employ special lodges, do not use inverted speech, and do not go to war.

Other data substantiate all of the parallels and remove some of the exceptions. The Iroquois do in fact use skin or cloth masks identical to those of the Plains Buffoons, and these are

---

[394] Grinnell The Cheyenne Indians, vol. 2s, pp. 204-206.

[395] *Idem* pp. 204-210, 329.

[396] *Idem* pp. 79-86. Cf. Dorsey, The Cheyenne, pp. 24-26; Mooney, The Cheyenne Indians, p. 413.

[397] Political Organization p. 504. Cf. Smith Witchcraft and Demonism, pp. 187-193; Parker Secret Medicine Societies, pp. 182-184; Fenton Masked Medicine Societies, pp. 415-418.

shared by the Algonkin adjacent to them. Furthermore, the association of the Plains Buffoon concept with cannibal clown is found here. Fenton explains: "The Iroquois and their Algonquin neighbors use buckskin masks to impersonate cannibal clowns who sometimes kidnap naughty children. The Seneca call this clown 'Longnose' because of his elongated proboscis." The Seneca long nosed cannibal clown frightens children; the Plains long nosed cannibal clown frightens disease spirits.[398]

Masks of the type described probably antedate the wooden masks of the Iroquois. Fenton suggests 1648 as the date of introduction of the latter. But a highly significant statement relating to the Huron, who live between the Iroquois and the Ojibwa, states that in the Midwinter Festival of 1636: "You would have seen some with a sack on the head, pierced only for the eyes; others were stuffed with straw around the middle, to imitate a pregnant woman." Here we have not only the typical mask but also the familiar type of simulated body deformation. And the following year, 1637, "... they donned their masks and danced, to drive away disease".[399]

Inverted speech is, indeed, not typical of the Iroquois dancer. Instead he uses grunts and gibberish. This is reminiscent of the Bluejay Character; the same interpretation holds.[400] The backward speech was added under Plains influence. Likewise the use of a special lodge is an aspect of the Plains pattern. The same may be said of linked warring activities. Bravery in warfare is too generally emphasized throughout the Plains to be of diagnostic value in the present case or in any of the other analyses here presented.

Thus Skinner's conjecture proves thoroughly sound. The specific events linking the eastern antecedents and ... Plains Buffoon complex are not yet known but the relationship cannot be doubted. As a working hypothesis we may assume that the Huron transmitted the basis of the clownish rituals to the Iroquois in the one direction and the Algonkin and Ojibwa tribes in the other; and that those Ojibwa who moved westward carried the practices to the Plains.[401]

The westernmost tribe included in the survey above of the Buffoon complex is the Crow. One step further west are the Shoshoneans. The Bannock are adjacent to the Crow; the Northern Shoshoni and Northern Paiute are not far distant. Associated with the socio-religious Circle dance of these groups are clowns which resemble those of the Crow. Costumes, masks, painting, and antics are similar. Park describes the Northern Paiute (Paviotso) performances under the name "Hump dance." The name is derived from the method of costuming by which a great hump on the back is simulated, exactly as by the Plains Cree Buffoons. Also, the effect of lumps is produced on the legs and belly, and men masquerade as women. Masks of the skins of animal heads are worn or the face is made grotesque with paint. The clowns dance during intermissions in the Circle dance. Apparently the whole object is to provide amusement for the spectators. Discordant dancing is performed; cripples, old people, and women are mimicked.[402]

---

[398] Quotation from Fenton *op. cit*, p. 418. For an Ojibwa mythological explanation of the origin of the cannibal trait see Coleman Religion of the Ojibwa, pp. 40-41.

[399] The statements, by Brebeuf, are quoted in Fenton *op. cit*, p. 414. Simulated anatomical deformation is found not only among the Plains Cree and Crow but also among the Paiute, as indicated below.

[400] See above.

[401] Fenton's data suggest that the Huron contributed the mask complex to the Iroquois (*op. cit*, pp. 415-416). Parker credits the Huron with introduction of masked shamanism to the Iroquois (Secret Medicine Societies, pp. 172-173).

[402] Park Culture Succession, pp. 188-190; Park's data refer generally to the Northern Paiute

Further parallels with the Plains Buffoon, found among other groups, are the use of cloth sacks for masks and the painting of the face with mud. The Basin distribution is limited but the distribution extends from the Bannock to California. At the latter point an area with another clowning complex is encountered.[403]

Thus the Basin practices may have come from either of the two areas. It may be stated categorically that similarities with the California complex are vague and scanty, whereas we have found those of the Plains to be highly specific. Furthermore, California clowning is apparently an old institution while Basin practices appear to have been introduced but recently. Steward's Snake River informants and some of Park's informants characterized clowning as a late innovation, perhaps not older than 1850 or even 1900. Park states that "In the pattern of exhibition dances the masked clownish performances of the Paviotso are unique and differ fundamentally from other Basin dances." These facts, together with the limited distribution, definitely place Basin clowning late in time. This is consistent with a Plains origin since the Buffoon complex did not reach the Crow until late. Since the conclusions as to source and age are based upon independent evidence of compelling character we may conclude that the source of the Basin clown was the Plains Buffoon.[404]

Thus we have shown an historical linkage of the Iroquoian masked dancer, the Plains Buffoon, and the Basin clown; a continuous line of diffusion from the Great Lakes to western Nevada; and a minimum time span of three hundred years.

Element Diffusion

From time to time in the foregoing discussions it has been necessary to utilize individual elements in making comparisons and interpretations. However the preferred method has been to trace concepts and logical complexes. One reason for this is found in the statement of objectives: to determine the structural and functional character of these rituals. The other reason involves historical methodology and the special bias of Plains culture where ideological tolerance permits almost any permutation of elements from the ritualistic stock in trade. The richness of detail in most of the Plains manifestations of the contrary concept is a reflection of general ceremonial wealth and the free exchange of elements from ceremony to ceremony, rather than elaboration of the concept itself.

This was found to be true even with respect to inverted speech. Furthermore this trait is found in

---

(Paviotso).

[403] Steward Culture Element Distributions: XIII, pp. 365, 334; Steward Culture Element Distributions: XXIII, pp. 287-288, 349: Stewart Culture Element Distributions: XIV, pp. 416-417; Curtis North American Indian, p. 85. Cf. Steward Ethnography of the Owens Valley Paiute, p. 320. The total distribution, as indicated by Steward and Stewart, follows: Northern Paiute of Snake River, Mill City, and middle Humbolt River near Winnemucca, Pyramid Lake, Carson Sink, Humbolt Sink, lower Walker Lake, and the Quinn River drainage near McDermitt, Nevada; the Lemhi and Fort Hall Shoshoni, and the Bannock. Clowning was denied by all Stewart's Southern Paiute and Ute informants (Culture Element Distributions: XVIII, p. 333), and all informants of eleven Northern Paiute bands.

[404] Steward *Culture Element Distributions*: XIII, p. 365; Park, *op. cit,* p. 190; quoted statement, *Idem,* p. 196.

Park discusses possible origins of Basin clowning at some length, weighing Southwestern, Californian, and Northwest Coast parallels, but finds none that are satisfying, He does not consider a possible Plains origin.

a number of Plains ceremonies quite unrelated to those here reviewed. It is probable that formal speech inversion is an older practice than contrary behavior. It certainly is not diagnostic of the latter; its use may involve mere irony. Wherever anti-naturalism is consciously sought the use of inverted speech is a reasonable practice and may be anticipated, especially if it be known already to the culture. However, if the contrary concept be the outgrowth of animal mimicry, for example, we need not be surprised at the absence of the trait. Reverse speech frequently has been confused with reverse reaction to instructions. While the two may be related they are nevertheless distinct practices.

Isolated elements may be used for historically valid interpretations only if they are culturally and environmentally arbitrary. The mere carrying of bows and arrows in a ceremony is of no interpretive value if these are customary weapons. But if the bow has a lance point on one end, this arbitrary and functionally useless object is an indication of diffusion wherever found. The same is true of crooked and useless bows and arrows which many contrary dancers carry. Again, the simple begging of food by the cults of two tribes does not prove that one borrowed the practice from the other, but when the food in both instances is thrown through the smoke hole of the lodge there can be no doubt of unity. Animal mimicry is an enlightening example. Culturally basic rather than arbitrary, it cannot be of historical use unless phrased more specifically. An historically useful variant of specific form is the perching of a dancer in the roof timbers of the dance lodge, as among Plateau tribes and the Arapaho. Costume details are generally indecisive if the basic garment pattern be the same. Also, costumes are apt to be shared by a number of societies, with but minor and variable differences. However, such arbitrary elements as the conical hat, the sack type mask, and the humped back, are clearly indications of diffusion when distributed contiguously.

The significance of environmental considerations is illustrated by the use of body paint. In some areas red is unavailable, but black is always available in the form of soot. Emphasis upon black in parts of the Plateau is thus explained. When both the Arapaho and Pawnee, for example, rub their hands on sooty kettles and transfer the carbon to the face, it may suggest borrowing, but it must be remembered that this is a logical and simple way to obtain and apply black paint.

More important, with respect to paint, is the limitation of colors. If in one area only black, red, and white paints are available, then all tribes and all societies of each must use one or a combination of these. Thus the emphasis by the graded societies on red paint, of the Bluejay and *Iruska* on black, and so forth, is of little significance. Another example of limited possibilities is the variation in the Plains in the wearing of a fur robe. It may be worn with the hair inside, or outside. Either practice considered alone, even though customary, means nothing,

The arbitrary trait is epitomized in the practice of ritual retrieval of small objects inadvertently dropped on the dance floor. Found among the Flathead, Kansa, Winnebago, and others, it strongly points to a common source.

Originally it was my intention to enumerate the linkages indicated by the distributions of these arbitrary elements. However, with the task completed, it is apparent that no new information is conveyed and a great deal of space would be required for presentation. We already know that extensive tribal interchange of ritual traits occurred in the Plains and on its borders during the recent period of intensive ceremonial growth. Lowie, Kroeber, Spier, and Wissler proved this long ago. Such an enumeration would throw no new light upon the contrary concept. In the accounts above the most useful details are presented and the general extent of overlap can be judged.

The Plains Indian Clowns, their Contraries and related Phenomena
John Plant
Vienna, Austria 2010

Table of Contents

Introduction 2
1. Ceremonial Clowns on the Plains.. .. 4
1.1. Contrary-Clowns of the Arapaho and Aa'ni Atsina........................... .. 5
1.2. Contrary-Clowns of the Lakota and Santee 7
1.3. Contrary-Clowns and Contrary-Shamans of the Plains Cree, Plains Ojibwa
    and Assiniboin 9
1.4. Contrary-Clowns and Clown-Doctors of the Cheyenne 11
1.5. Clowns of the Ponca 13
       1.6. Clowns of the Absarokee 13
2. *Contraries on the Plains* 15
2.1. *Contraries* of the Lakota and Santee.. .. 16
2.2. *Contraries* of the Cheyenne 19
2.3. *Contraries* of the Arikaree 21
2.4. *Contraries* of the Pawnee.. .. 21
2.5. *Contraries* of the Comanche.. .. 22
3. Reverse Reaction *Warriors*... .. .23
3.1. Hidatsa 25
3.2. Plains Shoshone 26
3.3. Kiowa.. .. 26
3.4. Kiowa-Apache 27
3.5. Absarokee 28
4. *Fools and Foolishness on the Plains* 30
4.1. Ceremonial Fool of the Mandan 30
Conclusion 31
Map 1. Native North American culture areas 34
Map 2. Approximate location of Plains Indian tribes c1850..................... .. 35
References.. .. 36
Endnotes.. .. 43

Introduction

Have you ever heard of Indian clowns or the *contraries* of the Plains Indians? Popular concepts of the North American Indian and, in particular, the Plains Indian leave no room for humor and laughter. The Indian is portrayed as a mounted brave wearing magnificent regalia and a war bonnet, or as a taciturn stoic, silent without tears or smile. For centuries, travel accounts, children's literature, Western novels and Hollywood films have propagated these rigid stereotypes. They deny Indians a sense of wit and a love for humor. These ideas of Indians are entirely misleading.

In reality, native North American cultures were surprisingly rich in organizations and traditions that were committed to laughter, clowning and acting in a foolish manner. Some of the best-known examples are from the Inuit of the Arctic region and the Pueblo Indians of the Southwest, but clowning and ceremonial foolishness were wide spread on the Plains. The clowns of the Plains Indians are ceremonial clowns since they performed primarily during rituals, dances and feasts. When Lakota Indians first saw European clowns, they instantly identified them with their own term for clowns, *heyoka*. In addition to ceremonial clowns, several Plains tribes recognized certain persons to be "crazy warriors" and others to be *"contraries."* The *contraries* were individuals devoted to an extraordinary life-style, in which they consistently did the opposite of what others routinely did. In adhering to the principle of contrary behavior in all seriousness, the *contrary* turned everyday routines and social conventions into their opposites. On a certain level, the *contrary* showed antagonism to his society. The "crazy warriors" were men who purposely abided by contrary, foolish or crazy principles in battle. Plains society thus harbored an unusual and wide array of foolishness and clowning.

In this essay, which draws on information gleaned from published and unpublished accounts, I seek to focus on the *contraries*, the clowns and related groups of the historical Plains Indians. The first authors to allude to the Plains clowns and *contraries* were pioneers, missionaries and ethnologists working among the Indian tribes in the nineteenth to early twentieth centuries, for example James R. Murie, George A. Dorsey, Robert H. Lowie, George B. Grinnell, Gideon H. Pond. A fuller account of the clowns, *contraries* and early references to them in the literature is contained in Plant.[405].

Important academic contributions to the study of North American Indian clowns and related groups were made by two American anthropologists of the mid-20th century, Julian Steward and Verne Ray. In 1929, Steward submitted his doctoral thesis at the University of California in Berkeley on the topic of clowning in native North America. Robert Lowie and Alfred Kroeber were members of the examination committee. A year later, Steward published the article, "The Ceremonial Buffoon of the American Indian," in which he further discussed contrary behavior. Steward was the first to use the phrase *contrary behavior* to describe the most dominant and characterizing traits of the clowns of the Plains Indians. These two traits were *inverse speech* and *acting by opposites*.[406] Steward viewed contrary behavior primarily as a comic device, a perspective that is challenged in this paper.

Ray initially became interested in contrary behavior through his own research on the Bluejay Dancer in tribes of the southeastern Plateau region. This dancer impersonated the mythological Bluejay Spirit for the duration of the winter ceremonial season and displayed foolish and anti-natural behavior.[407] Ray sought to clarify the historical distribution pattern of these behaviors in traditional North American ceremonialism.[408] He differentiated a third

---

[405] John Plant *Heyoka: Die Contraries und Clowns der Plainsindianer*. Wyk auf Foehr: Verlag für Amerikanistik 1994 http://www.anjol.de/documents/ 100703_heyoka_article_john-plant.pdf 1994.

[406] Julian H Steward *The Clown in Native North America*, Ph.D. dissertation, University of California, Berkeley 1929, p. 61, 62, 131, 133; *The Ceremonial Buffoon of the American Indian*, Papers of the Michigan Academy of Science, Arts and Letters, 14: 187-207 1930: 199, 202).

[407] Verne F Ray Bluejay Character in Plateau Spirit Dance, American Anthropologist n.s, 39: 593-601 1937.

[408] Verne F Ray *The Contrary Behavior Pattern in American Indian Ceremonialism*, Southwestern Journal of Anthropology, 1: 75-113 1945.

attribute in the contrary complex of the Plains: *reverse reaction*, which will be explained below. Steward and Ray aimed jointly to examine American Indian clowning and related phenomena; however, no publication resulted. Both considered contrary behavior in a broad sense, such that the concept included "anti-natural" and "unnatural" behavior, as in the Bluejay Character of the Plateau region, the Fire Dancers of the Plains and the Pomo ghost-clown of California.

Contrary behavior is used here in a narrower sense and refers to actions that arise from the stipulation or compulsion to act by opposites, whether in ceremony, ritual, on the warpath or in everyday life. Contrary behavior of the Plains *contraries* was always accompanied by the practice of "talking backwards" (*inverse speech*), in which one says the opposite of what one means. "No!" for example, expresses "Yes!" The utterance "Grandfather, go away!" becomes an invitation for him to come. *Reverse reaction* is further attribute in the contrary complex of the Plains. It represents a shortened form of contrary behavior, in which one understands the opposite of what one was told and reacts with the opposite behavior to instructions, commands or requests. To communicate with persons, who were *contraries*, one intentionally inverted the statement. For example, a grandmother, who wants her (*contrary*) grandson to gather firewood, would say to him, "Do not bring any more wood, we have plenty for the night!" *Reverse reaction* in combination with inverse speech was an abbreviated form of contrary behavior mainly used in military and dance societies.

This composition concentrates on historical sidelights of Plains Indian life and is not focused on the thriving practice of *heyoka* rituals and clowning of today, in particular among contemporary Lakota (Sioux). It is divided into four parts. Part (1) summarizes much of the available historical information on the ceremonial clowns of the Plains Indians. Part (2) is devoted to the individual *contraries* and part (3) to the reverse reaction warriors. Part (4) focuses on the ceremonial fool of the Mandan.

1. Ceremonial Clowns on the Plains

All sorts of humor and laughter permeated Plains society. Verbal jokes, practical jokes, wittiness, puns and pranks were widely enjoyed. They afforded amusement and brightened up camp life. Pranksters were long and affectionately remembered, such as Little Hawk, a Cheyenne, who once hid all the arrows in the camp during wartime. Comical occurrences were greatly applauded, and monuments were erected on the prairie to commemorate particularly humorous incidents.[409] The clowns and buffoons of the Plains, in contrast to the individual *contraries*, were ceremonial performers who after the performance removed their masks, headbands and costumes and resumed a normal life. They were unique in that inverse speech and contrary action were the predominant tools of their trade. They are termed *contrary-clowns*. Contrary behavior was an important comic device for them, in addition to other methods and techniques of clowning, such as exaggeration, imitation, absurdity, foolishness, inappropriateness, cleverness and wit. The clowns of the Plains belonged to different kinds of organizations (age-graded societies, dream cults), which served social or shamanistic duties. A *dream cult* was a loose association of persons together with their beliefs and rituals that revolved

---

[409]   John Stands In Timber, and Margot Liberty *Cheyenne Memories*, New Haven: Yale University Press 1967: 103-104n; Alexander F Chamberlain *Humor*, Handbook of American Indians North of Mexico, Frederick Webb Hodge, ed, Smithsonian Institution, Bureau of American Ethnology, Bulletin 30 (1): 578 1907.

around the same animal or spirit, which was encountered in a vision quest or supernatural dream. In contrast, a *society* was a more formally organized institution with important social and religious duties, as in the military, medicine and dance societies.

Many of the clown organizations practiced fire ritualism; however, fire was not an essential element for all groups. Fire ritualism was widespread on the Plains; there were Hot Dances, Fire Dances, Fire Walks and Hot Kettle Tricks. The dances sometimes called "tricks" since secret herbal preparations were applied to protect the skin against scalding water or hot embers. One medication was made from the root of *Malvastrum coccineum* (prairie mallow, Malvaceae) and another from dried leaves of *Dasiphora fructicosa* (Rosaceae).[410] The tricks and feats of magic were displays of shamanistic of power put on by a "trick-doctor." The Plains clown replaced the magic and levity of the trick-ceremony with humor and thus transformed the shamanistic Trick-Doctor into a Clown-Doctor. The "trick-doctors," like the clowns, formed an intrinsic part of ceremonies by inspiring awe and sacred amusement.

The clowns of the Arapaho and Aa'ni Atsina belonged to age-graded societies (and are treated in parts 1.1 - 1.2), while the clowns of the Sioux (Lakota and Santee) in part 1.2 had membership in dream cults. The clowns of the Plains Cree, Plains Ojibwa, Assiniboin and Cheyenne were at the same time medicine-men who employed contrary techniques in their shamanistic practices. They are spoken of as *clown-doctors* or *clown-shamans* (parts 1.3 - 1.4). Little is known about the clowns of the Ponca Indians (part 1.5); presumably, they acted by *contraries* and held their own ceremonies. The clowns of the Absarokee (part 1.6) were an exception to the dominant trend on the Plains. They came the closest to putting on a pure clown performance without the surrounding social framework of a permanent organization.

1.1. Contrary-Clowns of the Arapaho and Aa'ni Atsina

The ceremonial clowns of the Arapaho and Aa'ni (Atsina, Gros Ventre) were called the "Crazy Men" or "Crazy Dancers." They were the clowns in the latter half of the six-day ceremony, called the Crazy Dance or Crazy Lodge. Both these Algonquian-speaking peoples organized their important societies in a consecutive series according to age groups (i.e., the "age-graded" societies). The Crazy Dance (*hahankanwu* or *ahakanena*) of the Arapaho marked the third adult ceremony and consisted of men of about 40 to 50 years or older who were no longer expected to go to war. Among the Aa'ni Atsina, the Crazy Dance (*hahantyanwu*) was the second men's society. When a new group acquired the dance, several older men, called "grandfathers," were secured to serve as directors and instructors to the ceremony.[411]

---

[410] George Bird Grinnell *The Cheyenne Indians: Their History and Ways of Life*. Vol. II. New Haven: Yale University Press 1923: 176-177, 205 fnt; Edward Curtis The North American Indian, vol. 6, *The Piegan; The Cheyenne; The Arapaho*, New York: Johnson Reprint, 1970: 115 fnt); James H Howard *The Dakota Heyoka Cult*, Scientific Monthly, 78: 254-258 1954: 256.

[411] Arapaho: Alfred L Kroeber *The Arapaho*, Bulletin of the American Museum of Natural History #18 (1, 2, 4): 1-229, 279-454 1902-1907: 154, 188, 229; Curtis The North American Indian, vol. 6, *The Piegan; The Cheyenne; The Arapaho*, New York: Johnson Reprint, 1970 1911: 159); James Mooney, *The Ghost-Dance Religion and the Sioux Outbreak of 1890* Fourteenth Annual Report of the Bureau of American Ethnology 1892-93, Part 2 1896: 986, 988); Aa'ni Atsina: *Ethnology of the Gros Ventre* {Aa'ni},

Midway though the ceremony, the Crazy Dancers put on a spectacular Fire Trample dance, in which they extinguished a blazing fire by stamping on it with their bare feet. The Aa'ni Atsina clowns additionally put on the Flight of Arrows dance, at the conclusion of which they simultaneously shot their arrows as high up as they could. The clowns never tried to avoid the arrows as they fell back down and no one was ever hit. After the dances, the crazy period began. For the remaining days of the ceremony, the Crazy Dancers paraded as clowns and had the unbridled liberty to annoy anyone who was not within the safe confines of the tents and, in general, to do whatever they wished. Only the ceremonial grandfathers were exempt from annoyance.[412]

The Crazy Dancers used several herbal preparations. They rubbed one onto the skin to prevent burns during the fire dances. Another, the root of the poisonous wild parsnip, assisted in the ceremonial sexual licentiousness of the dancers. Their wives obtained the third medicine, which prevented tiredness in the dancers, from the "grandfathers" in a nighttime ceremony in which the grandfathers were required to practice sexual restraint.[413]

The Crazy Dancers used inverse speech and performed contrary antics. They effortlessly carried a heavy load, such as a full-grown dog, as if it were weightless; but to carry a puppy, they acted as if it were exceedingly heavy. To look at a person, they would put their head to the ground and pretend to look with their buttocks. They tossed buffalo dung into the tents and yelled "food!" They imitated animals, hunted buffalo chips, danced on lodge poles and shot backwards with bows and arrows. Arrows that fell in plain sight, they could not find; but if they fell in thick brush or tall grass, they could locate them at once.[414]

An essential part of the regalia worn by the Arapaho Crazy Dancers was a headband with a cluster of owl-feathers attached to the front. The clowns behaved in a crazy fashion, as long as they were wearing the owl-feather headband. The removal of the headband made them rational again.[415]

The Arapaho clown with the highest degree was the "white crazy man" or "white fool" (*nankhahankan*). He was painted entirely with white clay. Generally, there was only a single White Fool, occasionally two. He possessed strong "medicine" powers and was permitted sexual freedom during the ceremony. He carried a whistle and shot at spectators with soft tipped arrows. The White Fools, too, enjoyed the liberty to accost any non-participant they wished, and as a result, the people dreaded them.[416]

The White Fool clown is represented in Arapaho narratives about "Lime Crazy" or the "White Painted Fool" (*haaatinahankan*). Further, the Crazy Dance itself was also called the "Lime-Crazy" society. In the myths, Lime Crazy was portrayed as a good-for-nothing idler whose sexual excess and habitual laziness provoked jealousy and scorn. He thus presented the reverse image of his well-adjusted older brother, Big Chief, who forged plans to eradicate Lime Crazy.[417]

Anthropological Papers of the American Museum of Natural History, 1: 141-281   1908: 241-250).

[412] Kroeber, Arapaho: 190, 192), Aa'ni: 245.

[413] Kroeber, Aa'ni: 190-191, 193, 244).

[414] Kroeber, Arapaho: 188-196), Aa'ni: 246 fnt).

[415] Kroeber, Arapaho: 188), Aa'ni: 246 fnt).

[416] George A Dorsey, and Alfred L Kroeber *Traditions of the Arapaho*, Publication 81, Field Columbian Museum, Anthropology Series, vol. 5   1903: 30 fnt); Kroeber Arapaho: 188-191, 193, 227-229, Aa'ni: 246 fnt); Mooney *Ghost-Dance Religion*: 1033.

[417] Dorsey *Traditions of the Skidi Pawnee.* Memoirs of the American Folk-Lore Society, vol. 8   1904a: 339 fnt); Dorsey and Kroeber *Traditions of the Arapaho*: 18, 23-31); Claude Lévi-

Figure 1.   Arapaho Crazy Dancer in full regalia.   In the early stages of the ceremony, the choreography differed from other Arapaho dances in that the dancers held one hand over their eyes and extended the other hand out and slightly down.   As yet, nothing "crazy" happened in the ceremony.[418]   (Kroeber 1902-1907, plate 35).

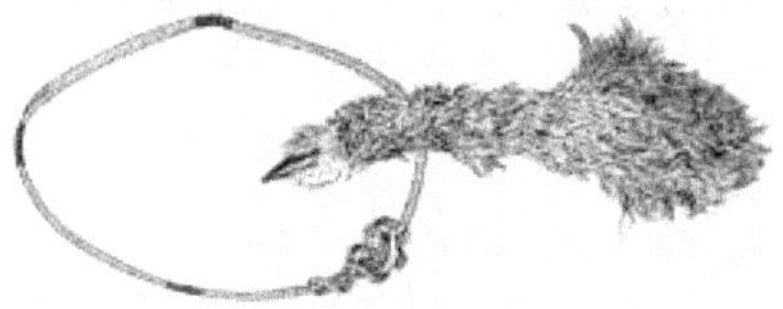

Figure 2.   Headband worn by an Aa'ni Atsina Crazy Dancer.   Attached to it is an owl skin with an owl beak.[419]   (Kroeber 1908, figure 36).
7

Mythological accounts of the origin of the Arapaho ceremonial lodges, including the Crazy Lodge, varied.   Some myths attribute the lodges to the First Man or to a sacred buffalo bull (*waxacou*), others to *Nihaca*.[420]   *Nihaca* was the traditional trickster figure of numerous tales and sometimes earth-maker and culture hero.   ("Culture heroes" were mythical figures who originated tribal institutions and ceremonies.)

1.2. Contrary-Clowns of the Lakota and Santee

The historical ceremonial clowns of the Lakota and Santee, possibly also the Yankton and Yanktonai (all four tribes are divisions of the Sioux), belonged to the *Heyoka* dream cult. Other dream cults were the Elk Dreamers, the Black-Tailed Deer cult and the Berdache.   The *Heyoka* dream cult was closely associated with the supernatural Thunder Beings or Thunderbirds.   A dream or vision of a dangerous form of them obligated one to become *Heyoka*. Like other spiritual people of the Lakota and Santee, the dreamers must act out the obligations, which arise from the dream or vision experience.   The minimum requirement for a member was to sponsor a *Heyoka* ceremony and to play the role of a clown who gets others to laugh at him on his own expense.   The lesson in humiliation felt by the dancer before his people was an important step in becoming a spiritual person.   If *Heyoka* dreamers neglected to perform the ceremony, they were often plagued by a great fear of thunder or of being struck by lightning, as was the experience of Black Elk (Lakota) in his youth.[421]

In preparation for a *Heyoka* ceremony, the clowns put up an old, smoke-darkened tipi (a contrary lodge) in the middle of the camp circle.[422]   The ceremony centered around the Hot-Water or Meat- Removal rite in which the dancers took dog meat out of a boiling kettle ... with their bare hands.   The Hot-Water rite was a *wakan* feat, a serious display of supernatural power.

After the meat was cooked and distributed, the clowning part of the ceremony began.

Strauss *The Naked Man: Introduction to a Science of Mythology*: Part IV 1981: 506).

[418] Kroeber *Arapaho* 1902-1907, plate 35.

[419] Kroeber Aa'ni *Gros Ventre* 1908, figure 36.

[420] Dorsey and Kroeber *Traditions of the Arapaho*: 1-8, 13-21, 22-23).

[421] John G Neihardt *Black Elk Speaks: Being the Life Story of a Holy Man of the Oglala Sioux*, Lincoln: University of Nebraska Press (First published 1932) 1979; Robert Lowie *Dance Associations of the Eastern Dakota*, Anthropological Papers of the American Museum of Natural History, 11 (2): 101-142 1913a: 114.

[422] James R Walker *Lakota Belief and Ritual*, Raymond J. DeMallie and Elaine A Jahner, eds. Lincoln: University of Nebraska Press 1980: 155-157.

The clowns would splash hot broth over themselves, complain that the broth was cold, play with the pots, knock them about, put them over their heads and chase each other. A special clown, who carried a crooked bow and arrows, danced between the beats of the song and out of time. The musical accompaniment was uncoordinated or the sound muted because the drumheads were deliberately loosened. The clowns sang together producing an unprecedented "riot of voices," since each sang their own individual song. Their songs were based on their own supernatural dream experience. Such practice was not known from other cults or societies.[423]

The clowns had a marvelous repertoire of tricks and stunts. They executed complicated sleight-of-hand rope tricks and could shoot a pin at 25 yards distance with an arrow. To step over a mud puddle, they proceeded with great gesture and pantomime as if traversing a wide river.[424] On occasion, the clowns shot steel-pointed arrows into the air causing the spectators to run away to avoid being hit by them as they fell back to the ground. The arrows, however, were innocently tipped with rawhide.[425] This stunt was practiced in several variations by other Plains tribes (Arapaho, Aa'ni Atsina, Absarokee, Kiowa-Apache and possibly Assiniboin). Only the *Heyoka* clowns, however, let it be known afterward that the arrows were soft-tipped, so that everyone knew they had been fooled.

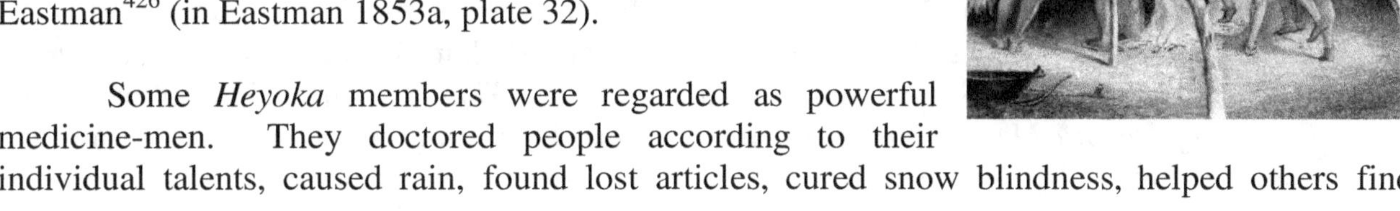

Figure 3. *Heyoka* feast of the Santee. One dancer removes a piece of meat from the kettle with his bare hands. Their dual pointed conical headdresses were made of birch bark and streaked with paint to represent lightning. Lithography by Seth Eastman[426] (in Eastman 1853a, plate 32).

Some *Heyoka* members were regarded as powerful medicine-men. They doctored people according to their individual talents, caused rain, found lost articles, cured snow blindness, helped others find

---

[423] Frances Densmore Teton Sioux Music, BAE B 61 1918:167 {no full citation in original text}); James Howard *The Canadian Sioux*, Lincoln: University of Nebraska Press 1984: 171-173); Lowie *Dance Associations of the Eastern Dakota*. Anthropological Papers of the American Museum of Natural History, 11 (2): 101-142 1913a: 115, 117; Lewis Henry Morgan 1959 *The Indian Journals, 1859-62*, Leslie A. White, ed, Ann Arbor: University of Michigan Press 1959: 146); Wilson D Wallis *The Canadian Dakota*, Anthropological Papers of the American Museum of Natural History, 41 (1) 1947:132-134, 138, 153); Clark Wissler *Societies and Ceremonial Associations in the Oglala Division of the Teton-Dakota*. Anthropological Papers of the American Museum of Natural History, 11: 1-99 1912: 83 84.

[424] Joseph Epes Brown *The Wisdom of the Contrary*. Parabola, 4: 54-65 1979: 57); Raymond J DeMallie *The Sixth Grandfather: Black Elk's Teachings Given to John G. Neihardt*, Lincoln: University of Nebraska Press 1984: 233-234; Lowie (1913a, p. 115); Neihardt (1979, p. 192); Wilson D Wallis *The Canadian Dakota*, Anthropological Papers of the American Museum of Natural History, 41 (1) 1947: 111, 134.

[425] Raymond J. DeMallie *The Sixth Grandfather* 1984: 234.

[426] in Eastman 1853a, plate 32

sexual gratification, protected others from lightning and forecasted events.[427] *Heyoka* medicine-men used their supernatural powers in a straightforward manner to affect cures and alleviate complaints. Their activities showed no relation to typical *Heyoka* traits, such as deceiving, fooling, clowning, talking backwards or acting in a contrary manner.

In the origin myths of the Lakota, the seven sacred rites, which form the core of their religion, were presented to them along with the sacred pipe by the mythic figure, White Buffalo Calf Woman. She taught them how to perform the Sweat Lodge, the Vision Quest, the Sun Dance and other important tribal institutions. However, the *Heyoka* ceremony or the Hot Water rite was not among the original rites.[428] The *Heyoka* tradition must have been acquired separately.

1.3. Contrary-Clowns and Contrary-Shamans of the
Plains Cree, Plains Ojibwa and Assiniboin

The ceremonial clowns of the Northern Plains were also known as the "Cannibal Clowns" or "Cannibal Dancers." They belonged to associations with various designations: the Cannibal Cult, Cannibal Dance, Masked Dance or Fools Dance. The Plains Cree named their clown group the *wetigokan*, the Plains Ojibwa *windigokan* and the Assiniboin *wintgogax*.[429] Although the names for the organizations are related to the Northern Algonquian term for the Cannibal spirit, *windigo*, neither cannibalism nor cannibal characters figured in the cult.[430]

---

[427] James Owen Dorsey *A Study of Siouan Cults*, Eleventh Annual Report of the Bureau of American Ethnology 1894: 469); Royal B Hassrick *The Sioux: Life and Customs of a Warrior Society*, Norman: University of Oklahoma Press 1964: 277); James Howard *Canadian Sioux* 1984: 172 173); John Lame Deer and Richard Erdoes *Lame Deer: Seeker of Visions*, New York: Simon and Schuster 1972: 237); Gideon H Pond *Power and Influence of Dacota Medicine-men*, In: Information Respecting the History, Condition and Prospects of the Indian Tribes of the United States, Henry R. Schoolcraft, ed, 1851-1857, 4: 641-651, Philadelphia: Lippincott 1854: 645); Luther Standing Bear Standing Bear *Land of the Spotted Eagle*, Boston: Houghton Mifflin 1933: 206 208); James R Walker *Lakota Belief and Ritual*, Raymond J DeMallie and Elaine A Jahner, eds, Lincoln: University of Nebraska Press 1980: 156); Wilson D Wallis *The Sun Dance of the Canadian Dakota*, Anthropological Papers of the American Museum of Natural History 16: 317-380 1919: 325;), (1947, p. 111, 118, 120, 140, 148, 166, 169, 171, etc.).

[428] Joseph Epes Brown *The Sacred Pipe: Black Elk's Account of the Seven Rites of the Oglala Sioux,* Norman: University of Oklahoma Press 1953; Williams K Powers *Lakota Religion*, In: The Encyclopedia of Religion, 8: 434-436, Mircea Eliade, ed, New York: Macmillan Publishing 1987: 435.

[429] 21 Plains Cree: Alanson Skinner *Political Organization, Cults and Ceremonies of the Plains-Cree*, Anthropological Papers of the American Museum of Natural History 11: 513-542 1914c: 528-529); David G Mandelbaum *The Plains Cree*, Anthropological Papers of the American Museum of Natural History 37: 155-316 1940: 274-275); Plains Ojibwa: Alanson Skinner *The Cultural Position of the Plains Ojibway*, American Anthropologist 16: 314-318 1914b: 500-505); Assiniboin: Robert H Lowie *The Assiniboine*, Anthropological Papers of the American Museum of Natural History 4: 1-270 1909: 62-66).

[430] 22 Mandelbaum *Plains Cree* 1940:274), Skinner *Dances and Societies of the Plains Shoshone*, Anthropological Papers of the American Museum of Natural History 11: 803-835

Figure 4. Activities of a *Heyoka* feast. The upper four figures collect "clown weed." Meat is cooked inside the tipi, and pieces of meat hang outside on a stand. Two dancers wear dual pointed headdresses with jagged lines that represent lightning. They carry bows and arrows with harmless tips. Several figures dance around the sacred stone in the middle and shake their deerhoof rattles. Modified after drawing by a Santee artist[431] (in Eastman 1853b, plate 36).

In addition to being ceremonial clowns who practiced inverse speech and contrary action throughout their dances, the cannibal dancers used absurd and contrary tactics in their function as shaman specialists. The leader of the cult was one who had a supernatural dream or vision of the Skeleton Being, *paguk* (at least among the Plains Ojibwa), which empowered him to be the initiator of the ceremony that lasted one to several days. For the ceremony, he drafted about ten men to be clown associates. They set up an old and tattered tipi (a contrary lodge) in the center of the camp. The costumes were designed to look as horrible and ragged as possible. The clowns wore masks with tubular noses, the leggings might be non-matching and their clothes turned inside out.[432]

To secure meat for the feast, the clowns sometimes set out on foot to hunt buffalo. After slaying an animal, they would dance around it, approaching it with displays of fear. Back at camp, the clowns staged absurd pantomimes of the hunt (mock hunting). In these skits, they stalked the fallen buffalo or strips of meat hung out to dry, as if they were wild buffalo. With elaborate gestures, they signaled to each other to lie down and crawl on their bellies. They would get up, peep, crouch and again crawl until they were absurdly close to the meat and shoot at it with their bows and arrows.[433]

The clowns would be terrified of stumps, or flee suddenly from dogs. One clown stood out in particular: the humpback clown. He would continue to dance in his comic way after the song had stopped, looking up in apparent confusion on discovering that he alone was dancing. The clowns afforded the camp a tremendous spectacle and always attracted a huge and dense crowd of onlookers.[434]

Figure 6. Assiniboin Clown wearing leather mask[435] (Lowie 1909, plate 3).

1916b: 911-912), Skinner *Political and Ceremonial Organization of the Plains-Ojibway*, Anthropological Papers of the American Museum of Natural History 11: 475-511 1914b: 503-504. A point reiterated by Lou Marano *Windigo Psychosis: The Anatomy of an Emic-Etic Confusion* , Current Anthropology 23 (4): 385-412 1982: 407.

[431] in Eastman 1853b, plate 36

[432] Mandelbaum *Plains Cree* 1940: 274-275); Skinner Plains Ojibway 1914b: 500.

[433] Skinner Plains Cree 1914c: 528.

[434] Skinner Plains Ojibway 1914a: 317 fnt); Mandelbaum *Plains Cree* 1940: 275.

[435] Lowie 1909, plate 3

Figure 5. Plains Ojibwa Clown masks. Tiny eye-slits contrast with the long crooked noses that are sewed on and stuffed with grass.[436] (Skinner 1914c, figure 6).

The leader of the clown organizations, at least among the Plains Ojibwa and Plains Cree, was a specialist in the removal of demons that caused illness or infection. His method of curing combined contrary behavior, inverse speech and (possibly) laughter and humor. The *contrary-shaman* is an appropriate term for him. He would call on a patient if one said to him "Don't let our friend get well, tell him to die at once." Thereupon, the contrary-shaman would bring his troop of clowns into the lodge of the patient and perform the exorcism rites. With ludicrous movements, the clowns approached the sick, while pounding their rattles, singing, whistling and dancing. They came up and looked at the patient, became startled and ran away frightened. If the contrary shaman announced that the sufferer would die, it meant that recovery was certain to occur by the next day.[437]

1.4. Contrary-Clowns and Clown-Doctors of the Cheyenne

The ceremonial clowns of the Cheyenne were members of the "Contrary Society" (*hohnuhka*),[438] the same word that was applied to the individual *contraries*. Both the individual *contraries* and the Contrary Society members bore supernatural relationships to the Thunder spirit and adhered to the principle of contrary behavior.

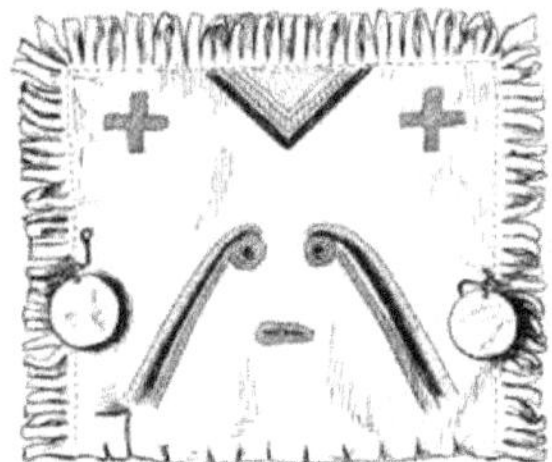

Figure 7. Two double-faced masks of Assiniboin Clowns. Front sides (left) and back sides (right) were made from canvas strips sewed together and fringed along the margins. Tin disks on the front sides represent earrings.[439] (Lowie 1909, figures 15-17).

The clowns of the Contrary Society performed a comical version of the Hot Water ritual and took part in the Massaum ceremony. The Contrary Society was one of several Cheyenne

---

[436] Skinner 1914c, figure 6

[437] Skinner Plains Ojibway 1914b: 501); Plains Cree 1914c: 529.

[438] Grinnell *The Cheyenne Indians: Their History and Ways of Life* ,Vol. II, New Haven: Yale University Press 1923: 204); Curtis The North American Indian, vol. 6, *The Piegan; The Cheyenne; The Arapaho*, New York: Johnson Reprint, 1970 1911: 115, 130; The North American Indian, vol. 19, *The Indians of Oklahoma; The Wichita; The Southern Cheyenne; The Oto; The Comanche.* New York: Johnson Reprint, 1970 1930: 129-131, 134 fnt); Karl H Schlesier *The Wolves of Heaven: Cheyenne Shamanism, Ceremonies, and Prehistoric Origins*, Norman: University of Oklahoma Press 1987; James Mooney *The Cheyenne Indians*, Memoirs of the American Anthropological Association, vol. 1 1905-1907: 415; Stands In Timber and Liberty Cheyenne Memories 1967: 58, 101.

[439] Lowie 1909, figures 15-17

medicine organizations. Its permanent members held their own ceremonies on an infrequent basis. Non-members that had pledged to take part for one reason or another earlier in the year, e.g. for the recovery of a sick child, a successful war expedition, were invited to participate. The clowns erected an inverted tipi with the covering on the inside, the poles on the outside, and the smoke-hole faced the direction opposite to convention (a contrary lodge). They smoked an inverted pipe in which the stem was inserted into the opening of the bowl, and the tobacco was stuffed into the hole meant for the stem.[440]

In their performances, the men and women clowns danced irregularly and clumsily, kicking and quarreling among themselves, butting backwards into others, overly dramatizing their motions and turning backward somersaults. Their antics were greeted by the spectators with loud laughter.[441]

The religious part of the Hot Water ceremony centered on the boiling of dog meat in a kettle of water as an offering to the Thunder Being. The clowns plunged their hands into the hot broth, rubbed soup on their chests, and pretended to enjoy themselves, to the great delight of the crowds. When the meat was cooked, the dancers snatched morsels out from the boiling soup with their bare hands and distributed them to the spectators.[442]

The other major public performance of the Contrary Society was in the Massaum, one of the most picturesque and amusing ceremonies on the Plains. The mythical culture hero, Sweet Medicine, had taught the Massaum ceremony to the people so that all the animals would be created. The ceremony was a reenactment of mythical occurrences. The clowns set up the contrary lodge inside the camp circle, and on the final day of the ceremony, they acted the part of *crazy hunters* (*emhoniu*). They did things contrary to ceremonial order, and armed with their tiny bows and arrows they hunted the Animal Dancers of other societies. The performance of the clowns was essential for the proceedings of the ceremony. In fact, the word Massaum is related to the Cheyenne term *massane* meaning foolish or crazy.[443]

The medicine-men of the Contrary Society treated illnesses and wounds with contrary protocol, humor and laughter. They could be considered *clown-doctors* or *clown-shamans*. They administered treatment and gave blessings during the Massaum ceremony, as did other shamanistic groups. The Deer Doctors and Buffalo Doctors, for example, would charge up to the patients, but the Clown-Doctors were scared by the patients and ran away. Slowly they would come back, walking on tiptoe as quietly as possible. Again, they would become scared and run away. Finally, they administered their treatment by vaulting high in the air over the patient.[444]

1.5. Clowns of the Ponca

The *Heyoka* dream cult of the Dakota-Siouan was adopted by the neighboring Ponca, who held the dance in the spring. The dancers used backward speech, took food from boiling

---

[440] Grinnell *Cheyenne Indians* 1923, p. 205-206); Mooney (1896, p. 1033).

[441] Grinnell *Cheyenne Indians* (1923, p. 207-208).

[442] Grinnell *Cheyenne Indians* (1923, p. 204, 208-209); Mooney (1896, p. 1033).

[443] Grinnell *Cheyenne Indians* 1923, p. 285-336; Curtis The North American Indian, vol. 19, *The Indians of Oklahoma; The Wichita; The Southern Cheyenne; The Oto; The Comanche.* New York: Johnson Reprint, 1970 1930: 129-135.

[444] Grinnell *Cheyenne Indians* 1923, p. 329-331; Stands In Timber and Liberty *Cheyenne Memories* 1967: 101.

kettles and poured boiling water over themselves.[445]

Entirely distinct from the *Heyoka* of the Ponca were the clowns of the "Mad-Men-Imitators" or "Those-Who-Imitate-Mad-Men" cult (*thanigratha* or *danibdada*).[446] They may have been contrary-clowns. However, information on the cult is meager and little can be said about the dream requirement, ceremonies and membership. We do not know if they acted by opposites, practiced inverse speech or if they were just "fun-makers," foolhardy and mischievous without much social or ceremonial significance.

What is known is that they were famous for their ridiculous stunts. To cross a stream without getting wet, people would customarily remove the moccasin and legging from one leg to hop across the stream bare foot. The Ponca Mad-Man, however, forded streams "by hopping on the clad leg and carefully protecting the bare one from moisture".[447] This stunt, in which common practice becomes inverted, was known among the Sioux,[448] where it appears in the context of contrary behavior.

1.6. Clowns of the Absarokee

The clowns of the Absarokee were called the *akbarusacaria*, which possibly means "woman-impersonator".[449] They may have been the only ritual clowns on the Plains who did not rely on inverse speech or contrary behavior, except perhaps for the Ponca Mad Men. Once a year in the spring, someone would decide to put on a clown show and would take the initiative and get his friends together. They attired themselves secretly and donned masks in order not to be recognized readily. After they disguised themselves, they approached the camp on a miserable looking horse, which they had abducted for the purpose. To conceal fully their identity, they altered their voices cleverly. The crowd of onlookers tried to figure out who the actors were and asked leading questions. If a clown was identified, the performance stopped immediately, which sometimes occurred as soon as they rode into camp.

Their performances resembled a comedy routine highlighted with quick wit, horsemanship and flare. They were noted for their equestrian antics. To dismount a horse, they would intentionally fall off and pretend to be seriously hurt. To get on the horse, they would purposely overleap it and fall off the other side. One clown would continue dancing without noticing that the song had stopped. As their name implies, one masqueraded as a pregnant woman. Sexual escapades were played out and the clowns shot harmless arrows to "frighten" spectators.

In contrast to other Plains clowns, the *akbarusacaria* performed no fire rites and had no religious or shamanistic duties. The clowns required no supernatural sponsorship, dream or vision. They were not a permanent organization with special duties and seem to have no

---

[445] Alanson Skinner *Ponca Societies and Dances*, Anthropological Papers of the American Museum of Natural History 11: 777-801 1915: 789.

[446] Skinner *Ponca* 1915: 789); James Howard *The Ponca Tribe*, Smithsonian Institution, Bureau of American Ethnology, Bulletin #195 1965: 124.

[447] Skinner *Ponca* 1915: 789.

[448] Luther Standing Bear *Land of the Spotted Eagle*, Boston: Houghton Mifflin 1933: 210.

[449] This summary of the Absarokee clowns is based on Lowie *Military Societies of the Crow Indians*, Anthropological Papers of the American Museum of Natural History 11(3): 143-217 1913b: 207-208). In the literature the Absarokee are also known as the Crow Indians.

mythological background. They resembled pure clowns more so than the other Plains clowns in that they lacked inverse speech and contrary behavior.

Figure 9. Absarokee clown in full costume with leather mask and shield (Lowie 1913b, figure 6). ←

Figure 8. A young Absarokee clown in disguise on horse (Lowie 1913b, figure 7). →

2. Contraries on the Plains

The *contraries* of the Plains Indians were individuals committed to doing the opposite of what others conventionally do, not merely in ceremony or when on the warpath, but on a permanent and daily basis. They were not always comedians or clowns whose job was not to lighten up austere camp life. Often they acted as antagonists to their own people.

Individual *contraries* were known from, at least, six Plains tribes. Three groups of *contraries* are differentiated: 1) The *contraries* belonging to the *heyoka-hohnuhka* complex of the Lakota, Santee and Cheyenne; 2) The *contraries* of the Caddoan speaking Pawnee and Arikaree; and 3) The *contraries* of the Comanche.

The *contraries* of the *heyoka-hohnuhka* complex of the Lakota, Santee and Cheyenne share several similarities. Their names are identical with their respective parent organizations, which were the societies dedicated to clowning. In addition, the *contraries* of the *heyokahohnuhka* complex belonged to dream cults. Many young men seeking spiritual meaning would undertake a vision quest. The experienced vision would be faithfully communicated to sacred elders, who were appointed to interpret its content and to provide advice on the future course of action. To live by the truth of the vision, even if it meant that one would become a *contrary*, was essential.

The dream or vision, which eventually would lead to membership in the contrary cult, had something to do with Thunder, the Thunderbird or the Winged One. However, not any dream or vision of Thunder would necessarily lead to becoming a *Heyoka*. Much depended on the details of the vision and what form of the Thunderbird was seen. The Thunderbird was a leading deity in most Plains religions. Many warriors obtained war medicine, protection and help from the supernatural Thunderbird without becoming *Heyoka*.[450]

Parallel to the contrary cults of the *heyoka-hohnuhka* complex, was the Berdache tradition, which like that of the individual *contraries*, sanctioned a socially acceptable alternative for those who, for whatever reason, could not conform to the typical male role. The "Berdache," a European designation, was a man who assumed the role of a woman in dress, work, marriage and use of speech ("woman's talk"). Among the Cheyenne, they were known as

---

[450] Clark Wissler *Some Protective Designs of the Dakota*, Anthropological Papers of the American Museum of Natural History 1: 19-53 1907, p. 46-48); Walker *Lakota Belief and Ritual* 1980: 276); James O Dorsey *A Study of Siouan Cults* , Eleventh Annual Report of the Bureau of American Ethnology 1894: 443); Colin Taylor *The Warriors of the Plains*, New York: Acro Publishing 1975: 38-42.

"halfmen/halfwomen" (*heemaneh*), since they were acquainted with both the male and female realms of existence.[451]

The *contraries* of the *heyoka-hohnuhka* complex were characterized by their close association to their respective clown societies and their membership in loosely organized dream cults centering on the Thunder Being. The institution of dream cults that sanctioned the *contraries* and berdache falls entirely within the ceremonial and religious pattern of the Cheyenne, Lakota and Santee.

The *contraries* of the Caddoan speaking peoples (Pawnee and Arikaree) and the Comanche differed from the *heyoka-hohnuhka contraries* in peripheral characters. They had no reference to the Thunderbird. They formed no part of a dream cult or society. Membership was by self-appointment. Names were used for the *contraries* in each tribe that referred to foolishness. The Caddoan *contraries* did not possess a medicine bundle and thus fall outside the ceremonial and religious pattern of the Pawnee and Arikaree. In fact, they disobeyed religious prescriptions. In the narratives of the Pawnee and Arikaree, the *contraries* are identified with the mythical Children of the Sun, who were homeless misfits possessing great powers but disrespectful of sacred animals.

Although the Comanche lacked the intricate ceremonialism (societies, dream cults, tribal dances) typical for most Plains Indians, among them was an association for the *contraries*. Parallel to them was a group of extremely brave men, called Large Red Buffalo Meat (*pia rekap ekapit*). These dauntless men were expected to act quietly and to practice uncommunicativeness (*naiimeapaiet*) (Lowie 1915 p.812). Mythological records for either the *contraries* or the Large Red Buffalo Meat of the Comanche are not known.

The *contraries* were unique and unprecedented; they existed in no other culture. At least, five Plains tribes had traditions in which men practiced vocational contrariness. They will be described for the Lakota and Santee (part 2.1), Cheyenne (2.2), Arikaree (2.3), Pawnee (2.4) and Comanche (2.5).

2.1. Contraries of the Lakota and Santee

Among the Lakota and Santee (possibly also the Yankton and Yanktonai), two kinds of *Heyoka* existed: the ceremonial clowns who belonged to the *Heyoka* cult and the individual crazy or foolish clowns.[452] Most *Heyoka* were satisfied with sponsoring a single clown feast, whereas others went beyond the minimum requirements and took on *Heyoka*-like attributes as a vocation. They were the *contrary Heyoka* or *individual Heyoka*.

To have to become a *contrary Heyoka* was considered a dreaded misfortune. Each lived alone in a depilated tipi and wore "foolish" clothing. They usually remained unmarried. However, sometimes contrary courtship led to marriage. Once, a young *Heyoka* man wooed a woman by pushing her away (to show that he was fond of her) and saying "Don't come with me," (meaning that she should accompany him). She followed him and became his wife.[453]

---

[451] Grinnell *Cheyenne Indians* 1923: 39-44.

[452] Clark Wissler *Societies and Ceremonial Associations in the Oglala Division of the Teton-Dakota*. Anthropological Papers of the American Museum of Natural History 11: 1-99 1912: 83; Wallis *Canadian Dakota*, Anthropological Papers of the American Museum of Natural History 41 (1) 1947: 111, 138, 170.

[453] Wallis *Canadian Dakota* 1947: 142.

When receiving a gift, the contrary *Heyoka* expressed thankfulness in reverse manner, for example, by hitting or kicking the donor and discarding the goods. Once, the sister of a *Heyoka* wanted to honor her brother by giving him a pair of decorated moccasins that she had made. Instead of wearing them, the *Heyoka* cooked them over a blazing fire.[454]

During extraordinarily hot or cold weather, the *Heyoka* substituted the behavior typical for one extreme with that of the other. During the hottest days of the summer, he might set up an awning to shade himself from the scorching sun, constructing it with meticulous care, only to sit beside the shade in the sun. In the worst winter storm, the *Heyoka* might sit naked behind a shelter of bushes to protect himself from the sun and gently fan himself as if perspiring from heat.[455] The blizzard dance, too, was an outstanding feat of contrary behavior and clowning. In the coldest winter blizzards, the *Heyoka* would prance about naked complaining only of the mosquitoes (i.e, the snowflakes). Gideon Pond, a Congregational missionary among the Santee in Minnesota, aptly summarized the main features of the solitary *Heyoka*, in 1854.

The traits of the *Heyoka* are the opposite of nature, i.e they express joy by sighs and groans, and sorrow by laughter; they shiver when warm, and pant and perspire when cold; they feel perfect assurance in danger, and are terrified when safe; falsehood, to them, is truth, and truth is falsehood; good is their evil, and evil their good.[456]

For the most part, the Lakota did not recognize *Heyoka* in the great collection of deities. However, among the Santee, a persistent and compelling force behind the *Heyoka*'s behavior was a supernatural or *wakan Heyoka*, who gave instructions. Santee *Heyoka* had their own guardian spirit-clown that was accessible only to them. The manifestations of the supernatural Clowns were thus seemingly endless: as a giant, a two-faced man holding a bow streaked with red lightning and a deer hoof rattle, a man with enormous ears carrying a yellow bow or a man with a flute.[457]

Figure 10. Representation of a supernatural *Heyoka* spirit in his lodge. Around his neck, he wears a very long whistle or flute. In one hand, he holds a deer hoof rattle and, in the other, a bow and arrow outfitted with a frog arrowhead. His pet bird emanates from his dual pointed headdress. He hangs elk and bird ornaments below (i.e, over) the doorway. The wavy lines around the lodge represent lightening. Drawn in 1840 by White Deer (Santee), in Schoolcraft[458] (1852, plate 55).

Many contrary *Heyoka* were compelled by their spirit-clown to lie about the hunt and deceive others against the *Heyoka*'s own wishes. Such predicaments were humiliating to the

---

[454] Hassrick (*Sioux* 1964: 152), for other versions of this incident, see Brown (*The Wisdom of the Contrary*. Parabola 4: 54-65 1979: 57) and Luther Standing Bear (1933: 210).

[455] Ella Deloria *Speaking of Indians*, New York: Friendship Press 1944: 53-54; Pond *Dakota Superstitions*, Collections of the Minnesota Historical Society 2: 32-62 1867: 45.

[456] Pond *Power and Influence of Dacota Medicine-men* 1854: 645.

[457] Dorsey (1894, p. 468-471); Lowie *Dance Associations of the Eastern Dakota*, Anthropological Papers of the American Museum of Natural History 11(2): 101-142 1913a: 113-117; Edward Duffield Neill *Dakota Land and Dakota Life*, Collections of the Minnesota Historical Society 1: 254-294 1872: 268).

[458] Schoolcraft 1852, plate 55

Heyoka. One man who was *Heyoka* was forced to assert to his family that he killed four moose (when he had not killed any). They all went out to find the moose, and instead found four rabbits. Everyone laughed at the *Heyoka*; the moment was embarrassing for him. At other times, the hunting methods of the *Heyoka* were astoundingly successful. One *Heyoka* was seen sitting backward on his horse during a buffalo chase, and all were amazed that he had killed several buffalo.[459]

Some *Heyoka* persons were instructed by their *wakan* Clown to go about camp singing all the time, to carry only a knife or stick into battle, to join a war party entirely naked, or even to murder a member of one's own tribe.[460]

The individual *Heyoka* were not war leaders, but they would accompany war parties, typically making no prior announcement of their intention.[461] One *Heyoka*, who was bedecked only with feathers, joined a war party. When the enemy was sighted, his comrades decided to retreat and gave the call to turn back. Since he was *Heyoka*, he understood the opposite of everything that was said to him. Instead of fleeing, he charged forward, and enemy shots killed him. The tragic event was symbolized in Lakota calendars (i.e *winter counts*) for the year 1787-1788 and is known as the "Left-the-*heyoka*-man-behind winter.".[462]

Figure 11. Calendar symbols for the *Heyoka* Clown who was deserted by his comrades in battle. The event was depicted in two different winter calendars both for the year 1787-1788. Winter count of The-Flame[463] (left, Mallery 1886, plate VII) and Battiste Good[464] (right, Mallery 1893, figure 344).

Sometimes, a *Heyoka* warrior was killed in battle because he suddenly changed sides and shot at his friends, who became confused and would shoot back.[465] On one occasion when the signal to charge the enemy was given, the *Heyoka* warrior ran in the opposite direction of the charge. To everyone's puzzlement, he arrived at the enemy first.[466]

---

[459] Wallis *Canadian Dakota* 1947: 142.

[460] Walker *Lakota Belief and Ritual* 1980: 155-157, 277-278, 279-280; Wallis *Canadian Dakota* 1947: 135, 164-166, 170-174; Clark Wissler *Societies and Ceremonial Associations in the Oglala Division of the Teton-Dakota*, Anthropological Papers of the American Museum of Natural History 11: 1-99 1912: 84-85.

[461] Wallis *Canadian Dakota* 1947: 140.

[462] Garrick Mallery *Pictographs of the North American Indians*, Fourth Annual Report of the Bureau of Ethnology, Smithsonian Institute 1886: 100; *Picture-Writing of the American Indians*, Tenth Annual Report of the Bureau of Ethnology, Smithsonian Institute 1893: 466.

[463] left, Mallery 1886, plate VII

[464] right, Mallery 1893, figure 344

[465] Martha Warren Beckwith *Mythology of the Oglala Dakota*, Journal of American Folk-Lore 43: 339-442 1930: 357; Edward Sheriff Curtis The North American Indian, vol. 3, *The Teton Sioux; The Yanktoni; The Assiniboin*, New York: Johnson Reprint 1970 1908: 159, 168.

[466] Wallis *Canadian Dakota* 1947: 115.

2.2. Contraries of the Cheyenne

The Cheyenne called their individual *contraries hohnuhka*, the same name as their clown society (the "Contrary Society"). The individual *contraries* were a loosely organized group of individuals bound by certain beliefs. At any one time, few men were *contraries*; there were never more than four or five.[467]

A supernatural dream or vision experience, which centered on the Thunder spirits, Thunderbirds or the Thunder-Bow was necessary before becoming a *contrary*. The dreamer could then purchase the right to carry a Thunder-Bow from one who was a practicing *contrary*. He paid horses, weapons, clothing or robes. Generally, one could only quit the contrary career and be relieved of the burden when another asked for the Thunder-Bow and thereby took over the office and the responsibilities of being a *contrary*.[468]

The Thunder-Bow was a bow-spear about eight-feet long and fitted with a sharp flint spearhead at one end to form a lance. The bow always remained strung. Furthermore, it bestowed the keeper great power and stamina in battle or while on the march.[469] Like other sacred objects of the Cheyenne, such as the Sacred Arrows and the Sacred Hat, the Thunder-Bow was renewed annually in the Sacred Arrows Ceremony. The bow was also carried by warriors of the military society, the Bow-String Warriors.

The Contrary Society, Bowstring Warrior Society and the individual *contraries* were three different Cheyenne organizations. They have been erroneously regarded as the same, starting with Dorsey who confused the inverted or Bow-String Warriors with the solitary *contraries*. Hoebel in his classic work on the Cheyenne united all three groups. Much confusion in the literature on the identities of these groups was cleared up by Karen Petersen's article on the Cheyenne warrior societies.[470]55

The role of the contrary warrior in battle was to blow his whistle and charge when his comrades retreated. If he were carrying the Thunder-Bow into battle, he would lead the charge alone. When he switched the Thunder-Bow from his left to his right hand from behind his back, the signal would be given for the other warriors to follow his charge.[471]

Figure 12. Cheyenne Bow-String Warrior draped in a red buffalo robe. He holds a Thunder-Bow that is decorated with owl and magpie feathers. Like the Bow-String Warriors, the *contraries* carried a Thunder-Bow. Drawn by a Cheyenne artist, in Dorsey (1905, plate x).

---

[467] Grinnell *Cheyenne Indians* 1923: 79-86.

[468] George Bird Grinnell MS unpublished Notebooks in Grinnell Collection, 1895-1902, Folders 204, 325, 328, 332, 333, 335. Courtesy of the Southwest Museum Library, Los Angeles. (MS Folder # 333, p.143).

[469] Dorsey *The Cheyenne: Ceremonial Organization*, Publication 99, Field Columbia Museum Anthropological Series, vol. 9 1905: 24-25); Grinnell *Cheyenne Indians* 1923:. 86; Powell, Father Peter John Powell 1981 *People of the Sacred Mountain ~ A History of the Northern Cheyenne Chief and Warrior Societies 1830-1879 with an Epilogue 1869-1934*, 2 Vols, Norman: University of Oklahoma Press 1981: 39.

[470] Dorsey *Cheyenne* 1905: 15-30); Adamson Hoebel *The Cheyennes: Indians of the Great Plains*. Second edition. New York: Holt, Rinehart and Winston 1978: 23-24; Karen D Petersen *Cheyenne Soldier Societies*, Plains Anthropologist 9: 146-172 1964: 146-147.

[471] Dorsey *Cheyenne* 1905: 25); Grinnell *Cheyenne* 1923: 83); Powell Sacred Mountain 1981: 39.

The life of the solitary *contrary* was said to be lonely and terrible. The *contrary* pitched his tipi away from the camp and spent his time alone, often on a distant hill, contemplating things. Dorsey observed, "They are the philosophers among their people." Their food was cooked separately and they ate apart from others. The *contrary* was not permitted to joke or have a good time with others. People could visit them, but could not stay long. They were treated with formality and respect. If asked to go, they came. The host had to clear things away to accommodate a *contrary* appropriately, since he could neither rest nor recline on a bed, only on bare ground. If invited, he left. If asked to ride, he walked. When traveling, he could not use the path but had to walk off to the side in the brush.[472]

Cheyenne *Contraries* were generally unmarried, however if married they spoke to their wives with inverted speech.[473]58 Some believed that the power of the Thunder-Bow was diminished if the owner was married. After they ceased to be *contraries*, they could return to a normal life and marry if they wished.

The Hollywood film, *Little Big Man* (1970), offered glimpses into the fictive life of a Cheyenne *contrary*, Younger Bear. He could be seen riding his horse backward, and on another occasion, he took a bath in the sand and dried off in the river.[474]

The Cheyenne Stump Horn was once asked to speculate what the legal consequences would have been, had a *contrary* killed a tribesman. Such a case was not known to have arisen, but clearly had the Cheyenne Council of 44 Chiefs told the *contrary* that he must leave the tribe, it would be taken not as banishment but as an invitation to stay. If they told him to give the family of the dead some horses as a form of compensation, the *contrary* would understand that the family did not want anything. The Council would have had to phrase its decree inversely and say, "Those people don't want you to send them any horses. They don't like your horses. They want you to keep them all." If two particularly good horses should be sent, the Council would have to say, "Don't send those two nice grays you have. They hate those terrible nags".[475]

2.3. Contraries of the Arikaree

The Arikaree called their *contraries* the Foolish Men or Foolish Ones *(sakhunu)*. They were self-appointed men or boys who in an initiation ceremony would receive instruction from an existing *contrary* regarding the mysteries of being a Foolish One. The young novice was made to drink a solution, after which he was considered dangerous. The people were warned to watch out for their children for if a child were to be frightened by the Foolish One and say, "Don't shoot me!" the Foolish One would not hesitate to shoot at the child.[476]

The Foolish Men probably numbered no more than two in a village at any time. They

---

[472] Dorsey *Cheyenne* 1905: 25); Grinnell *Cheyenne* 1923: 85-86.

[473] Dorsey *Cheyenne* 1905: 25).

[474] Based on the book by Thomas Berger *Little Big Man*, London: Eyre & Spottiswoode 1964.

[475] Karl N Llewellyn and E Adamson Hoebel *The Cheyenne Way: Conflict and Case Law in Primitive Jurisprudence*, Norman: University of Oklahoma Press 1941: 150.

[476] Robert Lowie *Societies of the Arikara Indians*, Anthropological Papers of the American Museum of Natural History 11: 645-678 1915a: 673-675); Douglas R Parks *Traditional Narratives of the Arikara Indians*, Lincoln: University of Nebraska Press 1991: 161-167, 936-938.

seem to have been companions. One was said to have died out of grief after his comrade was killed in battle. During the day, they played at their wheel game or went about blowing whistles and singing their song of death, "I am not afraid of anything except the Heavens".[477]

In battle, the Arikaree *contraries* were oblivious to danger. If one were asleep, when the enemy attacked the village, waking him was not permitted. Therefore, on one occasion, White Ear, who was one of two young Arikaree men who were *contraries*, was not aroused when enemy warriors were sighted. His comrade, however, was awake and had marched into the midst of the engagement singing merrily and blowing his whistle. He shot one of his precious black arrows at the enemy and set out to recover it, walking casually amid the enemy, who shot at him several times killing him. When White Ear arrived at the battle scene, he did exactly as his comrade; he discharged an arrow at the enemy and went among them to retrieve it. He, too, was struck by an enemy's arrow and was seriously but not fatally wounded.[478]

2.4. Contraries of the Pawnee

The Skidi Pawnee referred to their *contraries* as the "Children of the Sun" or "Children of the *Iruska*" (*iruska ipirau*). The name *iruska* may have reference to the old *Iruska* medicine society. The *contraries* were also called *saaro* or *saru*, a term used by elders when speaking to children to point out that they are acting in a childish or foolish manner. Indeed, the Children of the Sun had a mischievous element about them and tended toward foolishness. However, little is known about their organization. There were up to six to seven members, mostly young men. The two oldest were the most powerful.[479]

The tradition of the *contraries* were handed down to the Skidi Pawnee by the mythological Blackbird. Therefore, the members painted themselves black and wore the skin of a blackbird on their head.[480] Frequently, the Pawnee *contraries* went about the village in pairs and spoke inversely with each other. If someone said to them, "Do not go after water," they would immediately depart to fetch water saying to each other, "Let us not go after water".[481]

Their favorite pastimes were sitting around playing a wheel game and going about singing merrily and generally being unconcerned with the world. They never married and were disinterested in women. They sought to kill any strange or mysterious animal, which others feared.[482]

If an enemy attacked the village, the Pawnee *contraries* continued to play their wheel game. Someone had to come and say, "Do not go out to fight." Then they would immediately jump up and rush out to the fighting. In battle, they carried a quiver filled with valuable arrows made from dogwood. In a strange performance like that of the Arikaree, the *contrary* would walk toward the enemy, and without taking aim, simply shoot an arrow in the enemy's direction. He then marched into the midst of the enemy to search for his highly prized arrow. Whenever they shot an arrow, they went to retrieve it. On finding it, they would return and proceed to

---

[477] Lowie *Arikara* 1915a: 673.

[478] Lowie *Arikara* 1915a: 673-674.

[479] James R Murie *Pawnee Indian Societies*, Anthropological Papers of the American Museum of Natural History 11: 543-644   1914: 579, 580-581; Dorsey *Traditions of the Skidi Pawnee*, Memoirs of the American Folk-Lore Society, vol. 8 1904a: 24, 57-59, 339 fnt.

[480] Murie *Pawnee* 1914: 580-581.

[481] Dorsey *Skidi* 1904a: 57-59.

[482] Murie *Pawnee* 1914: 581).

repeat the act (provided they were still alive or not wounded).[483]

In the mythologies of the Pawnee and Arikaree, the Children of the Sun were mischievous youths with no home or family, living in the wilderness, literally, under the sun. They would simply help themselves to any food they found and, in general, did what they wanted to do. In mythological times, the villages of the Pawnee and Arikaree were once plagued by an attack of snakes because the *contraries* had interpreted matters inversely and violated observances set up to respect the sacred red snake by shooting it to pieces.[484]

2.5. Contraries of the Comanche

Comanche society lacked the intricate ceremonial life of other Plains tribes. There were no warrior societies, no police groups to control the communal hunts, no Sun Dance (at least, not until 1874) and no marriage ceremony. However, they did have *contraries*.[485]

The *contraries* of the Comanche were named *pukutsi*, which referred to foolhardiness, especially in battle, and meant as much as "crazy warrior." The *pukutsi* were self-appointed; anyone brave and daring enough could become a *contrary*. They delighted in being mischievous and disobedient according to the principle of opposites. If asked to fetch water, they would bring fire. They smeared ashes or white paint over themselves and went about camp singing all the time. In cold weather, they complained of the heat and removed their clothing. The *pukutsi-contraries* did not marry, and women tended to avoid them. Their method of courtship was self-defeating. One *contrary* composed love songs, but sang them in isolated places where they could not be heard.

The *contrary* of the Comanche was a "no-flight" or "sash" warrior. He wore a long sash over his shoulder and rolled up under his arm. In battle, the sash was unrolled and staked to the ground with an arrow, and he was obliged to stand on that spot. Instead of fighting from this defensive stance, he held a bow in one hand, shook a buffalo-scrotum rattle in the other, and sang resolutely until victory or death came. He was severely forbidden to release himself; only a comrade could free him.

The term of the Comanche *contrary* lasted for years. If he had not died in battle and he attained prestige owing to conspicuous acts of bravery, then a respectable middle-aged man could terminate his career by taking away his rattle. Former *contraries* were important men in their family and village.

---

[483] Murie *Pawnee* 1914: 580-581); Dorsey *Skidi* 1904a: 59.

[484] Dorsey *Skidi* (1904a, p. 57-59), *Traditions of the Arikara*, Carnegie Institution of Washington, Publication No. 17: 1-202 1904b: 125-126.

[485] This summary of the Comanche *contraries* draws on accounts from E Adamson Hoebel *The Political Organization and Law-ways of the Comanche Indians*, Memoirs of the American Anthropological Association, Number 54 1940: 33-34); Ernest Wallace and E. Adamson Hoebel *The Comanches: Lords of the Southern Plains*, Norman: University of Oklahoma Press 1952: 275-276); and Abram Kardiner *The Psychological Frontiers of Society*, New York: Columbia University Press, First published 1945 1963: 62-63, 84-85, 88. In addition to the Sun Dance, the Mud Men clowns, *sekwitsit puhitsit*, were a late acquisition of the Comanche, probably acquired from their visits to the nearby Pueblos (Wallace and Hoebel *Comanches* 1952: 321-322).

3. Reverse Reaction Warriors

The warpath was an important station in traditional Plains manhood. War honors increased one's rank and status. Military ambitions were intense, and men strove continually to surpass the achievements of others. Bravery obligations, in particular, regarding commands to charge and hold ground, were demanded of many Plains warriors that went beyond raw courage and that stood outside the coup system of counting military honors.

The *no-flight warrior* was an outstanding example of such a bravery obligation. He tethered himself to the ground at a particularly precarious location in the fight and was committed to stand and either fight or encourage his comrades. No matter how extreme the danger, he was not allowed to retreat even if the others had abandoned him. Such were the Crazy Dogs of the Pawnee and the Dog Soldiers of the Cheyenne. The Crow Lance warriors of the Pawnee were obligated to bind themselves together with a buffalo skin rope when under enemy attack; if one was killed, the rest dragged the body about with them.[486]

The *advance warrior* represented another outstanding example of a bravery obligation. He was committed to charge at the foe in a direct approach at any cost, not stopping, retreating or hiding until he engaged the enemy. Such were the Dogs of the Oglala (Lakota); they always fought to the end, as did the warriors of the Omaha Make-No-Flight Society and the leader of the Crazy Dogs of the Absarokee.[487] The four leaders of the Club-Men Society of the Arapaho were required to ride forward and strike the enemy with their clubs and then ride back.[488]

Many bravery vows were transformed into pledges of outright foolhardiness. When the Brave Dogs of the Blackfeet (advance warriors) approached the enemy, they never turned back, regardless of the consequences. However, their duty was not to fight, but to sing and dance their songs while standing in front of the enemy.[489] Often, the behavioral rules were extended to non-military occasions, in particular during dance ceremonies and when on the march. The Cheyenne Crazy Dogs were obliged to continue dancing in the direction ordered by their ceremonial leader until he commanded them otherwise, even if it meant to march into the river.[490]

In an incident recorded by Lewis and Clark, the advance warriors of a Yankton organization, who numbered about twenty extremely well respected men, were crossing the frozen Missouri River in February 1805, when a gaping air-hole appeared in the ice straight ahead in the path of the warriors. The opening in the ice could have been avoided by walking

---

[486] Murie *Pawnee* 1914: 570-573, 580); George Bent to George Hyde Correspondence, Letter of February 23, 1904, William Robertson Coe Collection, Yale University, Courtesy of the Beinecke Library, New Haven, Connecticut MS 1904.

[487] Wissler *Societies and Ceremonial Associations in the Oglala Division of the Teton-Dakota*, Anthropological Papers of the American Museum of Natural History 11: 1-99 1912: 54; Lowie *Dance Associations of the Eastern Dakota*, Anthropological Papers of the American Museum of Natural History 11 (2): 101-142 1913a: 193; *Plains Indian Age-Societies: Historical and Comparative Summary*, Anthropological Papers of the American Museum of Natural History 11: 877-984 1916b: 889.

[488] Mooney *The Ghost-Dance Religion and the Sioux Outbreak of 1890*, Fourteenth Annual Report of the Bureau of American Ethnology, 1892-93, Part 2 1896: 989.

[489] Clark Wissler *Societies and Dance Associations of the Blackfoot Indians*, Anthropological Papers of the American Museum of Natural History 11: 359-460 1913: 397-399.

[490] Grinnell Cheyenne Indians 1923: 790.

around it, but since their duty was to advance toward the enemy in a direct and undeviating line, the first advance warrior marched straight on right into the hole. He disappeared under the ice, never to be seen again. The rest of his group would have followed him, but were hindered and finally had to be dragged around the hole.[491]

This part describes the military and dance organizations that practiced reverse reaction with respect to commands, requests and instructions during their ceremonies and warfare. The warriors and particularly the leaders of these societies were usually married men with military honors. They inverted the meaning of battle commands and responded accordingly. The order to retreat signified "Charge!" They could only fall back, when commanded to attack. The practice of using reverse commands in battle was not associated with humor. Reverse reaction warriors represent an abbreviated form of the *contraries*. They will be discussed for the Hidatsa, Kiowa-Apache, Kiowa and Plains Shoshone (parts 3.1 - 3.4). The Absarokee, too, had a group that was devoted to contrary behavior, although the group was less formally organized (part 3.5).

3.1. Hidatsa

The Real Dog (*macukaike*) of the Hidatsa practiced an abbreviated form of contrary behavior. He was the leading officer of the Dog Society, an important organization for mature men with war experience. The society belonged to the series of age-graded societies and membership was customarily offered to the next age-group in a big transfer ceremony. Each Hidatsa village had a Dog Society with four officers, as well as the rank and file members, i.e., the "Dogs." The Real Dog was usually a middle-aged married man of good judgment and high repute. He was obliged to use inverse speech and to do the opposite of what was requested of him, even with his wife and family. If she said to him, "Come, Real Dog," then he would turn and go away. If she told him not to come, then he would race up to her.[492]

The Real Dog relinquished his office in the transfer ceremony to a new occupant. The retiring Real Dog prayed (converse prayer) for the short life, immediate death and eternal dissatisfaction of the new leader. The other three officers of the society and the "Dogs," addressed the Real Dog with inverse speech. All officers were distinguished by their magnificent magpie feather headdress made well known from the brilliant watercolor portrait of *Pehriska-Ruhpa* completed by the Swiss artist Karl Bodmer.[493]

In addition to speech reversal and reverse reaction, another element in the Real Dogs' behavior was dog imitation, a feature that was widespread in Plains ceremonialism. The "Dogs" of the society had rites of sexual license, meat stealing and howling. One Real Dog was known to walk bare foot about the village and the woods in the winter carrying only a whistle and a flint knife, yet his feet never froze.[494] The same feat was performed by the *Heyoka* of the Lakota,

---

[491] Meriwether Lewis and William Clark *History of the Expedition under the command of Lewis and Clark*, Elliott Coues, ed, New York: Dover Publications 1965: 95-96) [Original Journals, vol. I, p. 130]

[492] Lowie *Societies of the Hidatsa and Mandan Indians*, Anthropological Papers of the American Museum of Natural History 11: 219-358 1913c: 285-289.

[493] Lowie *Hidatsa and Mandan* 1913c: 286, 289.

[494] Lowie *Hidatsa and Mandan* 1913c: 288-290); Alfred Bowers *Hidatsa Social and Ceremonial Organization* Smithsonian Institution, Bureau of American Ethnology, Bulletin 194 1965: 195.

however, in the context of clownery and contrariness. As dogs need to be taken care of, the Real Dog was assigned an attendant to look after him, to dress him for dances and to accompany him into battle. The attendant acted as an interpreter and using speech reversal communicated the commands meant for the other warriors to the Real Dog. If the general command was to retreat, the attendant told the Real Dog, "Go now!" or "Go ahead, and jump at the enemies!" If the attendant said, "Well, there is great danger," or "Come back, don't go near the enemies!" — the Real Dog would advance.[495]

Figure 13. Initiation of a Dog Soldier symbolized on a Yanktonai calendar for the year 1846. He carries a deer hoof rattle and wears a long collar scarf.[496] (Mooney 1898, figure 96).

One officer of the Dog society represented *Yellow Dog*, the mythical figure who instituted the various dog societies of the Hidatsa, including the custom of "backward speech." Further, Yellow Dog instructed Real Dog to act as he wishes and regard nothing as sacred.[497]

In village life, the consequences of such behavior could be tragically fatal. Once, a Real Dog ignored the prescriptions of the medicine-men, who were preparing a counterattack on the enemy for the next day. At that time, the Hidatsa people did not know how to address the Real Dog correctly and he had no attendant. Thus, no one was able to prevent him from violating the orders of the medicine-men. The Real Dog took from the food offerings and said, "Tomorrow is the day for me to die, I do not care whose food this is. If I want it, I'll have it." At daybreak the next day, the Real Dog rushed straight into the enemy's encampment before the Hidatsa warriors attacked. Later his body was found all cut to pieces.[498]

3.2. Plains Shoshone

All members of the "Yellow Noses" society of the Plains Shoshone were deeply committed to backward speech (*nanoma ponait*) and reverse compliance in not only ceremonies and war activities, but when addressed as a group and possibly even in their own family.[499] They were a military organization and additionally served to police communal hunts and marches. They may have applied the contrary principle in ordinary circumstances. If a Yellow Nose dropped something, he was not allowed to pick it up; yet, others could take ownership of it. A thirsty Yellow Nose would say, "Don't give me a cup of water" and mean the opposite. If a woman wished to marry a Yellow Nose, she knew that his refusal meant acceptance and vice versa. The first whites to encounter the Shoshone asked the Yellow Noses if they desired to be friends. The Yellow Noses replied, "No!" In battle, the Yellow Noses acted in unison using

---

[495] Lowie *Hidatsa and Mandan* 1913c: 285, 288-289.

[496] Mooney 1898, figure 96

[497] Lowie *Hidatsa and Mandan* 1913c: 285.

[498] Lowie *Hidatsa and Mandan* 1913c: 289.

[499] Lowie *Dances and Societies of the Plains Shoshone*, Anthropological Papers of the American Museum of Natural History 11: 803-835 1915b: 813-815, *Notes on Shoshonean Ethnology*, Anthropological Papers of the American Museum of Natural History 20: 185-314 1924: 283.

backward commands. If directed to charge, none would move. If the chief called out, "Don't charge the enemy," they would answer, "No, we shall not charge," and launch an attack.[500]

3.3. Kiowa

The *Kaitsenko* Society (*koitsenko, qoitsenko*) was one of several military societies with bravery obligations, but the only one that used inverse speech during their ceremonies and in battle.[501] All members were men of the highest military order and served to police the communal buffalo hunts. The meaning of the society's name is uncertain: Real Dogs, Principal Dogs, Chief Dogs or Horses. Often, they were simply referred to as "Dogs" or "Dog Soldiers." The society had a leader and up to ten members. Initiation occurred during the Sun Dance by presentation of a pipe. In ceremony, the dancers were painted red, and they wore bone whistles.

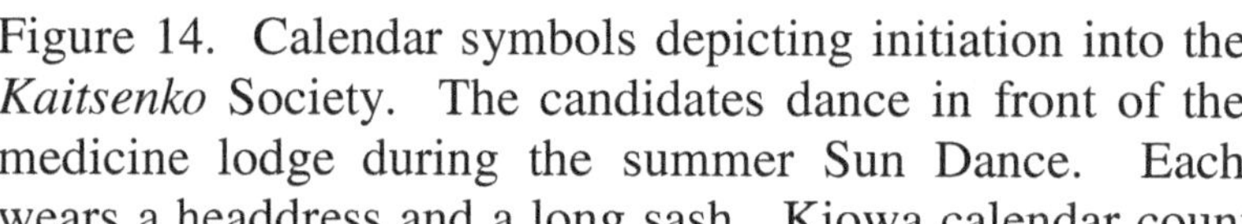

Figure 14. Calendar symbols depicting initiation into the *Kaitsenko* Society. The candidates dance in front of the medicine lodge during the summer Sun Dance. Each wears a headdress and a long sash. Kiowa calendar count for the summer of 1846 (left), for summer of 1848[502] (right) (Mooney 1898, figures 95, 100).

Aside from inverse speech, no examples of reverse battle commands or reverse compliance to instruction are known. The *Kaitsenko* soldiers were "sash" warriors. In battle, one might anchor himself to the ground by fastening the free end of his long black scarf into the earth with an arrow. Regardless of the danger, he was under solemn oath never to retreat. His duty was to stand there with his reddened dewclaw rattles and sing the death-song of his society. "O sun, you remain forever, but we *Kaitsenko* must die. O earth, you remain forever, but we *Kaitsenko* must die." He could only be released from his station if someone withdrew the arrow, which held the sash.

3.4. Plains (Kiowa) Apache

The *Klintidie* society of the Kiowa-Apache was a men's society with 10 to 16 members.[503] It contained only the bravest and oldest men still capable of fighting. New

---

[500] Lowie *Plains Shoshone* 1915b: 815.

[501] This account of the *Kaitsenko* is based on Lowie *Societies of the Kiowa*, Anthropological Papers of the American Museum of Natural History 11: 837-851 1916a: 847-849); James Mooney *Calendar History of the Kiowa Indians*, Seventeenth Annual Report of the Bureau of American Ethnology 1895-96, 17, 1, Part 1 1898: 287-288); *Military Societies*: 861-863, In: Handbook of American Indians North of Mexico, Frederick Webb Hodge, ed, Smithsonian Institution, Bureau of American Ethnology, Bulletin 30 (1) 1907: 861-863; and Mildred P Mayhall *The Kiowas* , Norman: University of Oklahoma Press 1962: 329.

[502] Mooney 1898, figures 95, 100

[503] This account of the *Klintidie* is based on J. Gilbert McAllister *Kiowa-Apache Social Organization*, Social Anthropology of North American Tribes: Essays in Social Organization, Law, and Religion, Fred Eggan, ed, Chicago: University of Chicago Press.

members would be asked to join the meetings, which lasted one to four days. Although being a member was honorable, many men were reluctant to join and would leave camp for the duration of the meetings.

At their dance gatherings and when in battle, the *Klintidie* were committed to inverse speech and reverse compliance to commands, instructions and requests. On one occasion the dancers were all painted and dressed for a dance gathering, when they had to march straight into the creek because someone said to them, "Don't dance in that water!"

Of the four leaders, the most outstanding was the Owl-Man (or Ghost-Man). The owl was revered to be the most mysterious and the most sacred spirit-animal, even more so than the buffalo. The word for owl also means "spirit" or "ghost." The Owl-Man was dressed in full regalia, and he prayed for the health and happiness of all. He had the privilege to engage in sexual intercourse with any woman during the public ceremony. Women who knew of his customs could avoid his approaches by saying to him, "Do it to me." In that case, he could not touch them.

In battle, certain warriors of the society took a stand at a dangerous spot by driving an arrow through the free end of their sash. They could not retreat or release themselves. Only another warrior could release them by pulling out the arrow and telling them to stay there. If the Kiowa-Apache were losing a fight and a general call for retreat was sent out, the *Klintidie* warriors had to charge. Only if someone noticed their predicament and commanded them to charge could they retreat.

3.5. Absarokee

The Absarokee had two associations called Crazy Dogs. One was a military society with rank and file members and four officers; the other was a cult or club that used inverse speech. To differentiate them, the first were called the long Crazy Dogs (*micge wara'axe hatskite*) because of their long tradition, and the latter the Crazy-Dogs-Wishing-to-Die (*micge wara'axe akcewiuk*).[504] The Crazy-Dogs-Wishing-to-Die amounted to a club for death-seeking young men, who, for various reasons, no longer wished to live. The motive to declare oneself a member, at least in several cases, was personal (insurmountable grief, weariness of life). All practiced inverse speech, and they were expected to do the opposite of what they said. They showed a deliberate indifference for life and limb that would lead to their death. Anyone who would adhere to the death pledge could announce that he was a Crazy-Dog-Wishing-to-Die. Usually, only one or two persons declared themselves in the course of a year to be Crazy-Dogs-Wishing-to-Die. However, in some years, no one volunteered and in other years up to five or more would.

1937, p. 153-156.

[504] Accounts of the Crazy-Dogs-Wishing-to-Die are found in Lowie *Military Societies of the Crow Indians*, Anthropological Papers of the American Museum of Natural History 11 (3): 143-217; 1913b: 191, 193-196, *Myths and Traditions of the Crow Indians*, Anthropological Papers of the American Museum of Natural History, 25: 1-308 1918: 299-304, *Notes on the Social Organization and Customs of the Mandan, Hidatsa, and Crow Indians*, Anthropological [39] Papers of the American Museum of Natural History 21: 1-99 1922a: 31-33, and Curtis The North American Indian, vol. 4, *The Apsaroke, or Crows; The Hidatsa*, New York: Johnson Reprint, 1970 1909a: 13-14.

During the day, the Crazy-Dogs-Wishing-to-Die rode about camp on their horses. They wore a sash, carried a rattle, and danced and sang their distinctive songs (death songs) proclaiming that they were here for only a short period and that all women were invited to visit them.[505] Elderly women cheered lustily when the Crazy-Dogs-Wishing-to-Die rode by in camp. At night, women, including married women, visited the Crazy-Dog-Wishing-to-Die to comfort them. One of them, Spotted Rabbit, was said to be the most handsome Absarokee who ever lived.[506] [29]

People had to stand clear of the Crazy-Dogs-Wishing-to-Die when they rode through camp for they might shoot at anything. One shot himself in the foot with a Hudson's Bay horse-pistol. Another rode off a cliff with his horse. However, most Crazy-Dogs-Wishing-to-Die awaited the season's first opportunity to make their foolish charge at the enemy. If, by lucky circumstance, he survived his attack, he ceased to be a Crazy-Dog-Wishing-to-Die.[507]

The family of a Crazy-Dog-Wishing-to-Die would attempt to dissuade the candidate, but without success. If he acted cowardly and refused to sacrifice himself at the critical moment in battle, he would become a laughingstock and fall into disrespect. One Crazy-Dog-Wishing-to-Die lost heart and cried at the decisive moment when he was to fulfill his pledge to die. His friend, Hillside, reminded him of his vow and shoved him along, admonishing him to go on and die.[508]

A famous Crazy-Dog-Wishing-to-Die, who was alive while Lowie was working with the Absarokee, was Young Cottontail Rabbit. He became a Crazy-Dog-Wishing-to-Die because he had been shot in the knee when he was young and, therefore, could not go afoot on war parties. He was envious of other young warriors and wished to be dead, even though the entire camp loved and admired him. He was handsome and rode a vigorous horse. He did not participate in camp activities like marching or hunting instead, he went about singing or dancing, and he spoke "backwards." The women particularly liked him. When enemy warriors were discovered and driven back to their fortification, Young Cottontail Rabbit recklessly rushed up to the breastwork of the enemy and shot inside at them. They shot back and he fell. It rained violently all night and Young Cottontail Rabbit lay dead in the rainwater. His people could not recover his body until daybreak. They wrapped him up and carried him back to camp. Everyone cried and mourned his death. His body was placed on a four-pole scaffold and the camp moved on without him.[509]

---

[505] Curtis The North American Indian, vol. 4, *The Apsaroke, or Crows; The Hidatsa* 1909a, p. 13.

[506] Lowie *Crow Military Societies* 1913b: 196; *Notes on the Social Organization and Customs of the Mandan, Hidatsa, and Crow Indians*, Anthropological Papers of the American Museum of Natural History 21: 1-99 1917: 84; *Myths and Traditions of the Crow Indians*, Anthropological Papers of the American Museum of Natural History 25: 1-308 1918: 299); *The Material Culture of the Crow Indians*, Anthropological Papers of the American Museum of Natural History 21 (3): 201-270 1922b: 267, *The Crow Indians* , New York: Farrer and Rinehart 1935: 18, 331-332.

[507] Curtis The North American Indian, vol. 4, *The Apsaroke, or Crows; The Hidatsa* 1909a: 14); Lowie *Crow Military Societies* 1913b: 194.

[508] Curtis *Apsaroke, or Crows; The Hidatsa* 1909a: 13-14; Lowie *Crow Indians* 1935: 331.

[509] Lowie *Mandan, Hidatsa, and Crow* 1917: 84-85); *Crow Indians* 1935: 331-332.

Figure 15. Music to a song sung by a Crazy-Dog-Wishing-to-Die. "I am merely staying on earth for a time; all women look upon me!"[510] (Recorded by Curtis 1909a: 13).

4. Fools and Foolishness on the Plains

Historical Plains society was interspersed with many forms of "foolishness" and "craziness." Native words used to identify the clowns and *contraries* are most often translated as "foolish" or "crazy." These terms are not intended in a derogatory manner, and they were widely used in other contexts. Many of the extremes to which the ambitious Plains warrior resorted were called "crazy," "reckless" or "foolish." In addition to war craziness and foolish warriors, Plains culture knew "love craziness." The words *foolish* and *crazy* also depicted exaggerated conditions or extremely wrong persons, such as women with improper sexual behavior and cruel despotic men. The terms were also part of the names of numerous individuals; examples are Fool Chief, Crazy Mule, Crazy Horse, Crazy Bear, Foolish Woman and Fools Crow.

The roles played by the ceremonial and mythological figures, such as the sacred Clown Hunters of the Cheyenne Massaum ceremony and the Okipa Fool of the Mandan (discussed in part 4.1) further show that foolish and irrational elements were deeply established in Plains religion.

4.1. Ceremonial Fool of the Mandan

The Okipa Fool (*Okeheede*) was a mythological figure who was impersonated by an actor during the largest and most colorful annual religious ceremony of the Mandan — the Okipa. He was neither a *contrary* nor entirely a clown. The complexity of the figure is reflected by the variety of names assigned to him in translations, e.g. the owl, Evil Spirit, Foolish One, clown, a monster or devil.[511]

The Okipa Fool turned his excessive sexual energy into sacred amusement. He bursts into the ceremony during the proceedings of the all-important Bull Dance. He provides for the

---

[510] Recorded by Curtis *Apsaroke, or Crows; The Hidatsa* 1909a:13.

[511] George Catlin *O-Kee-Pa: A Religious Ceremony and other Customs of the Mandans*, John C Ewers, ed, New Haven: Yale University Press, First published 1867 1967: 59); Curtis The North American Indian, vol. 5, *The Mandan; The Arikara; The Aa'ni Atsina*, New York: Johnson Reprint, 1970 1909b: 48-50); Lewis Henry Morgan *The Indian Journals, 1859-62*. Leslie A White, ed, Ann Arbor: University of Michigan Press 1959: 194-195); also spelled *Oxinhede* (Alfred W Bowers *Mandan Social and Ceremonial Organization*, Chicago: University of Chicago Press 1950: 132, 152, 153), *Ochkih-Hedde* (George Will and Herbert Spinden *The Mandans*: *A Study of their Culture, Archaeology and Language*, Papers of the Peabody Museum of American Archaeology and Ethnology, Harvard University, Cambridge, 3 (4): 79-219 1906: 133, 143) and *Ochkih-Hadda* (Maximilian, Prinz zu Weid *Reise in das innere Nord-Amerika in den Jahren 1832 bis 1834*, Vol. II, Colbenz: J. Hoelscher. Maximilian 1841: 68, 91).

highest excitement by running about uncontrolled and chaotically. He was entirely naked and painted pitch black using pounded charcoal and bear's grease, except for several small white rings over his body. He was outfitted with a most distinguishing utensil, a colossal wooden phallus suspended between his legs that he could raise and lower since it was tied with a string to a long staff, which he held over the ground before him. He would play mischief on the women spectators and desperately rush at them with the phallus raised.[512]

The Okipa Fool was necessary to ensure the welfare of the people. He entered the ceremony during the all-important Bull Dance, which was a dramatization of the mythical occurrence of first attracting the [31] buffalo (and ensuring the winter food supply). The "disruption" of the dance by the Okipa Fool and his unrestrained sexuality were essential parts of the ceremony as attested to in origin myths of the Bull Dance. The yearly return of the buffalo was attributed to the Fool mounting and mating with the Bull dancers, which he acrobatically did while keeping in perfect time with the dance.[513]

The spiritual power of the Okipa Fool was transmitted through sexual intercourse. The women thus awaited opportunity to defeat the Okipa Fool and capture the symbol of his powers. The one who triumphed and took possession of the phallus made claims to powers of fertility and took over as the director the remaining ceremonies, including "Walking with the Buffalo Bulls," a sex ceremony in which the ~~squaws~~ chose from the "buffaloes.".[514]

In the mythological accounts, Okipa Fool's father was the Sun or a sun spirit, and his mother was a good young woman who never went out with men (solar impregnation). As a child, the Okipa Fool was black in color with white circles, always leaping and running about, even up the sides of the lodges. Because he killed sacred snakes and the Holy Woman, who lived in the ash thicket, conflicts arose and the culture hero, Lone Man, killed the Okipa Fool.[515] The Mandan worshipped and paid honor to the Okipa Fool since he was an ancient and powerful force who infused serious matters with foolishness.

Conclusion

The *contraries* are an extraordinary example of the richness of Plains Indian culture. The few individuals in several tribes, who were known as the *contraries*, were committed to doing the opposite of what others normally do in their society. To understand better the *contraries*, it is necessary to tease them apart from related Plains phenomena. In this essay, I have thus endeavored to formulate a classification that distinguishes the individual *contraries* from the ritual clowns, clown doctors, contrary-shamans, reverse-action warriors and ceremonial fools.

The *contraries* are related to the ritual clowns, i.e the *heyokahohnuhka* complex, but should not be lumped entirely with them.

Clowns in many cultures serve to promote the maintenance of the social and ethical

---

[512] Catlin *O-Kee-Pa* 1967: 59-62.

[513] Bowers *Mandan* 1950: 156); George Catlin *Letters and Notes on the Manners, Customs, and Condition of the North American Indians, Written during Eight Years' Travel amongst the Wildest Tribes of Indians in North America, in 1832-1839*, Vol. I, Third Edition, London: Tilt and Bogue 1842: 168, 1967: 84).

[514] Catlin *O-Kee-Pa* 1967: 61, 69-71, 84-85; Bowers Mandan 1950: 131, 144-166, 348.

[515] Bowers Mandan 1950:. 352); Catlin *Letters and Notes* 1842: 179 fnt, 1967, p. 73-74.

structure by playing out flagrant violations of it. Clowns cultivate creativity, open new social avenues and serve as emancipators of the downtrodden. After a performance, actors and clowns remove their masks and costumes and return to normal life. Not so, the *contraries*. The position of a *contrary* was full-time, he was not restricted to performances yet he was seriously bound to special rules of behavior. The term of an individual *contrary* lasted years if not forever, especially among the Lakota and Santee. Sometimes when the career of a *contrary* ended, the position would be replaced by a younger candidate. Ex-*contraries* could return to a normal life, achieve [32] social recognition and marry. While they were *contraries*, however, they were generally unmarried. The *contraries*, unlike the clowns, foolish warriors and ceremonial fools, had no special sexual privileges and never participated in public sex practices.

The *contraries* are similar to the foolhardy and crazy warriors of the Plains, but should not be mistaken for them. Their actions in battle were sometimes identical. The Comanche *contrary*, for example, was a sash-bearing "no-flight" warrior, who in the midst of a battle instead of fighting, shook his rattle and sang his songs. The actions of the Caddoan *contraries* in battle put their lives in direct danger. (By the way, these examples should dispel opinions that the *contrary* sought to escape tradition masculine obligations.) The Cheyenne *contrary* had special obligations in battle only when carrying the Thunder-Bow. The *contrary Heyoka* abided by his inner compulsion to act by opposites at all times, even in battle. In some cases, he even switched sides and shot at one's own comrades!

The *contraries* have a logical affinity not only to Clowns, but also to the Trickster character. All admit to being disruptive, disrespectful, mischievous, counter-productive, absurd and taboo-breaking. Yet, the Plains *contraries* should not be viewed as the earthly descendent of the Plains trickster. Like the Clown, the Trickster is a cross-cultural category that has generated multiple suggestions for scholars. Tricksters, for example, reflect an early undifferentiated stage in the evolutionary development of human consciousness. They show the vagueness of religious boundaries, the limitations of the human condition, and the human tendency to err and be destructive. Certainly, the Trickster was the most popular folkloric character on the Plains to judge by the number of recorded fables. Particularly youngsters loved hearing tales of that ingenious, deceiving and cunning Coyote (or Spider or Rabbit) who was always doing things wrong. Trickster stories generally conveyed lessons of morality through negative example. Yet, in the oral traditions of the Absarokee, Arapaho and Lakota (as well as Winnebago and Ojibwa), the Trickster sometimes appears in human form and replaces the traditional world creator, culture hero and first man. In general, however, the Trickster played no part with the clown organizations, with Plains warfare or the *contraries*. Nor did the mythological background of the clowns and *contraries* rely on trickster tales. The principle of contrary behavior is far too restrictive for the Trickster. His talent was to deceive (i.e. fool) others purely for the sake of self-advantage. In doing so, he all too often became entrapped by his own scheming.

The diversity of the *contraries* prevents general statements regarding their relationship as a whole to the clown organizations, foolish warriors and ceremonial fools of the Plains. For example, only the contrary cults of the *heyoka-hohnuhka* complex were characterized by a close relationship to clown societies. The Arikaree and Pawnee had no clown organizations, and their *contraries* were probably rooted in mythologies connected to the Okipa Fool myths of the Mandan. In their respective mythologies, they share several features. They were begotten by the Sun. They had a tendency to violate religious precepts by killing sacred animals. Further, they were foolish already in childhood and managed to persist in their practice into manhood.

In conclusion, the *contraries* are not to be identified as ritual clowns, earthly tricksters or foolish warriors. They were not part of society just for laughs, lessons or daringness. Only the *contraries* lived permanently by the contrary principle. The clowns, warriors and shaman, who practiced contrariness either did so temporarily or in abbreviated form. This composition thus sought to shed light on the *contraries* by disentangling them from related categories, such as Clowns, Fools, Tricksters. It is hoped that a significant step has been taken toward understanding the phenomenon of the Plains *contraries*.

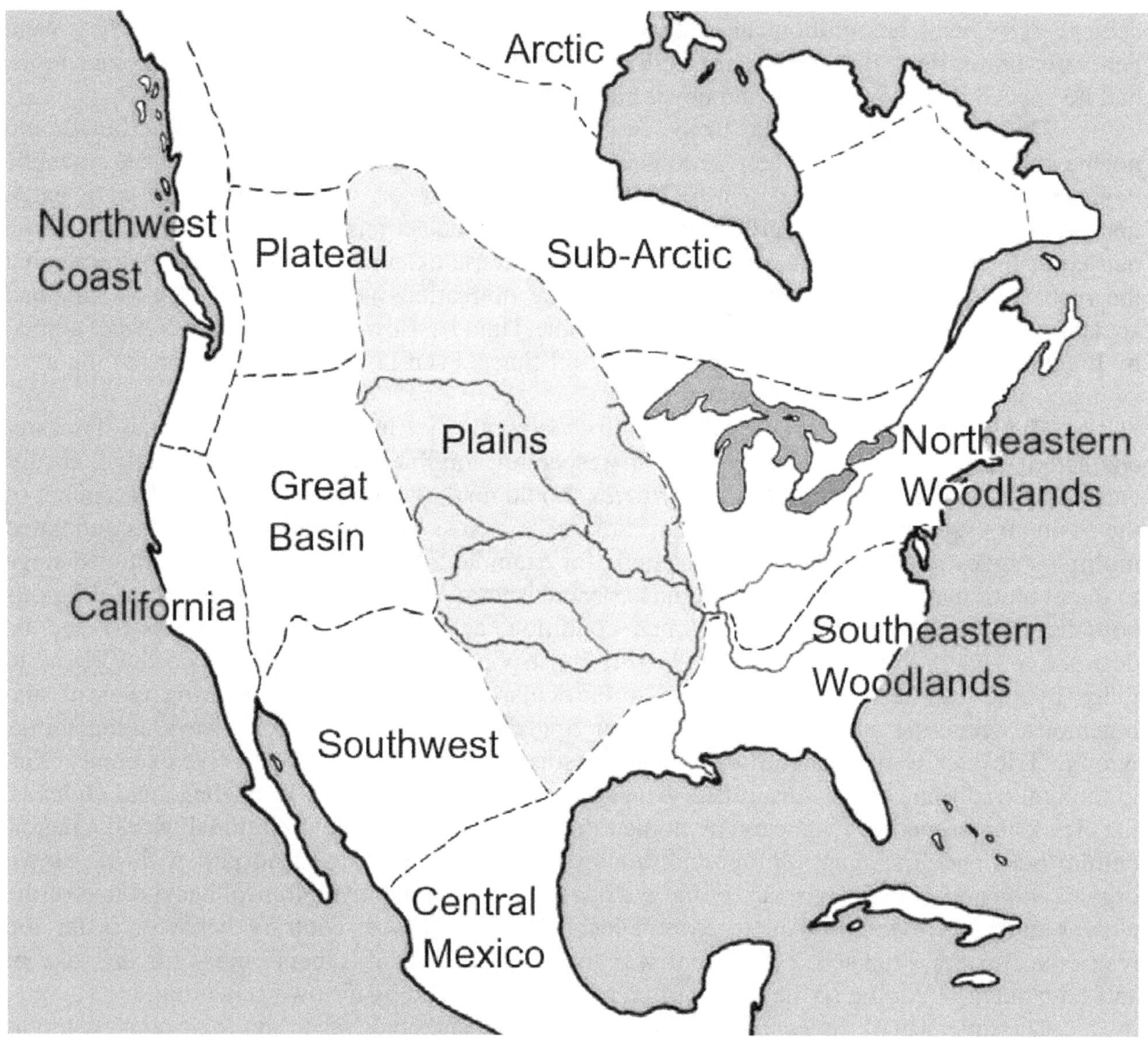

Map 1. Native North American culture areas.

The Plains culture area covered the heartland of North America. Plains economy was primarily based on the buffalo. The culture area consisted of the nomadic bison hunters, who roamed the short-grass High Plains in the west, and the bison hunters on the tall-grass Prairie in the east who farmed, harvested maize and dwelt in villages.

Map 2. Approximate location of Plains Indian tribes ca. 1850.

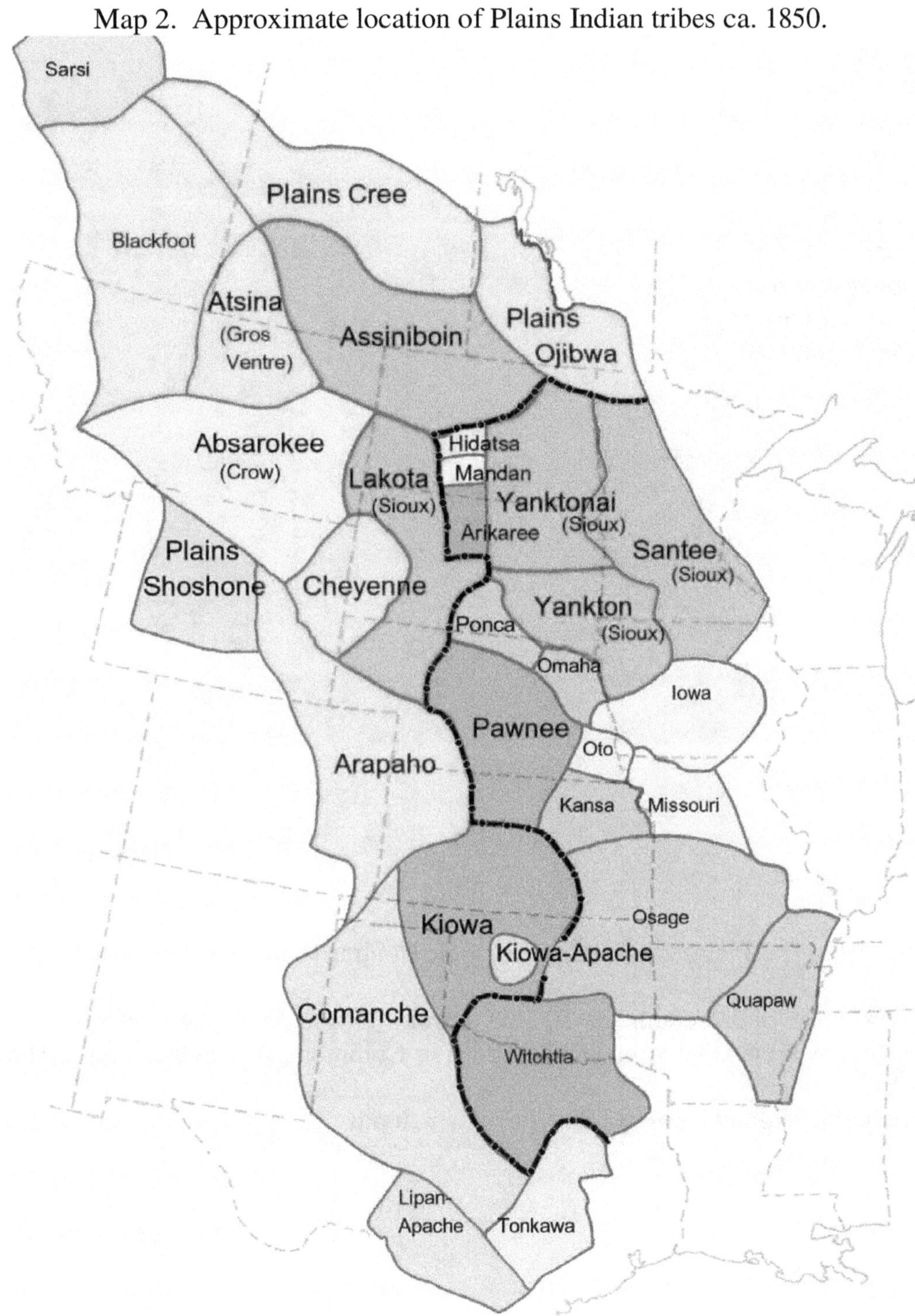

Thick black line marks the separation of the nomadic tribes of the Plains in the west and Plains farmers in the east. Colors of tribes correspond to language groups

(coded in box insert).
Language Groups
Algonquian = green
Athapascan = brown
Caddoan = rose
Kiowa Tanoan = purple
Chiwere Siouan = lime
Dakota Siouan = blue
Dhegiha Siouan = drab
Missouri Valley Siouan =
Proto-Siouan = yellow
Tonkawan = tan
Uto-Aztecan

Please cite this article as

Plant, John 2010. The Plains Indian Clowns, their Contraries and related Phenomena. Vienna, Austria.
URL: http://www.anjol.de/documents/100703_heyoka_article_john-plant.pdf
The text and maps are available under the Creative Commons Attribution-Share Alike License (CC-BY-SA).
 https://www.anjol.de/documents/100802_heyoka_neu.pdf

Arapaho, Age Grades, Lime Chief

Table 9.1 Social and Political Functions of Arapaho Men's Age Sets

AGE GRADE	FUNCTION
Kit Foxes and Stars	Servants for other lodges
Clubboards and Spears	Appropriation of value from outside camp circle and police force for controlling camp movements, use of physical force
Crazy Men	Ritual agency and use of medicine to control others
Dogs	Chiefship, as following others
Old Men	Learning sacred knowledge
Seven Old Men	Painting, guiding all other lodges

The Crazy Lodge[516]

The next grade [153] an age set passed into was the Crazy Lodge (*hohooko 'oowu'*). The men who entered this lodge were around thirty to forty years old and were called *hohookeenenno'* Crazy Men.[517] As discussed in chapter 3, the stem for 'crazy' (*hohookee*) is a general descriptor of behavior that is foolish, immature, or without proper knowledge. Mooney[518] (1896: 988) states that the Crazy Men did not go to war; they served only religious functions. The lodge and the ceremony were similar in form to the Clubboard and Spear rituals. One member of the age set pledged out of pity for the life movement of a family member or the tribe, and then other age-set members had to follow. Ceremonial grandfathers and elder brothers were also called upon to assist. Again, the elder brothers were drawn from the Old Men's society, and the grandfathers had to be very old men, likely from the Seven Old Men, who had passed through all the lodges. As in other lodge ceremonies, three days of preparation were followed by three days of dancing with similar exchanges throughout.

In the Crazy Lodge there was only one dancer of highest degree, called *nookohookee* 'white crazy man'. His quiet and still leadership behavior exaggerated that of the lead Spear man: "As the dancers move about the camp-circle, he always goes last, being markedly slow in his actions in contrast with the lively and untiring movements of all his companions".[519] In this grade, leadership required yet slower movement and stronger duty to follow others. Whereas the white crazy man wore an all-white cape and was painted white entirely, the other dancers wore white and red capes. In this dance the men carried small bows with specially prepared arrows, which they shot backward in a contrary way.

On the evening of the first day of the ceremony, the Crazy Men danced before their grandfathers, but then they performed a crazy ritual act. With bare feet they entered a prepared

---

[516] Jeffrey Anderson The Four Hills of Life ~ Northern Arapaho Knowledge and Life Movement, Lincoln: University of Nebraska Press 2001: 153-7.

[517] Sister M Inez Hilger, Arapaho Child Life and Its Cultural Background, BAE B 148 1952: 118.

[518] James Mooney The Ghost-Dance Religion and Sioux Outbreak of 1890, BAE AR 14 1892-3: 641-1110 1896: 988.

[519] Alfred Kroeber, The Arapaho, Bulletin of the American Museum of natural History 18 (1, 2, 4) 1904: 189; reprint, Nebraska 1983.

fire, "stamping or dancing on it until they have trampled it out".[520] The dancers thus mimicked the behavior of the moth *hohookehe'* 'little crazy', which often flies into fire or light. Following the fire dance, the men spoke and acted contrarily for the remainder of the three-day ceremony.[521] [154]

Throughout this time, the men wore a medicinal root attached to their owl-feather headdresses and capes. Kroeber[522] identifies the root as *tcectäätcei* (*ceceecei*). Any living thing touched by the root or by a dancer's cape was paralyzed. Even passing the cape over an animal's track would immobilize it. According to Kroeber, the same root with this power protected the men themselves from its paralyzing effects. Each lodge in the *beyoowu'u*, along with the old women's quill ceremony, used different roots from a set of seven sacred Arapaho medicines. The crazy root was used only in the Crazy Lodge and the Offerings Lodge. In the arrangement of medicines for the Offerings Lodge preparations, the crazy root was also placed in the center, as the "heart".[523] According to Dorsey the crazy root was really a mixture of medicines and signified "law and order" as well as "everything reversed".[524] The connection is that by the time men had reached age, they had acquired their medicine power and could be initiated to using beetee power to control others' behavior. The use and symbolism of the crazy root embodied the appropriation of medicine power for maintaining "law and order" that is, doing things in a good/correct way. In other words, the Crazy Men had control over life movement itself, a power that culminated in old age.

While wearing their regalia and root, the Crazy Men acted as "contraries," saying the opposite of what they meant and doing the opposite of what they were asked. For instance, "When one of the dancers is carrying a comparatively heavy load, such as a dog, he acts as if it weighed almost nothing".[525] There are two symbolic aspects of the crazy practice. One is that the men at this stage in life have become immune to harsh conditions, that is. unaffected by or "closed" to the external world. The second is that the men have by this time acquired medicine power to immobilize, that is, suspend the life movement of others.

Kroeber adds that the Crazy dancers also put a root, *haakahaa*, in their ears that made them deaf and thus "crazy".[526] As discussed in chapter;), the practice of craziness implies "not listening" or having one's senses blocked up so that one cannot hear what others advise and cannot sense what is going on in the environment. Adding to their closed senses, the men also danced with their hands over their eyes. The Crazy Men enacted blindness as well as deafness, then, both of which contribute to crazy behavior, or not being able to see or hoi dangerous situations approaching.

The owl-feather circlets they wore were also believed to make them act foolish. The color white, dominant in the Crazy Lodge, is associated with the owl and winter. The Crazy Men annoyed everyone in camp with their foolish behavior, except their grandfathers,

---

[520] Alfred Kroeber The Arapaho, Bulletin of the American Museum of natural History 18 (1, 2, 4) 1904: 189; reprint, Nebraska, 1983.

[521] Alfred Kroeber The Arapaho, 1904: 190.

[522] Alfred Kroeber The Arapaho, 1904: 190.

[523] George Dorsey Arapaho Sun Dance: The Ceremony of the Offerings-Lodge, Chicago: Field Columbian Museum Publication 75, Anthropological Series 4 1903: 64-65.

[524] George Dorsey Arapaho Sun Dance, 1903: 66.

[525] Alfred Kroeber The Arapaho 1904:192.

[526] Alfred Kroeber The Arapaho 1904:192.

grandmothers, and others who perhaps had [155] more powerful medicine.[527] When it came to old people, the prescription of respect superseded even the foolish behavior of the Crazies. Ritualized craziness thus allowed a temporary and limited suspension of respect. It is interesting to note that the crazy behavior was confined to the space outside the tents and tipis. When eating or entering a tent, the Crazy Men removed the owl circlets. In doing so, they could not harass people while they were in their tipis, perhaps because of respect for children or other vulnerable persons inside. The symbolic content of the regalia and articles used, according to accounts compiled by Kroeber, connoted abundance and long life, or life movement in general.

In the story called "Lime-Crazy",[528] recounting the origin of the lodge, a man is banished from the tribe for foolish laziness and spending too much time with women. Thus, he acts immaturely by violating the value of being useful through doing and by crossing the boundaries of gender segregation that accompany adulthood. As a result of complying with the people's wishes to banish the man, his brother, the Chief, becomes increasingly poor and thus pitiful. To relieve his difficulty, while on a buffalo hunt the Chief leaves his younger brother, instructing him to walk in circles around a buffalo carcass to drive off the flies. When the Chief does not return, the younger brother continues to walk around the meat. After three or four years, the people shun the Chief and his wife for having abandoned Lime-Crazy. The Chief then goes out to look for his brother and finds him in a pit formed by years of walking in circles. Lime-Crazy then returns to the people with the knowledge of the lodge and the power to immobilize and remobilize others through use of the crazy root.

As in other stories, a person acquires knowledge after being estranged from camp circle and enduring a difficult, pitiful ordeal. In all such stories, the individual must return to the camp circle and give back the knowledge to the people so that it can be channeled into blessings for collective life movement. In that way the power of craziness is appropriated within ceremonial lodge and camp circle, where it can be kept within right age groups and ritual boundaries.

Consistent with other American Indian cultural contexts, craziness or contrariness is not intrinsically evil or threatening to the order; rather, within boundaries, it provides a source of energy for life movement itself. The Crazy Lodge circumscribed "craziness" in a ritual context and thus channeled the power into the desire for abundance and life. It also brought together in the age grade three key dimensions: craziness, maturity, and medicine. It is about at the age of Crazy Men that elders and the tribe could recognize a person as an adult [156] in Arapaho terms. Ironically, just as men were reaching full adulthood, they passed through the Crazy Lodge.

As suggested by the mythical character Lime-Crazy, medicine power is acquired through fasting or apprenticeship at or by this time in the life cycle. Hilger's informants agree that very young men did not fast for personal medicine: "There was no such thing as young men fasting. Men at 30 went out on hills or mountains to fast".[529] Kroeber corroborates: "The custom of more easterly tribes, for young boys to go out soon after the age of puberty, and fast in a given way for a certain number of days, is not known by the Arapaho. The men who go out to obtain supernatural power are usually fully adult, and sometimes of middle age".[530] It is clear, then, that by the time men moved from the Spear to the Crazy Lodge they had been allowed access to medicine in one form or another. Furthermore, the acquisition of medicine as one moved through the life cycle was associated with increasing exposure to heat, as in the sweat lodge set up for a person who was fasting and the heat of the fire into which the Crazy dancers danced. Recall

---

[527] Alfred Kroeber The Arapaho 1904:192

[528] George Dorsey and Alfred Kroeber Traditions of the Arapaho, Chicago: Field Columbian Museum Publication 81, Anthropological Series 5 1903: 23-30. {Read it below herein}

[529] Sister M Inez Hilger Arapaho Child Life 1952: 128.

[530] Alfred Kroeber The Arapaho 1907: 418.

the association with heat in the Arapaho life-cyclical model that required the separation of children and medicine.

The use of the crazy root ritually expressed the acquisition of power to immobilize others through the use of medicine, thus anticipating the power older men exerted for social control. As age sets moved from the junior lodges into the Crazy Lodge, they progressed from the use of direct physical force to the use of indirect medicine power to control the movement of others. Power was a matter of paralyzing other people and animals by using roots and other medicines along with the knowledge to cause others to become sick. As in the Crazy Lodge dance context, when Arapahos did have medicines of that sort, it was necessary to be careful not to cause arguments or act improperly toward people who had such power, for they could cause illness or even death.

The association of owl feathers with the ability to paralyze is related to the idea mentioned above that dead people turned into owls. Objects shot into people were called ghost/skeleton arrows (*3iikono3ii*), and illness was thought to be the result of arrows or other objects shot by ghosts into people.[531] The Crazy dancers in this way personified ghostlike behavior. Their bows and arrows paralleled those that ghosts use. The white paint of the highest-degree dancer suggests a ghostlike appearance. In the story describing the origin of the Crazy Lodge, the younger brother "dies" in a sense, for the tribe believes him to be dead. Then, because his people and his brother wronged him, he returns to use his power over others.

The Crazy Lodge, then, was a rite of passage in Van Gennep's terms, as a [157] reversal and a reincorporation back into the total life movement system. In previous age grades, young men were oriented outside the camp circle to form peer groups for horse care, war parties, police duties, and hunting. The strong warrior message of the Clubboard Lodge and the Spear Lodge is replaced by the use of "medicine" in the Crazy Lodge. The crazy behavior of the lodge was an inversion of maturity and a symbolic death in order to mark the transition to adulthood. In a sense, the ritually bounded expression of craziness aimed at a culturally constituted catharsis to preempt or at least discard ahead of time subsequent crazy behavior by adult men outside the ritual context. In the Arapaho theory of practice, that is homologous to the ritual expression of suffering as sacrifice in order to preempt future suffering. There is thus "reversed" rather than "sympathetic" logic at work in the Crazy Lodge and elsewhere in Arapaho ritual. Fasting averts hunger, sacrifice brings abundance, alienation brings knowledge to the tribe, enduring an illness makes it possible to cure that illness oneself, opening effects closure, and craziness effects maturity.

In the ear piercing ceremony discussed in chapter 5, the expression of pain by the child was good, for it would avert future pain. Among the old medicine men, swallowing objects that they removed from others made it possible for them to cure illness. For the Crazy Men, their inappropriate behavior instilled future appropriate knowledge as they took on more and more ritual and social responsibilities. They had to become like the white crazy dancer of highest rank.[532] As in the Spear, Dog, and women's Buffalo Lodges, the leader's actions were opposite to those of the lower-ranked dancers. Leadership required immobility, not moving ahead of all others. In the Clubboard Lodge, the leaders charged ahead of everyone else, activating the motion of youth. In the Spear and Crazy Lodges, the leader moved slower than the others.

---

[531] Alfred Kroeber The Arapaho 1907: 437.
[532] Alfred Kroeber The Arapaho 1904: 189.

The Sacred Dances

General Features

In the Aa'ni public cult, as contrasted with more or less private cult concepts and observances, next after the sacred Pipe ceremonies, in order of rank and importance in the native view, were the Sacred Dances or Lodges, — the terms are used interchangeably, and while etymologically "Lodge" is correct, our informants preferred usually "Dance."

There were eight of these Sacred Dances: the Sacrifice Dance (commonly but incorrectly called the Sun Dance), the "Law Enforcers" or Old Man's Dance, the Drum Dance, the Kit-Fox Dance, the Dog Dance, the Crazy Dance, the Fly Dance, and the Old Women's Dance.[533] Of these eight, the Sacrifice Dance was more generally regarded as the "greatest," ranking first in order of importance and dignity, but somewhat outside of the others which have been mentioned in descending order. All eight were regarded as sacred rites, not merely social or good-time occasions, although such elements entered into them or were associated with them.

Ordinarily a person participated in or vowed during his life first the Fly Dance; only after this the Crazy, Kit-fox, Dog, Drum and Sacrifice Dances, and finally the Old Man's Dance.

Our chief ~~informants~~ on the Sacred Dances were The Boy, Turn Toes, Thick, Charles Buckman, Coming Daylight, and Singer. Lame Bull, from whom The Boy got most of his information on the Dances, had gone through all of them except the Drum Dance. He had even been selected as one of the two outstanding [174] men who had roles to play in the Old Women's Dance. Turn Toes (b. ca. 1860) had taken part in the Sacrifice Dance (about four times) and in the Crazy, Dog, Fly, and Old Men's Dances, having joined the Crazy Dance first and participated in the Fly Dance when he was already an old man. The Boy had witnessed the Sacrifice, Fly, Crazy, Old Men's and Old Women's Dances, and his contemporaries. Thick and Charles Buckman, knew something of them too. The others had disappeared before their time. Coming Daylight and Singer (b. ca. 1854) witnessed some of the Dances. Coming Daylight as a small girl participated as one of the "calves" in the Old Woman's Dance. Our other informants were able to supplement accounts as given by these from what they had heard from their relatives and others of the older generations.

Today the Sacred Dances survive only in memory. Dates when the respective Dances were last held are: Drum Dance, when Lame Bull (b. 1824 or 1825) was a boy, hence probably in the 1830's; Kit-fox, ca. 1870, when Turn Toes was a small boy; Dog Dance, after the last Kit-fox, apparently in the late 1870's because Turn Toes had gone through it; Turn Toes did the Old Men's Dance, at which time he was only about 20 years old, therefore about 1880, at the junction of Beaver Creek and Bear Gulch on the east side of the Little Rockies; Sacrifice Dance, 1884; Crazy Dance, twice after the establishment of the Fort Belknap Agency, — the last time right after the Sacrifice Dance of 1884; Fly Dance, about 1907 (the one in which Turn Toes as an old man participated). Since that date none of the Sacred Dances has been held.

The Sacred Dances were held, not as part of a seasonal cycle, but only (with one exception to be noted later) in fulfillment of a vow by some individual. The vow itself, even in the case of the Fly Dance, was made to the Supreme Being, not to any other being. Which of the

---

[533] Kroeber, Ethnology of the Gros Ventre Aa'ni 1908, pp. 227-268, gives an excellent account of these Dances, gotten at a time, nearly half a century ago, when tribal memory was fresher. Our data may help to fill out some of the picture.

dances an individual chose to vow would depend on circumstances. If, for instance, he were in sore straits, surrounded by the enemy and in imminent danger of being killed, he would vow the Sacrifice Dance which cost greatly in suffering and goods, or else the Crazy, Dog, Kit-fox, or Drum Dance. Usually, however, a boy was supposed to go first through the Fly Dance, and only the aged could go through the Old Man's [175] Dance.[534] Women could vow the Old Women's Dance, but no other Dance could be vowed by women of any age.

The vower would call upon his company or age-society to help him fulfill his vow. As elsewhere explained, when the young boy was about 15 to 17 years old he together with others of his age joined in a body one or other of the two Soldier Societies, the Stars or the Wolves. Each such newly joining group of youths would be incorporated in the larger society of Stars or Wolves, but would keep its own identity through life as a subdivision of the Stars or Wolves, would have its own name (such as Potbellies, Calves, Holding-On-to-Dogs-Tail), and would hang together in common loyalty, protection and helpfulness.[535]

The vower's company, not all the Stars or Wolves, would help him make provision for the Dance, would be in charge of the affair and, during it and only during it, could exercise certain definite authority over other members of the tribe. If the tribe were on the march toward the spot where the dance was about to be held, that company came immediately after the Flat Pipe, according to The Boy, and during the Dance the band chiefs and Pipe keepers stepped aside and yielded to the company the authority to run the camp, compel attendance, give orders, and punish disobedience. If during a Sacred Lodge an individual hunted buffalo out of turn, before the communal hunt began, his lodge would be destroyed, his clothes cut up, and so forth. A like punishment might be meted out to any who might refuse to come into camp, at the time the dance was held.[536]

The two Soldier Societies, the Stars and Wolves, and their respective constituent companies were permanent organizations. The specific individuals who vowed or joined in any given Dance [176] did not constitute such. Their grouping was a purely temporary one, lasting only for the duration of the Dance. During, for instance, the Crazy Dance, all who Joined in it, both members of the vower's company and others, were called Crazy Dancers, but once the Dance was over, they ceased to be such; there was no permanent organization or society of Crazy Dancers.

A first step which a man who had vowed a Sacred Dance had to take was to fill an ordinary pipe, go to a man who had gone through the rite in fulfillment of a vow and who knew the rite well, and offer him the pipe, saying: "Here is the pipe. You will be my 'grandfather.' " By accepting the pipe, — and he could hardly refuse, — the latter became the vower's ritual "grandfather." At the same time the "grandfather's" wife became the vower's "grandmother," and both the vower and his wife (or wives) became "grandchildren" of the "grandfather" and his wife, and they addressed one another respectively by these names. The vower himself was in

---

[534] In 1948, The Boy indicated that probably the Crazy, Dog, Kit-fox and Drum Dances would have been vowed in order, that is, that a man would vow a Dog Dance only if he had been previously a Crazy Dancer, and so on. He was none too sure on this point. He was quite emphatic, however, that any man who belonged to either the Stars or Wolf Men could vow the Sacrifice Dance. [R.F]

[535] For a description of the whole ceremonial organization, so far as it can be reconstructed, sec Flannery The Aa'ni Gros Ventre of Montana, Part I: Social Life, Catholic University of America Anthropological Series #15, DC 1953, pp. 49-51.1953, pp. 36-43.

[536] See Flannery Social Life 1953, pp. 43-44.

charge of the Dance and of the preparations therefore. The "grandfather's" role was that of liturgist, to instruct the vower in the ceremonies and observances proper to the given Lodge, and to see that they were carried out correctly. By way of exception, for the Old Women's Dance there were "grandmothers," but no "grandfathers."

When a given individual vowed one of the Sacred Lodges, other individuals could join with him in the rite, and each of these others would also choose a "grandfather," — one who had participated in the given Dance, — with whom he (and his wife) would contract the same sacred relationship and who would perform the same offices. No person could be "grandfather" to more than one vower or associate on the occasion of any one dance.[537] The "grandfathers" would usually be older than the participants but not by any means necessarily very old men.

If, however, a younger man offered a pipe to a very feeble old man whose memory of the rites was poor, the old man might accept the pipe and so become the younger man's "grandfather." [177]

The old man, however, might and commonly would appeal to another old man, who knew the Dance rites well even though he might never have vowed the dance, to double for him in seeing that the rite was properly carried out.

A keeper of one of the sacred Pipes, or at least of the Flat or Feathered Pipe, could not, during his term of office, function as "grandfather" at a sacred Lodge, but an ex-keeper could.

The relationship between ceremonial grandfather or grandmother and grandchild was a sacred one. Between such grandparent and grandchild a certain respect behavior had to be observed, and either was obligated not to refuse a request of the other.

Gambling, for instance, between them, or apparently even playing on opposite sides in a non-gambling hand game, was improper. Between blood grandparents and grandchildren a distinct joking relationship obtained,[538] not however between ritual grandparents and grandchildren, although our field evidence is not entirely consistent. According to one good informant, between these latter, telling vulgar jokes and stories, teasing about lovers, and so forth, were taboo; according to another, a little freedom in such matters was allowed, but not as much as was allowed and practiced between blood grandparents and grandchildren.

As regards, however, the much more significant mutual obligation of ceremonial grandparents not to refuse requests of grandchildren, our field data are entirely consistent and clear. This mutual obligation was rigidly lived up to and played a very important role in Aa'ni social life. This role may best be illustrated by the following actual case.

Once Iron Woman, Crow Bull's wife, ran away with Kitfox. When people noticed she was gone, they said: "Oh, she must have run away again with somebody." Before she ran away this time, Crow Bull had said: "If she runs away again, there will be trouble." So people went to Black Raven, Kitfox's father, to tell him that his son was suspected and that there would probably be trouble. When Iron Woman and Kitfox came back, Crow Bull seized his loaded gun and dashed out as if he were going to kill [178] them. Crow Bull's ceremonial grandson, whom he had instructed during the Crazy Dance and who was a relative of Black Raven, heard about this and ran in front of Crow Bull, saying; "Grandfather, don't do anything," and grabbed him just when he was about to fire. So Crow Bull said: "All right, because my grandchild stopped me." Then the relatives of Black Raven collected horses and blankets and other valuables, the young man himself contributing a blanket, and they all marched to Crow Bull's lodge carrying the

---

[537] In 1948, The Boy indicated that for the Crazy Dance at least two younger men might together approach an older man and have him act as their ritual grandfather if he accepted them. [R.F.]

[538] See Flannery Social Life 1953, pp. 121-22.

goods and leading the horses. On arrival at the lodge, the guilty lover went in first with the fine blanket he was giving and did a great thing. He covered White Skunk, Crow Bull's "dearly-loved child"[539] with this blanket. So Crow Bull could hardly do or say anything. He just said, "Well, I will leave it up to my son White Skunk, whatever he says, I will do." White Skunk then said: "Just give her (Iron Woman) to that man (Kitfox). Just let her go," and that is what Crow Bull did. He got all these horses and blankets and other things in payment.[540] Thus even though Crow Bull was so angry, his "grandchild" could stop him.

If a woman left her husband, and her "grandfather" went to her and told her to go back to her husband for she had nothing to get mad about, she would have to do so no matter how much she dreaded it.

If one Aa'ni had murdered another, and the relatives of the murdered person were afraid to approach the victim's father to offer indemnity, they could offer a pipe to any one of the father's ceremonial grandfathers. If the grandfather accepted it, he prayed with it and smoked it. When the murderer's relatives were ready with horses and clothing for payment, the grandfather would lead the relatives to his grandson, the murdered person's father, and say to him: "I have brought these people who ask your forgiveness. They are bringing these horses and blankets to you. I am asking you as my 'grandchild' to accept." The father could not refuse, for if he refused, some evil would overtake him. Actually refusals to such requests by a "grandfather" did not occur, to our ~~informants~~' knowledge. [179]

Two general aspects of this socio-ceremonial relationship were discussed in detail with The Boy: the obligation not to refuse requests, and the possibility of abuses arising under the system which for the rest had obvious social values in solving conflicts and preventing bloodshed.

What lay back of the sense of obligation to grant requests? The offered pipe was the central symbol, whether offered once for all at the time the ceremonial relationship was first contracted or offered on a specific occasion to a "grandfather" or "grandson" not the offerer's own. The ordinary pipe as offered in either case was looked upon as a sacred thing, as symbolic or representative of the sacrosanct Flat Pipe and/or Feathered Pipe which had been given by the Supreme Being as the most powerful media to pray with, as the most assured means of getting a hearing from the Supreme Being. The offered common pipe was a sort of substitute in the case for the sacred Pipes themselves. The "grandfather" or prospective "grandfather" on accepting the offered pipe, would always pray reverently with it to the Supreme Being before smoking it. If he once accepted the office of "grandfather" to another, he realized that he was assuming all the responsibilities that went with it, among them that of never refusing a request made by his "grandson" without a pipe, or by another with a pipe to intercede with his grandson. It was a sort of implicit sacred pledge into which the Supreme Being himself entered, at least indirectly. He knew that if he ever refused such a request, harm would come to him in some form: he would have to pay the price of his refusal, to suffer the consequences. Whether such consequences would follow automatically or by action of the Supreme Being or other beings is not clear from our field data, but in any case they were in some sense "supernaturally" caused. If people heard that a "grandfather" had refused a request made to him by his "grandson," they would say: "He (the 'grandfather') has sealed his fate." They would immediately lose their good opinion of him, — a social sanction added to the supernatural one, — and would look for some misfortune to

---

[539] For details on the dearly-loved child, see Flannery The Dearly-loved Child among Gros Ventre of Montana, Primitive Man 1941, pp. 33-37.

[540] For a discussion of indemnity in case of adultery see Flannery Social Life 1953, pp. 185-88; for indemnity in case of murder, *Idem*, p. 45.

befall him sooner or later. If soon after the refusal, evil did befall him, death or other grave mishap, they would say: "That's because he refused his grandson." [180]

The problem of possible abuses of the system was explained by The Boy along the following lines. "First of all if an old man had become my 'grandfather' only recently, say Just last week and I were a young man, no one would ordinarily ask me to appeal for him to my 'grandfather.' By strict right I could do so, and if no one else were available, I might be asked, but as an 'amateur,' as one lacking in experience, I would not be a good person to ask. An older, more experienced 'grandson' would be asked."

Besides choosing a "grandfather" the vower also selected, as a herald or crier for the Dance, some intelligent old man gifted as an orator. The crier's main task was to walk or ride around the camp before and during the Dance announcing to the people whether the group would move, other decisions, and agreements covering preparations for and procedure during the dance.

If the bands happened to be scattered at the time a sacred Dance was to be held, runners were sent by the vower to bid them foregather for the Dance. All members of the tribe were obliged to attend the Sacrifice and Crazy Dances, and pretty surely the Drum, Kit-fox and Dog Dances. As regards the Fly Dance, this was ordinarily held in connection with one of the other Dances, so everybody would be present anyhow. As regards the Old Men's and Old Women's Dances, they were not so lively or colorful, and were held a little apart and the people did not take much interest in them and "did not go much" to them; attendance was apparently not required.

If any individual or group failed to come when summoned, the vower would request the soldiers of the Stars or Wolves as the case might be, compel attendance.[541] Even a war party could not start out if some one had vowed a dance and it was about ready to begin. So much for the types or personnel, — vower, associates, age-groups, ceremonial "grandfathers," criers, police, and "congregation," — more or less common to all the Sacred Lodges. Personnel peculiar to particular Dances will be taken up later when each is described. Before describing the Dances one by one, some ritual observances common to all or many of them may be noted.

After the vower of a Dance had chosen his ritual grandfather [181] and before any further ritual step toward fulfillment of his vow had been taken, he arranged to have formal and public announcement of his vow to the people, even though he had already told some of his relatives or friends quickly or confidentially of it. In some instances the actual making of the vow took place at the public announcement rite. In either case the vower would call together in his own lodge all the "holy" men and women, such as ex-keepers but looked upon as holy, powerful, great. When all had gathered and were properly and solemnly seated, the vower filled a common pipe, offered it to one of the men present to have him pray with it and announce the vow. The one to whom it was offered could not refuse. If he were already in the place of honor in the circle he would remain there; else he would take it, and the occupant would vacate it. The chosen announcer would next make a smudge with sweet grass, and smudge the pipe in it. Then carrying the pipe he would go outside the lodge, stand in front of it, and in a loud voice call for order and command attention. After all was quiet, he would hold up the pipe und say; "So-and-so (the vower's name) has made a vow to do such-and-such (the content of the vow), you, *Ixtcibani:həhat*," ending with a prolonged "Yo ho ho ho." Then he prayed, addressing first as always, the Supreme Being and next to the other supernatural beings such as the Four Holy Beings, Those-who-follow-each-other, but not the Last Child, that the vow might be carried out

---

[541] For a detailed illustration of this point, see Flannery The Gros Ventre, Social Life 1953, pp. 49-51.

well, that its purpose might be attained (if not already attained), and that no sickness or other misfortune might come to the tribe during or after the ritual fulfillment of the vow. During the prayer, the announcer would mention the name of the person whom the vower had chosen as ritual grandfather. After ending the prayer, the announcer re-entered the lodge, and gave the pipe to this grandfather, and the latter took the place of honor which the announcer had momentarily occupied. Before or after the handing over of the pipe, all would smoke it, and some of those present would, of their own choice and without being invited, say a short prayer for themselves or for the vower.

Throughout the Sacred Dances, any ritual praying and smoking to be done with a pipe was done with an ordinary black stone pipe. Apart from the bringing of the Flat Pipe to the erection of the [182] Sacrifice Dance center pole, the sacred Pipes did not enter at all into the Sacred Lodges.

In all the Sacred Dances, the ritual number was four and movement was clockwise.

A sweat-lodge rite was held in connection with the Sacrifice and Crazy Dances, but we could obtain no details on it; whether also in connection with the others our informants could not say.

The Sacrifice, Drum, Kit-fox, Dog and Crazy Dances regularly lasted four nights and days; the Fly and probably the Old Men's and Old Women's just one day.

The sacred Dances were not held in the winter time when the bands were usually widely scattered, but in the period from about May or June when the bands foregathered to September after which the bands tended to scatter for the fall buffalo hunt.

The lodges for the Old Men's and Old Women's Dances were very simple and were put up outside the camp circle toward the south thereof. The lodges for the other Dances were erected inside the camp circle, near the center.

Feasting daily during the four-day dances was customary, except during the Sacrifice Dance which entailed much fasting on the part of the participants.

The alternation of reverent tension and pleasurable free release that characterized the sacred Pipe rites was even more characteristic of the Sacred Dances. [200 The Gros Ventres {Aa'ni} of Montana: Part II, Religion]

CRAZY DANCE

This dance was called *haha:tcau'wə* "crazy or silly lodge" (cf. Sifton, *hahachena*, adj. "crazy, silly"). The dance was also called in common parlance the "miller dance," and the dancers, "millers," — the reference being to the origin of the rite and to the fire ceremony of the fourth day, to be described presently. Millers or moths are also called by the Aa'ni "Crazy Men."

The Crazy Dance was last held immediately or shortly after the last performance, in 1884, of the Sacrifice Dance. Our chief informants on the Crazy Dance were: The Boy and Thick who had witnessed it three times and participated once respectively in the role of "little Crazy Dancers"; Turn Toes who had taken part as a regular "dancer"; Coming Daylight and Singer, both of whom had witnessed the dance, the former several times, although neither had actually joined it. Our information on the Crazy Dance is considerably more extensive than on the Drum, Dog, and Kit-fox dances, but is still far from complete. It confirms many details of Kroeber's account[542] and adds a number of others.

We did not obtain the full origin story of the Crazy Dance. The Boy stated that this rite had been first given (to the Aa'ni) by a miller (moth), that the Crazy Dancers when they jumped in the fire on the fourth day, were imitating the millers who fly around (and go into) the fire at

---

[542] Cf. Kroeber, Ethnology of Gros Ventre 1908, pp. 241-50.

night, — an interpretation confirmed by Coming Daylight, — and that the old cloak donned in the how rites on the fourth day was "in imitation of millers" but neither he nor Thick knew any origin story of the dance, nor did they know why the badger and owl (see infra) entered into the rite.

The Crazy Dance was, like the other Sacred Dances, held in fulfillment of a vow made by a man in case of his own, or a relative's serious illness or other grave emergency. Unlike any of the other Sacred Dances, it was also held under the following circumstances, without previous vow proper. [201]

Between times, during the summer months, that is, when no sacred dance was in progress, the two soldier societies, the Stars and the Grass dancers (Wolves), would compete with each other in foot races or other sports or in gambling bouts.[543] The losers would have to "cook" or to do other things for the winners. The losers in formation, with one of them in front carrying the Crazy Dance badger pelt trimmed and fixed up and tied to one end of a stick, might go to where the winners were sitting in a sort of semi-circle. On arrival there, the man carrying the pelt would say: "We are also bringing the badger pelt. It, too, we lost in the bet," — although actually the pelt itself had not been wagered. This was a dare or challenge to the winners to put up the Crazy Lodge, a challenge which they were "compelled" to accept. Some great man among the winners would then get up, take the badger pelt from the man who brought it, and make an exclamation meaning that he was glad and that he accepted the challenge. He and his fellow-winners of the same age-group would then at once send criers to announce their acceptance of the challenge and, to give notice that they would without fail carry through their acceptance, would get in formation and sing. When the Crazy Dance was so carried out it had the same prestige and it was performed with the same rites and observances, as when carried out to fulfill a vow.

Each of those men who joined the Crazy Dance Joined with one of his wives or with a substitute for her. The chief although not the only role of these women was participation in the ritual grandfather sex-test to be described later. Some husbands were so jealous of their wives that they would do all possible to avoid joining the dance or having their wives join. This appears to have been the case with the husbands of Coming Daylight, who was a belle in her day. In other cases, as The Boy remarked, "the husband knew his wife's character and disposition, and if she were weak he did not put her to this test as he would be pretty sure that she would fail." Singer had never joined although some wanted her to do so at the time. "My husband," she said, "was advised not to let me do so because I was too young and I might make [202] a mistake [ritual?] and besides it was a hard thing to do. I Was too crazy yet, they said. At the time my husband's other wife was about to have a baby, and some wanted me to Join so she would have a safe delivery, but the others did not let me do it," Then, too, if a wife were in her menses at the time of the dance, she to her embarrassment would have to say so and she would have to be substituted for. If a Crazy Dancer did not have a wife of his own he could borrow one, a sister-in-law or other woman with whom an avoidance or respect relationship did not obtain. Thus Little Man, Coming Daylight's husband, once gave permission to his unmarried younger brother, Spotted Bird, to Join the Crazy Dance with her, but Spotted Bird declined on the ground of his being too young, although actually Spotted Bird took part in that Dance as an attendant, which made Little Man so angry that he would not give anything away during the Dance for Spotted Bird. "A man," said The Boy, "who loaned his wife to another man for the Crazy Dance had to be a strong man. And before he would lend any of his women he was pretty sure he was lending away the right one who had strong character because it was tough."

When a man made a vow or accepted a challenge to perform the Crazy Dance all and

---

[543] Cf. Flannery Social Life 1953, p. 42.

only the members of his own company such as Calves, Holding-on-to-dog's-tail, Having-breast-for-a-pillow, or other, — within the Stars or Wolves as the case might be, joined or were expected to join the dance with him. Actually, on at least some later Crazy Dance occasions, not all the members of the given age-group joined. When the crier announced the coming Dance, some of the men of the age-group involved might make remarks such as: "Well, these old men [the ritual grandfathers] are getting hungry for good times again! They want to play around! They are agitating for the Crazy Dance." And some might bypass that particular dance even though at the risk of being looked upon as jealous weaklings. "If," said The Boy "a man belonging to the age-group to which the vower of the Crazy Dance belonged failed to join the dance, without good excuse, he and his wife would catch it; this would be published, because he did not want to have his wife go through this [the ritual grandfather sex-test]." [203]

For the duration of a Crazy Dance, political as well as ritual authority was vested in the age-group giving the Dance, and the ordinary personnel of government ceased for the time being to function. The Crazy Dancers ran everything; their word was law; they decided what was and was not to be done, even regarding the hunt.

The vower himself was for the time being in supreme command. He selected, as his councilors, however, four outstanding men, of middle age, older than the actual participant dancers, but not too old, men of prestige who had won recognition through merit, who had made their mark and were known as "chiefs," "successful and with good homes, good men." These four, according to Turn Toes, were chosen from among the next older age-group of the society, Stars or Wolves, to which the participant dancers age-group belonged, and were "elder brothers" of the dancers. Turn Toes emphasized more the ritual functions of these four "elder brothers." While the dancers themselves were in authority during the dance, and paid the expenses thereof, they would be helpless without knowledge of the proper rites and observances. The four "elder brothers" who had previously gone through (he Crazy Dance, would be instructors in procedure to the group of younger dancers and would give the decisions thereon. The Boy emphasized more the political functions of the four "elder brothers." The vower together with these four constituted a sort of council or governing body. The five consulted and advised together on arrangements preparatory to and during the Dance, the "balance of power" resting with the vower in case of a deadlock among the four "elder brothers."

After these five got together they selected as their crier an intelligent old man who was known for his command of language. He sat in on their meetings, but without vote, so to speak. It was his duty to listen carefully and keep abreast of proceedings, and when decisions were made by the council of five he was told "Go around the whole camp and announce that such-and-such shall be done." The five also chose as attendants or servants two young men, apparently two who had not previously joined the Crazy Dance. These two had no initiative; their task was to do what [204] the council told them to do. Before the Dance actually started, the participant age-group split up into two divisions, the "talls" and the "shorts," probably organized as in the Sacrifice Dance but we did not obtain details, except that the "talls" and "shorts" each selected a "tall" and a "short" old man respectively to be older brother to them and assistant to the above-mentioned chief crier. The two groups competed and on one occasion in connection with a Crazy Dance indulged in a contest of supernatural power, according to the following story narrated by The Boy.

"On one occasion, while preparing for a Crazy Dance, the 'talls' and 'shorts' besides engaging in games and sports against one another, played a game of magic, of exhibition of power. They put up a double lodge, like the one used in the Flat Pipe transfer rite, and started in to show their power, the 'talls' were against the 'shorts.' The contest went on and on, and a big crowd of spectators was attracted. The 'shorts' were losing and got mad. One of the 'shorts' made a snake, and it crawled around. At this the 'shorts' all cheered for their side, and said; 'You "talls" can't match that.' But the 'shorts' did not reckon with their opponents. 'All right,' said the 'tails, 'We'll show you.'

"One of the 'talls' then stepped out in the middle. He used to wear in his hair a piece of rawhide cut out in the figure of an elk. He said to his comrades, 'Sing this song,' and he taught them a song to sing. Then he said: 'I'll lie down. You cover me up with a robe. Continue singing, and after a while uncover me. After everybody has seen what you uncover, cover me up again. Then sing again, and after a while uncover me again.' They proceeded to do as he told them. Meanwhile news of the making of the snake by the 'short' had traveled fast, and some of the principal men of the tribe had come over to the double lodge.

"The 'tall' then lay down and his comrades covered him, sang a while and uncovered him. When they lifted the cover, there sat an elk. The 'talls' cheered loudly. Then they covered him, sang a while, and uncovered him, and he got up smiling.

"But the 'shorts' said; 'That's nothing. We too can do things like that.' So one of the 'shorts' did just as the 'tall' had done. He told his comrade to sing a certain song, cover him, sing, [205] uncover him and so forth. This they did. When they uncovered him, there lay a human skeleton. They then covered, sang, and uncovered, and there was the 'short' himself. And all the 'shorts' cheered and shouted.

"At this point the principal men present stepped in: 'There is danger in this kind of contest. After a while there may be a fight.' So the contest came to an end.

"The Aa'ni talked for a long time about this contest, and they still talk about it and wonder what would have happened if the principal men had not stepped in and stopped it."

The Crazy Dancers had to be, or by age or custom were, younger men, married or unmarried, fully adult but not yet middle-aged, "mature." They chose their ceremonial grandfathers from among those who had previously been through the Dance. From one to four, — but not more than four, — dancers could choose the same ceremonial grandfather, lest they should run out of grandfathers. Only those could be grandfathers who had never had sex relations with the wives or substitute women joining the dance with the respective grandson or group of two to four grandsons, and an actual shortage of grandfathers meeting this requirement was apt to he more than a theoretic one, at least in the later days when the Dance was given. In one case, in fact, still well remembered, the prospective Crazy Dancer had to hunt all over the tribe to get his ceremonial grandfather. According to Coming Daylight a man who joined the Crazy Dance a second time had to have the same grandfather whom he had had on the first occasion. Where two to four men combined to choose the same grandfather, one of one group served as a sort of leader for it. Apparently if the age-group putting on the dance belonged to the Stars, the grandfathers and grandfathers' helpers were chosen from the Wolves, and vice versa.

There was great reluctance on the part of older men to serve as Crazy Dance grandfathers, although, to judge from the previously quoted remarks of some of the younger men, there were probably exceptions to this rule. The reluctance shown was real, not make-believe, as the older men approached to be grandfathers might have to make embarrassing confessions and refuse, or if they accepted had to undergo a severe test of character, failure in which entailed grave penalty, as will be explained infra. [206]

When, consequently, a Crazy Dance was in the offing, older men who learned that they might be asked to be ritual grandfathers were very apt to run away and hide. But they could not sleep forever out on the hills, and when they came home, they would be stalked and caught by surprise, by day or night, and offered a pipe by an individual or group of two to four who intended to participate in the coming Dance. The group had secretly convened and decided on their grandfather. Finally bringing a filled pipe with them they would go to his lodge and walk in. The older man would then be practically trapped, for in accordance with the general Aa'ni pattern an offered pipe could hardly be refused. He might wilt and long hesitate, sitting with bowed head while the visitors entreated him to accept and to help them carry out their part in the Dance.

If on any occasion in the past he had had sex relations with any of these men's wives, either before or after their marriage to them, he would, when offered the pipe, be sacredly obligated to make indirect confession of the fact by refusing the pipe and saying to them (or to the individual young man, if the latter was alone), "My grandchildren, you are stillborn. I' cannot serve as your grandfather," or "Go to somebody else. She is not your wife," or using some similar circumlocution. Such a reply might cause great embarrassment and worry to the young man, who perhaps had never suspected his wife.[544] Failure to confess would be "something wrong, a violation of belief or important custom" and would be followed by misfortune, even early death.

If when offered the pipe, stem first, the older man accepted it, and with it the office of grandfather, he would get up and say to the offerer: "All right, we will go outside." After they got outside the lodge the old man would say; "Now, young man, face east." The older man would stand behind him, holding the pipe stem up, and pronounce the vow, "A womun is being offered so that such-and-such a person will recover from sickness and get well. We are going to have a Crazy Dance. He [the young man] [207] says this to You [Supreme Being]," and at the end would say four times, "Yo-o-o-o-o-o." Then (or perhaps before this pronouncement rite) the older man smoked the pipe. The grandfather was free to recruit an assistant, usually a younger man than himself, to help him paint the vower and the vower's wife. The several functions of the grandfather, — instructing, painting, feeding, gift-making, and especially the sex test, — will be described as we go along.

If the chief vower or any members of the groups of two to four dancers had younger brothers of, say, about 7 to 10 years of age, these latter could be brought into the dance as "Little Crazy Boys." These young boys were painted, were present all through the rite, and served as pages or messengers. If, for instance, a grandfather did not know exactly how body painting at a particular juncture should be done, the Little Crazy Boys would be sent around to get the information. They did not, however, participate in major features of the rite, such as jumping in the fire and so forth.

The making of the vow to hold the Crazy Dance and the securing of the ceremonial grandfathers were done quietly and privately. The public phase of the dance began with the formal announcement.

A crier (or criers) would go around the camp advertising the dance and talking it up, with exhortations such as; "Now you young men who are going to dance, fix up your hearts, be men, be strong, be men and join the dance, go through with it. Be men, don't be weaklings. But think it all over well before you join. This red paint is rough (said figuratively to imply: your wife is involved, you will have to give her away, to expose her to a severe test.)" As previously mentioned there was apt to be a certain resistance on the part of the younger men, to this "sales pressure," and a touch of cynicism as well.

---

[544] The Arapaho custom in this matter was quite similar, we were told by an Arapaho woman, the widow of a Gros Ventre, who was present while we were discussing the point.

The Crazy Dance was usually held about June when the buffalo had fattened up well, or else a little later, about August. In case the people happened to be scattered at the time, runners were sent out to bid them foregather. The chief vower or the one who accepted the challenge put up his lodge in the center of the camp circle, and this served as executive headquarters of his council and age-group until and during the dance. [208]

The main rites of the Crazy Dance extended over four days and four nights, and were followed by a period of "talking backward" and other "crazy" behavior by the dancers. Dancers did not fast during the dance, as did vowers during the Sacrifice Dance, but ate heartily. Large quantities of food were procured beforehand, and many puppies were killed and cooked to provide the delicacy, dog meat. The dancers, however, were not allowed to swim, bathe, or "touch water" during the Dance. If any dancer did so, Bha'a {Thunderbird} would get angry and there would be a big storm. On each of the four nights of the dance, the dancers slept in the Crazy Dance lodge, but after each night they went back home in the morning to paint up.

The Crazy Dance lodge was erected in the center of the camp circle, not far from the chief vower's tipi and executive headquarters. The "lodge" was an open roofless circular corral made of upright poles about 6 or 7 feet high stuck in the ground, with a wide opening to the south according to Coming Daylight, to the southeast according to The Boy and Thick. To the top of the poles were lashed tipi poles to make a railing. Over this railing were hung tip! covers, which lapped over on the ground inside the corral as a place on which to rest and sleep. The tipi covers needed — two, or three, or more, depending on the number of the vower's age-group who participated and hence on the size of the corral — were taken, without asking permission, by the dancers from enemy-friends belonging to the next older age-group of the dancers' own society, Stars or Wolves as the case might be.

Inside the corral, at the place of honor immediately to the right of the opening, according to The Boy, or opposite the opening according to Coming Daylight, a little sort of wickiup was put up. Here, as the ceremony started, sat the chief vower and here was kept the ritual badger skin. The crier(s) (and council of four?) also were in the wickiup, according to The Boy and Thick. Very little of what went on inside the wickiup was known to our informants.

The participant dancers sat in the corral on either side, the "talls" on the west, the "shorts" on the east, with their respective ritual grandfathers and wives, — the dancers in front, the [209] grandfathers back of them and the wives back of the grandfathers, according to one statement by Coming Daylight; the grandfathers in front, and the dancers and their wives back of them according to another by her. The bows of the "talls" and "shorts" were stuck upright in the ground in two crescents in front of the two respective divisions; the bows of the ritual "elder brothers" (the four councilors?), a little apart near the south or southeast ends of these two crescents.[545]

The chief ritual paraphernalia used in the Crazy Dance were the badger pelt, hoof rattles, whistles, bows, and poisoned arrows. The stuffed badger hide, "trimmed and fixed up," figured prominently in the rites. The bone whistles, hung on the neck of the dancers, were blown by them when dancing. The rattles, $\theta a\theta anas$, sticks about five feet long, with deer hoofs attached in a row along the upper third, were used by the grandfathers who sang, sitting in a row and pounding the ends of the rattles on the ground to beat time.

Each Crazy Dancer treated one of his arrows with poisonous wild parsley, and tied the poisoned arrow to his bow. If the dancer "got mad or any serious situation arose" he would unfasten the arrow and shoot to kill. If the arrow penetrated the skin of the victim or even

---

[545] Kroeber Ethnology 1908, p. 242, gives a different arrangement, with which still another statement by Coming Daylight that "the women sat on the west side" insofar agrees.

scratched him, he died. This extreme measure was very rarely resorted to. We were told of no actual instance. When the dance was over these poisoned arrows were carried away to a spot where no one could find them and were buried.

The ceremonies on each of the four days of the Crazy Dance began with the painting of the bodies of the dancers and their wives, the pattern of the painting differing each day. The painting was done in the respective lodges of the leaders of the groups of two to four dancers. Here they gathered with their respective ceremonial grandfathers and "Little Crazy Dancers." The dancer and his wife, or borrowed surrogate, would sit there naked, the woman with legs close together and stretched out in front. This was a source of serious embarrassment to all concerned. The bodies [210] of the two, even the soles of their feet, were painted all over, — in red, at least on the first day. Coming Daylight, although she herself had never joined the Crazy Dance, used to hear that the women would say: "Grandfather, I cannot paint my back. Now you paint my back." The grandfather, according to The Boy, commonly recruited a younger man than himself as helper in the painting and would direct him how to paint the various parts of the couple's bodies. At some time in this painting rite, the grandfather prayed in a short quick way with a pipe for those being painted.

After the couples were painted, all proceeded to the Crazy Dance lodge or corral, the dancers whistling on the way with their bone whistles in their mouths. On arrival at the lodge, the chief vower and the 4 councilors took their places inside the smaller wickiup, or enclosure within the corral, and the rite proper began.

A smudge was made, — according to The Boy, of a certain large flat or bulbous semispherical mushroom the "fuzz" of which "flies out when it is stepped on," — a smudge song was sung (but The Boy did not remember the melody), and a solemn prayer was said.

After the prayer came the "feeding" of the badger. Someone would suggest: "Sing the feeding song, so the badger can eat." Then someone would take the badger skin and walk with it clockwise around the lodge, inside between the bows and the outer wall. He walked very very {ok} slowly, barely moving, and while he did so song No. 59 was sung. He made the complete circuit four times, and the song was sung once at each circuit. If at any time he were not holding pelt down low enough to the ground, he would be told in backward talk (see infra); "Raise him up!" When at the end of the fourth round he reached the wickiup, he would lay the pelt down. Then song No. 60 was sung, four times in succession, and at the end of each singing the pelt was given a hard blow with a stick by "the old man" (the chief vower's grandfather?). All this singing and striking was done seriously and reverently, without levity. The Boy had asked his father, Lame Bull, the meaning of the blows, but the latter had answered; "I do not know." The two above songs, both wordless, were sung without accompaniment of rattle or drum. The drum note in song No. 60 was introduced by The Boy in his recording merely to represent the blow struck on the badger. Both songs were sung by The Boy for the recordings. Apparently at other times during the Crazy Dance rites,—about 10:00 a.m, 2:00 p.m, and 5:00 p.m, according to Coming Daylight, — the badger skin was given a blow, but clear details were not obtained by us.

Between whiles during the Crazy Dance, when no specific ceremony or observance was going on, there was very lively good-time dancing, the dancers "jumping up and down" to the accompaniment of the above-mentioned deer hoof rattlers. One such song. No. 61, was recorded as sung by The Boy, it has just one word in it, meaning: "I poured water all over him." The song is supposed to have been composed by the enemy-friend of some Crazy Dancer and sung about him. The reference in the case is to the prohibition against bathing and "touching water" by Crazy Dancers.

What rites, if any, were peculiar to the second day of the Crazy Dance we did not discover. The third day, according to The Boy and Thick, was the day on which payment of horses, robes, clothes and so forth, "the best of everything" was made and in generous quantity, to the grandfathers. The goods would be piled up and the horses picketed nearby, for all to see. Participants who "brought no presents then were looked down upon as no good." Singer mentioned only the presents given to the grandfathers, but The Boy and Thick stated that the grandfathers on their part also gave "presents" to the Crazy Dancers and that the transaction was "really a trade." In accord with the general Aa'ni pattern of trade and gambling as well as of remuneration for ritual services rendered, payment to the grandfathers was expected to be made on the spot and in full; promises to pay at some future time and payment by installment were barred.

Before we take up the rites and observances peculiar to the fourth and last day of the Crazy Dance, it seems advisable to cover certain ones whose exact place in the ceremonial sequence we are unable to determine from our field evidence. These are: the ceremonial feeding of the dancers, the giving of presents in honor of the dancers, the sweat-lodge rite, talking backward, and the sex-test.

There was no fasting during the Crazy Dance; on the contrary [212] all ate plenty. Both the dancers and the grandfathers, and the latters' helpers, brought food. When the grandfathers brought food each would say to his respective grandson or team of two to four grandsons; "All right, my grandson(s), here is your milk". The grandsons or one of them would then get up, give the exclamation of thanks (according to Coming Daylight), and would kiss the "grandfather" and would "nurse."

In the course of the Crazy Dance, as at most other social and ritual large gatherings, it was customary for relatives of the dancers to give away presents in their honor, not to the dancers themselves, but to third parties.[546]

According to The Boy, a sweat-lodge rite was held in connection with the Crazy Dance, but we obtained no details. Presumably it followed the general pattern of the rite as carried out for the sacred Pipes.

"Talking backward" was characteristic of the dancers' behavior during the day or days immediately following the four day rite, but also, according to our informants, during the four-day rite itself. If the dancer said "Hit me real hard," he would be barely touched; if he said, "Don't hit me hard," he would be hit very hard. "Go away" meant "Come here"; and vice versa. An answer "yes" meant "no." "Raise it up," meant "Lower it down." "All right," a dancer would say "you fellows will not dance"; then he would sing and they would dance.

The sex-test calls for more extensive explanation. It was a major, in a sense the major, feature of the Crazy Dance, the "sacrifice" about which the dance centered. The dancers were in a sense "throwing away," offering as a quasi-sacrifice, their wives or substitute women. In the sacred Pipe rites, the costly offerings were in material things, sacrifices in the strict sense of the term, in the Sacrifice Dance, the main offerings were the physical sufferings of the participants, "sacrifices" in an extended sense of the term; in the Crazy Dance, the "sacrifice" consisted more in the mental suffering of the dancers who submitted their wives or substitute women to a severe sex-test, a test which at best brought acute anxiety and embarrassment to all concerned. From the [213] content, — the announcement and other prayers, — it seems fairly clear that the "sacrifice" by the Crazy Dance chief vower and his associates was offered to the Supreme Being.

---

[546] For example, see Flannery Social Life 1953, p. 108.

Just on what night or nights in the rite the test or tests took place was a point we did not clear up. Information regarding the form of this test was not revealed by elders to children, and actual happenings when given grandfathers and granddaughters were alone were commonly kept more or less secret by the two parties concerned, though the facts might leak out and founded or unfounded rumors were apparently often topics of gossip. The test itself took the following form.

Late at night the crier would go around the camp and bid all the people to go inside and shut their lodges and stay in, and not even stick their heads out because the grandfathers were going to come out. Anybody who disobeyed this order would be chased, caught, made to dance, kicked, and apparently hit with cactus-armed sticks. When all was quiet and all the people were indoors, the ceremonial grandfathers would go out beyond the camp circle, halting four times on the way, and would sit down in the dark scattered here and there, each a distance from the others. The men dancers stayed in camp, in the Crazy Dance lodge, and "sang brave songs" until their wives returned. Their wives or substitute women, — whether one for each individual dancer or successively one for each team of two to four is not clear — then went out to the grandfathers, one woman to each respective grandfather. The women were naked, except for a blanket or robe covering their bodies and leaving only their heads sticking out. Each carried with her a filled common pipe.

If at the last moment a dancer would not allow his wife to go out and meet his and her grandfather, or if she failed to do so, or if after going out she did not submit to the body-to-body test, the fact would be published and tongues would wag, and there might be other consequences. On one occasion, the story runs, among the women going out to the grandfathers was a pretty one who had a lover. The lover intercepted her on her way out, took her home, and eloped with her. He died soon after, his body having just shriveled and wasted away. On another occasion, a certain woman, [214] a noted singer well known to Coming Daylight, appears to have declined to submit, after she had gone out, to the body-to-body test, or at least to have resisted advances. On the way out she was heard to say: "Oh, I won't have this old man just for this little root [see infra]. If I wanted to own some medicine I could go and dig it out of the ground.'*

Each woman, when she had located her particular grandfather in the dark, would say: "Here, my grandfather, is a pipe." The grandfather would act as if hesitating to accept. He would not accept it right away. After he finally had accepted it, he would rub his palms on the ground and rub the pipe itself, "sort of cleansing it." Then he would pray with the pipe to the Supreme Being, for the woman, after which he smoked it alone. Then he rubbed his hands again on the ground and "felt (rubbed?) her all over, and cleansed her body."

After this she would lie down on the ground, supine and naked, and the "grandfather," likewise naked, would lie on her. In this position the ritual grandfather who had been chewing the powdered blackish medicine or sacred root, of a plant (unidentifiable by us) growing in the Rocky Mountains and not found in Aa'ni territory proper, touched his lips to hers, and passed the chewed root from his mouth to hers. All this, as Coming Daylight put it, was considered "something holy" and "no sin whatever." Either the act or the root or both — we did not clear up this point — was supposed to impart what she called "life everlasting" (she probably meant "long life") to the woman. This root was chewed by the Crazy Dancers.

The ritual code which prescribed this body-to-body ceremony for the wife and her ceremonial grandfather, at the same time rigidly prescribed sexual intercourse between them. By code, the ceremony was not ritual license but on the contrary a test, one set for the husband, the wife, and the ritual grandfather. "The husband," as The Boy put it, "was sending his wife to his ceremonial grandfather and giving her to him. It was figurative. It was giving but it [intercourse] was not supposed to happen but if it did, well it just did." As Mathilda Cuts-the-rope expressed it, "the test was for the husband to allow his wife to go out with the grandfather. [215]

The husband would have to be a man of strong heart." The husband would be gravely anxious, and in a sense deeply embarrassed and humiliated, but could not show temper or "get mad"; "he would however have gotten mad," said Coming Daylight, "if his wife actually had had intercourse with the grandfather."

The character test of the wife and grandfather was equally severe or even more so, but was, as is obvious, of a different nature. "These women [the wives or substitutes]," The Boy commented, "were usually young women, just enjoying life to the fullest measure. They were of that age, and to make the test more severe their husbands kept away from them before it so that the temptation would be greater, more intense. And the 'grandfathers' were not harmless old men." Apropos of this test, The Boy remarked: "It was known by the Aa'ni that the female sex is the weaker one, but in such matters it is the stronger one ... of old the Aa'ni held this [sex] a great weakness of mankind."

Penalties for failure in the sex-test were either supernatural or social or both. One ritual grandfather, who on one occasion could not stand the test and who had intercourse with his granddaughter, was found dead in his bed before four nights had passed. If the couple succumbed, the fact was very apt to become known. "The woman," said The Boy, "would sometimes tell, or else the couple would give themselves away afterwards by their actions.... They would naturally brood over it [their failure], ... It would prey on their minds and they would blunder and make mistakes, and it would drive them downward, afraid to Join in social life. People would begin to comment: 'What is the matter with these two?' The Aa'ni were very inquisitive and would want to know what was the matter. The couple would be driven to make a confession and get it over with. Or something would happen anyway to confirm the suspicion that people had of them, ... Even if the two were lovers, it would have been hard to do this [fail in the ritual] test and yet keep it quiet."

There was, as would under the circumstances be suspected, appreciable differences of attitude toward this feature of the Crazy Dance on the part of husbands, wives and grandfathers. Some husbands, as we have seen, would not, for jealousy or for fear of [216] sexual mishap, join the Dance at all or permit their wives to join, even though such refusal was apt to entail a certain loss of face or status, to subject those who refused to the charge of being over-jealous weaklings, of not having "strong hearts," of not being able to take it. Most at least, perhaps all, who joined, suffered grave anxiety or humiliation or both. Some of the wives and ritual grandfathers, probably the majority, were, it is clear, very reluctant to submit themselves to the test, for fear of the penalties for failure. and, so far at least as these wives were concerned, for dislike of the anxiety, embarrassment and humiliation involved. Some other wives and grandfathers, probably a majority, were, it seems equally clear, quite the reverse of reluctant.

A certain air of secrecy surrounded this whole matter of the sex-test, and actual occurrences connected with it and, when the test and occurrences were talked about, they were commonly discussed in hushed tones. It was consequently very difficult for us to discover what proportion of failures occurred. The Boy seemed to think that failures were somewhat less frequent than did Coming Daylight and Singer, but all agreed that some failures did occur. Many stories and rumors ran the round of gossip. A younger, middle-aged informant, Cora Chandler, used to hear these stories. One of them, heard by Coming Daylight and told us, was that one couple said: "Let's lie here longer. There is nothing to worry about." "Some of the women," she stated, "liked it all right, but some of them didn't ... Some returned (from their grandfathers to their husbands) quickly and others would take a long time."

After the test the ceremonial grandfathers and the women would get up and the latter would go back to their husbands in the Crazy Dance lodge. The attendants on watch at the door thereof would announce their arrival. Each husband would go to meet his wife who would give him back the pipe that she had taken with her and would give him the root (or some of it) that she had gotten from her grandfather. Then she went home to her lodge.

The purpose for which the root was used was not known to The Boy. To judge from a short dialogue recorded from Coming Daylight, it may have had something to do with fertility, [217] child-bearing, or child begetting. She had said to her husband on one occasion; "If I had joined it [the Crazy Dance] and had been given it [this root], I would use it." To this her husband replied: "You should not talk that way. You already have children. You should pray to the Supreme Being." In this connection it may be recalled that some once wanted Singer to join the Crazy Dance in order that her husband's other wife, pregnant at the time, would have a safe delivery. The root may also have been a medium through or by which long life was imparted to the woman.

The chief events of the fourth and last day of the Crazy Dance proper were, after the preliminary body painting, the fire dance and the bow rites,

According to The Boy and Thick, on this last day in their respective lodges the Crazy Dancers were painted up to represent owls, — why, we could not discover. Their bodies were painted yellow all over, to the elbows and knees; the forearms, and the legs from the knees down, solid black. On the chest was painted an owl, with wings spread, the wings represented by black strips extending along the arms. The dancers' left ears were daubed and plugged with white clay (and apparently a mushroom), so that hearing was blocked on that side. From the left side of the headband there hung an owl head (not a skull) over the left ear.

In preparation for the fire dance, the ritual grandfathers treated the soles of the dancers' feet, according to The Boy and Thick, — their whole bodies, according to Coming Daylight, — with medicine. The dancers also. Coming Daylight implied, chewed this root during the fire dance.

A prominent warrior "chief," from an age-group other than the one giving the dance, was then asked to make shavings out of a lodge pole for the fire. He would tell four of his outstanding war-deeds, and at each would make a motion as if starting to cut the shavings. After the fourth deed was told, he actually began making the shavings, continuing until he judged he had a pile big enough for the fire. Then he would light them. The fire was made in the middle of the Crazy Dance corral or lodge.

After the fire was started, there were four songs and four dances. One of these four, or else a song sung to the accompaniment [218] of the deer hoof rattles as the dancers jumped in the fire, was recorded, number 62, as sung by The Boy. It contains just one word meaning: "I wonder what makes me so crazy" (i.e, so crazy that I will jump in the fire). After the singing of the four songs, when the fire was blazing well, the Crazy Dancers said "Ya" and leaped barefooted into the fire and trampled it out with their bare feet. No case is on record of a dancer's feet being burned. As noted previously, the dancers in some way represented millers (moths).

It was a common custom for enemy-friends, male or female, of the dancers to rope them Just as the latter were about to jump in the blazing fire and to release them only after the fire had died down or been stamped out. On release, the dancers would step only in the coals or ashes. Coming Daylight had so held back an enemy-friend on one occasion. Some women were quite strong enough to so hold men dancers back. At other times the men would break loose from the women. All this was done as a practical joke on the enemy-friend. Sometimes a wife would so hold back or try to hold back her husband, with a rawhide rope tied to his belt, apparently out of fear for his safety.

After the fire dance came a series of rites or observances which we are calling the bow rites, as the bow enters prominently into them. They consist of a dance, a race, bow-tightening, arrow-shooting, and moccasin plundering.

Before the dance began the Crazy Dancers selected two prominent men from another age-group than their own to act as referees for the race that followed the Dance. These two, one for the "talls" and one for the "shorts," took their places on either side of the dance lodge door. Then the grandfathers took the bows of their respective grandsons and, to the accompaniment of the deer hoof rattles, sang four times a wordless song, number 63, — sung by The Boy and recorded by us. The dancers did not join in the singing as they had their whistles in their mouths. During the singing, the Crazy Dancers, in a mass, "talls" and "shorts" mingled, but with each team of two to four led by its grandfather carrying its bows, moved clockwise in a sort of dancing walk around the inside of the dance lodge, beginning at the left of the entrance. The singing and dancing were so synchronized that the [219] mass of dancers would reach the right entrance at the ending of the fourth singing. On arrival there, the dancers said "Ya" and grabbed their bows from the hands of their grandfathers and started their race.

They ran pell-mell toward a mound far outside the camp circle, rounded the mound clockwise, raced back to the dance lodge. All the dancers, "talls" and "shorts," had to take part in the race. Their grandfathers did not accompany them, but the two old men criers, of the "talls" and "shorts" respectively, ran along with them.

Each of the "talls" and "shorts" on reaching the dance lodge gave his bow to the respective referee at one entrance. The losing side, "talls" or "shorts," had to give a smoke to the winners.

While the dancers were racing, the two old criers were having a race of their own, a race which provided "lots of fun" for the spectators. Along the way the boys would in fun pick up buffalo chips and throw them at the two old men. At one Crazy Dance, the two racing criers were The Boy's father, Lame Bull, and another old man, both crippled. The latter was outdistancing Lame Bull, but the boys bothered him so much that he left off the race to chase them, while Lame Bull kept going and came in the winner. The other old man accused Lame Bull of framing him. According to Turn Toes, the four "elder brothers" or councilors were the ones who raced and were pelted with buffalo chips, but we did not have opportunity to discuss the point in detail with him.

After the race and the subsequent smoke to the winners, came the bow-tightening rite, for which some poor old man was chosen. The referees re-distributed the bows to the dancers. The dancers then each put on their best moccasins and an old robe with a hole in the middle to be worn like a poncho, the old robe being "in imitation of millers".[547] The old man would get ready well away from camp, lying face down on the ground with his head covered with a robe. Each dancer would tighten his bowstring, bracing [220] the bow on the old man's back, and would push in under the old man's robe moccasins or other goods, as presents or payment. "The old man's back," Coming Daylight remarked, "would get higher and higher and he would go home with a pack [of these presents] on his back."

After this, each of the dancers moved away from where the old man had been lying,

---

[547] In 1948 The Boy stated that this robe made from discarded lodge covers hung down the back, with only enough in front to hold it on. It was painted red at the four corners and at the neck; owl "pelts" were attached between the shoulders, the large feathers having been removed, and hung down the back, When the garment was worn it looked as though the dancer's shoulders were painted. [R.F]

mounted an arrow, and danced four times. At each of the four dances, they motioned as if to shoot the arrow. At the end of the fourth song, they said "Ya," and released their arrows. The boys then grabbed the arrows; whoever grabbed one could keep it as his own.

Then the dancers started running back to camp, with men, women and children chasing them. Any pursuer who succeeded in grabbing a dancer — and throwing him down, according to Coming Daylight — would take the moccasins of the latter, who would submit without struggle. On one occasion Coming Daylight chased a dancer who was "kind of queer" but who "could run like an antelope." He made for a high hill, calling back at her repeatedly: "Why don't you make your own moccasins if you want them?" She could not overtake him.

This moccasin-plundering apparently marked the end of the Crazy Dance rite proper. After it the dancers would mingle barefooted with the people throughout the camp and "talk backward," and the whole camp would move, if only a little way off.

But for some time after the end of the rites proper,[548] the dancers would go around giving orders in "backward talk" to any one they met to dance or sing, chasing and "shooting" members of other age-groups as "imaginary enemies," and indulging in other forms of horseplay. If any victim was commanded "I suggest that you don't dance," he would have to dance. If told, "Don't sing," he would have to sing four times any Crazy Dance song he remembered. If the victim said, "Don't kick me hard," he would be kicked hard, and vice versa. The "imaginary enemies," especially enemy-friends and members (and their wives) of the opposite society, Stars or Wolves as the case might be, were shot with arrows the ends of which had been chewed to blunt them, as there [221] was no intention to really hurt the "enemies." Dogs, too, would be shot at. The poisoned arrow was of course never used in such good-natured shooting. The horseplay could, however, at times be pretty rough. On one occasion, a Crazy Dancer put his foot on the chest of an old man returning from berry-picking in the mountains, and pushed him over the edge of a cutbank. The old man fell over and also spilled all his berries. The Crazy Dancer was avenging the old man's inordinate boasting against "imaginary enemies" in an earlier Dance in which the latter had been a crier, On another occasion, when Coming Daylight's husband, Deafie, was coming back from hunting with deer meat piled on his horse, Crazy Dancers chased him clear to his lodge, although he had been their ritual grandfather. Coming Daylight at risk of being herself "shot" by them, went out of the lodge and upbraided them roundly, throwing in to boot a coarse remark, and making an insulting noise. They went off without "shooting" her but with the parting remark: "My, we have a crazy grandmother!"

---

[548] Four days, according to Kroeber Ethnology 1908, p. 247.

THE CEREMONIAL BUFFOON OF THE AMERICAN INDIAN
JULIAN H STEWARD

THOSE who are accustomed to thinking of the American Indian as sober and stone-faced will be surprised to learn that he not only laughed as frequently as his white-skinned cousin, but actually introduced into his most sacred ceremonies a comedian whose primary business was to delight the spectators.

The subject of laughter has long been an open field for all manner of students of human nature. Rarely have two bagged the same game. All have made the serious mistake of attempting to formulate a type stimulus to laughter from the humor of a single culture, namely, our Euro-American civilization, although a few rash theorists have fancied a "racial" difference in what things are funny.

It cannot be supposed that an anthropological approach to laughter can solve all the subtleties of this manifestly difficult problem. A review of humor in distinctly different cultures, however, may provide a least common denominator to the humor of the world and thus clear the ground for sounder psychological theorizing. The problem then may be restated in anthropological terms, To what extent does culture predetermine what is laughable?

The American Indian furnishes abundant material for a tentative answer to this problem, but it must be remembered that our attention is to be centered upon the institutionalized humor exhibited by the ceremonial buffoon. Humor of everyday occurrence, to be sure, was much in evidence in native life, but this is not available for our purpose because observers have paid little attention to it and made less record of it. The antics of the buffoon, on the other hand, have been well described.

The ceremonial buffoon, however, did not have universal occurrence [188] in North America. The idea of setting aside one person or a group of persons to act as both sergeant-at-arms and comedian seems to have originated, as an historical complex, but once, either in Mexico or among the ancestors of the Pueblo tribes of New [189] Mexico and Arizona, and from its early source to have diffused to several culture areas of North America. The clown was especially prominent in the Southwest, the Plains Area, California and on the Northwest Coast.[549] What diffused, however, was the idea of setting aside a special person as buffoon, not a particular set of notions about the comic. In other words, a "pattern" diffused whose content was to be filled in somewhat differently in each culture area.

A classification of the themes of humor employed by the ceremonial buffoon permits a twofold division: (1) traits of comedy common to all peoples regardless of culture, and (2) traits of comedy peculiar to each culture area.

COMIC THEMES OF UNIVERSAL OCCURRENCE

The greater number of the comic devices employed by the clowns of native America are based upon situations which are regarded as humorous in every culture. Although as employed by the Indians these devices are rude and smack strongly of the soil and are not comparable to the fine-spun themes of the highly intellectualized European comedies, they are nevertheless

---

[549] See Map 2 for the distribution of the clown. Julian H Steward *The Ceremonial Buffoon of the American Indian*, Papers of the Michigan Academy of Science, Arts and Letters, 14: 187-207 1930: 199, 202 based on *The Clown in Native North America*, Ph.D. dissertation, University of California, Berkeley 1929.

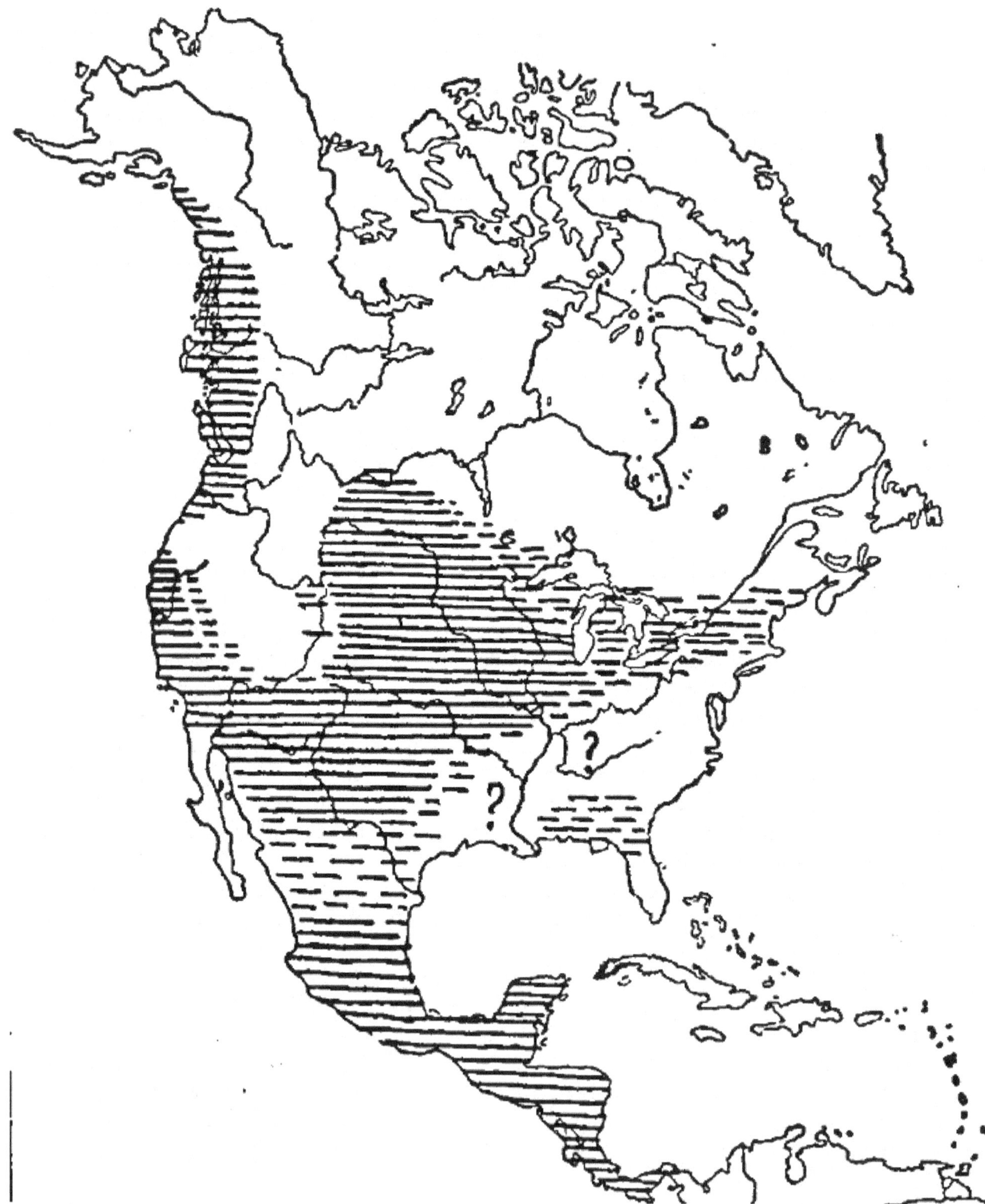

MAP 2. Distribution of the ceremonial buffoon in North America. Full lines indicate the presence of a strongly developed "clown complex"; broken lines, that the complex is weakened or that adequate data are not available.

basic in all cultures. They center about matters which possess the greatest emotional appeal in any cultural group; they are "human interest" themes.

These may be grouped in four main categories; (1) themes of humor in which sacred and vitally important ceremonies and sometimes persons are ridiculed and burlesqued, or, at times, themes of the nature of practical jokes, which riotously disregard those folkways and mores which are so essential to the smooth functioning of society; (2) themes of humor based upon sex and obscenity; (3) themes based upon sickness, sorrow, misfortune, etc, and important activities in daily life; (4) caricature and burlesque of foreigners.

1. Burlesque of the sacred

This class of comic situations comprises one of the most common themes of buffoonery. The clown is the person *par excellence* who is privileged to ridicule, burlesque and defile the most sacred and important ceremonies, persons and customs. He is licensed to [190] behave as no ordinary mortal would dream of behaving.   He is held accountable for nothing.   In his transgression of custom lies much of his comedy. Those mores which are ordinarily observed most rigorously and which are held in great esteem are the subjects of the most pleasurable comedy. As Bandolier says of the Koshare, the "delight makers" of the Pueblo Indians, "nothing is sacred; all things are permitted so long as they contribute delight to the tribe".[550]

A few illustrations from the wealth of material at our disposal will exhibit the clown in this role in different cultures.

Among the Pueblo Indians of the Southwest, clowns are present at the god-impersonating dances to perform comic side-plays on the central theme of the ceremony. They burlesque the *kachina* dancers, dancing out of time, stumbling, grimacing and doing things ordinarily taboo. At a Jemez Pueblo dance a clown is reported to have irreverently sprinkled his fellows with sand and ashes in imitation of the ceremonial sprinkling with corn-meal and pollen;[551] at Zuñi the Newekwe clown society speaks in Spanish or English before the gods, a thing strictly taboo to ordinary people.   The latter once rigged up an imitation telephone and pretended to converse with the gods, although gods are not supposed to speak.[552]   The Hopi Koyemsi or "Mudheads" perform separate dances of their own in ludicrous imitation of the *kachina* dancers. The clown of the Navajo Night Chant dance joins the masked dancers in a wholly erratic and unorthodox manner. He gets in their way, dances out of time and awkwardly, sits on the ground, rocking to and fro peering foolishly at people. When the other dancers have departed lie continues dancing until he discovers his mistake and then runs after them. Sometimes he imitates the leader, trying to anticipate him in giving signals for the dance.[553]   Even sacred sleight-of-hand performances are burlesqued so as to reveal the secrets.[554]

The buffoon of the religious dances of California performs in a similar manner. Among the Northwestern Maidu his chief [191] stock-in-trade is to parody the ceremonial leader and burlesque the dancers.   He enters the dance house after the dancers have come in, munching food. The leader reprimands him and asks him to take part in the dance. A bantering dialogue

---

[550] 1890a, p. 137.

[551] Reagan, 1915, pp. 423-27.

[552] Parsons, 1917, pp. 229-233.

[553] Matthews, 1902, pp. 150-151.

[554] Matthews, 1887, pp. 443-444.

ensues. Whenever the shaman tries to make a speech, the clown parodies his remarks. He steals tobacco and is again reprimanded. When he finally joins in the dance, he does so languidly, frequently stopping to eat.[555] In the Wintun Hesi ceremony, the acme of Wintun ceremonialism, the clown directs his comic assaults at the leader. "When the captain of the host village was singing as he marched slowly about the inside of the dance house, one of the clowns stationed himself before the captain and marched slowly backwards in step with him, while delivering joking remarks concerning the latter's ability to sing and the particular song he was voicing. This did not seem in the least to disconcert the singer who continued to sing in his gravest manner; but his song was not received with the usual seriousness.[556]

In general, the Northwest Coast religious concepts imposed a pattern of behavior on the buffoon which was too rigid to permit this type of clowning, but instances of this kind have been reported from the Quinault[557] and the tribes of eastern Puget Sound.[558]

The same thing was true in large measure of the clown of the Plains, as among the Cree,[559] Ojibway,[560] Arapaho,[561] and others, especially in the northern Plains, where the pattern was less clear-cut.

Even in Central America, where drama tended to be divorced from religious ceremonies, the Maya are said to have had at their feasts and entertainments jesters who were clever in mimicry and caricature and did not spare even the chief men,[562] while the priests of the Aztec sometimes contributed to the fun of religious ceremonies by blowing mud balls at the actors and praising or censuring the performances in a jocular manner.[563] [192]

That this type of humor is not unique in America is apparent at once from brief reflection on comic themes in our own culture. Even among other primitives it was prominent. Thus in Samoa a jesters dance is performed by men and women of rank to provide comic relief to the dance of the very sacred *taupo* (the woman of highest rank and divinity).[564] The African Masai dances had similar frivolity.[565] The primitive Konds of India actually permitted ridicule of the goddess to whom human sacrifice had been made.[566]

In the foregoing examples the keynote of the comedy is what is commonly called "comic relief." Indeed, in nearly every instance it is the very thing which is regarded with greatest reverence or respect which is ridiculed.

A great deal of ruffianism is also exhibited by clowns. Things and persons are not at all respected. The Zuñi Newekwe and Koyemshi indulge in all manner of acts of physical violence. The Hopi clowns have tussles, tormenting each other with cactus branches, stripping breech-clouts and such-like.[567] The Papago clowns visit people's houses, upsetting things,[568] and, like

---

[555] Dixon, 1905, pp. 315-317.

[556] Barrett, 1919, p. 457.

[557] Olson, personal communication.

[558] Gunther, personal communication.

[559] Skinner, 1015, PP. 528-529.

[560] Skinner, 1914. pp. 494-504.

[561] Kroeber, 1907, p. 192.

[562] Bancroft, 2: 711-712.

[563] *Ibid*, 2: 291-292.

[564] Mead, pp. 114-115.

[565] Barrett, personal communication.

[566] Chambers, 2: 266-270, from Elliot, *The Indian Village Feast*.

[567] Fewkes, 1808, pp. 293-294.

[568] Mason, 1920, pp. 17-23.

them, the Miwok clowns run about after dances, prying into houses and wrecking what they can lay hands upon.[569] The Cahuilla "funny man" of Southern California annoys people by throwing water on them or dropping live coals down their backs.[570] And in like manner the Huichol clowns of Mexico torment people with "botherations" and prevent their sleeping by shaking rattles near their ears, or by tugging at their clothing.[571]

To a very large extent, rowdyism characterized the clowns of the Northwest Coast. The Haida often greeted their feast guests at the shore, "playing pranks" with their baggage, bursting it open, and doing similar things, all of which the visitors "expected and were prepared for".[572] The Kwakiutl Fool dancers, when excited by their possessing spirits, ran about with lances, knives or clubs, hitting people, or in serious cases even stabbing and killing them. Disliking clean and beautiful things, they attempted to break, [193] destroy and soil them.[573] The Nootka,[574] {Nuxalk} Bella Coola[575] and Haida[576] had clowns who behaved largely in this manner.

2. Humor of sex

The prominence of sex humor in our own Euro-American civilization need not be pressed. It is equally, sometimes more, prominent in American Indian cultures. The importance of sex humor is the inevitable result of the powerful biological sex drive. Closely associated are matters of obscenity and the excrementitious.

The Koshare and Newekwe societies of the Southwest are preeminently associated with sex. They are in fact specifically phallic societies. The Jemez clowns make advances toward women[577] and the Zuñi Koyemshi, who wear imitation penes,[578] encourage sex license during the Shalako ceremony.[579] The Hopi clowns, who are said to be very fond of women, caper with female impersonators. The Hehe's *kachina* mask, in fact, is decorated with phallic symbols.[580] Obscenity and handling of filth run riot in certain ceremonial occasions in the Southwest.

Among the non-Pueblo tribes of the Southwest there was also a considerable preoccupation with sex in the activities of the clown.

In California, among the Yokuts, obscene and pretended phallic advances toward young girls formed part of the stock-in-trade of the clown.[581] The Yuki clowns hold each others privates in their frolics.[582]

---

[569] Gifford, manuscript.

[570] Strong, 1929, p. 166.

[571] Lumholtz, 1907, pp. 185-186.

[572] Swanton, 1909, p. 168.

[573] Boas, 1897, pp. 468-471, 664.

[574] Sapir, 1911, pp. 22-27.

[575] Boas, 1892, p. 917; 1897, p. 469.

[576] Swanton, 1905, p. 173.

[577] Reagan, 1915, pp. 423-427.

[578] Parsons, 1917, pp. 321-322.

[579] Stevenson, 1904, pp. 224-227, 235-236, 276-277; Cushing, 1920. pp. 601-607; Parsons, 1917, pp. 187-188.

[580] Fewkes, 1900, pp. 128-129.

[581] Gayton, field notes.

[582] Kroeber, 1925, p. 186.

Obscenity, although not prominent, was not lacking on the Northwest Coast. Elliot has described scatological practices of various groups of Alaskan Eskimo.[583] During a comic interlude of a Kwakiutl ceremony a man jests with a chiefs daughter, making pointed references to sex.[584]

The clown in the Plains was much concerned with the phallic, [194] which constituted a frequent theme of humor. The Arapaho clown was permitted sex license and obscene behavior. His phallic activities were facilitated by the use of a root by means of which he magically paralyzed and thus secured the women of his fancy.[585] The Ponca clowns were said to crawl up and touch a woman's genitalia in full daylight,[586] and the Hidatsa clowns were permitted incest, despite the usual strength of the incest taboo.[587]

Among the Fox, east of the Plains, a mule dance in which a man imitating a stallion performs indecent antics was a great amusement. Other dances and songs of the Sauk and Fox were highly obscene.[588]

By the Eastern Dakota phallicism was intimately associated with the Heyoka complex.[589] The Heyoka clowns were believed to have great supernatural power which, among other things, enabled them to satisfy their libido. As part of the Winged Head complex, this belief runs eastward all the way to Maine.[590] Among the Iroquois and various tribes of the Southeast, certain dances furnished occasions for sex license.[591]

Themes of sex and obscenity were common in the ceremonies and performances of the tribes of Middle America.[592]

Lewdness was also highly typical of the humor of cultures other than those native to the new world. The Samoa jester's dance, for example, was in large measure salacious.[593] The Feast of Fools, which survived in Europe until the middle of the sixteenth century, included a licensed desecration of the church and riotous buffoonery which was largely of an obscene, nature.[594] In fact D.M Robinson has derived the earliest Greek comedies from the phallic songs of the Bacchic dancers and revellers.[595] [195]

3. Misfortune

This class of humor is based upon situations and activities which are fundamental to human existence and which are frequently sources of pain, trouble and unhappiness. The clown often pretends to be crippled, infirm or destitute. He is clad in rags and goes about as though

---

[583] Bourke. pp. 142, 207-209, 391-392.

[584] Boas, 1897, p. 546.

[585] Kroeber, 1907, pp. 188-189, 191-106.

[586] Skinner, 1915, p. 789.

[587] Lowie, 1913, pp. 284-290.

[588] Michelson, personal communication.

[589] Pond, p. 232.

[590] Speck, personal communication.

[591] Speck, 1907, pp. 138-140; 1909, pp. 129-130; 1911, pp. 204-205; Swanton, 1928, p. 534.

[592] Bourke, 1891, pp. 435-136; Brinton, pp. xxii-xxvii; xli-xliv.

[593] Mead, pp. 114-115.

[594] Bourke, pp. 11-23.

[595] In J. Hastings, *Encyclopaedia of Religion and Ethics*, s.v. *Greek Drama*.

starving, begging for food. He enacts scenes of household strife and marital difficulties. He burlesques activities of hunting and fishing, food-gathering and horticulture. Gluttony, too, is employed, for it is an exaggeration of an extremely important daily activity.

In the Southwest, the Jemez Koshare dress in rags, carry crooked wands and wear corn husks in their hair.[596] The clowns of the Jemez Pinon dance perform in rags, begging for food. One of these beggars is impersonated by the governor of the Pueblo.[597] A Navajo stunt on the last day of the Mountain Chant ceremony is the impersonation of a dull-witted, decrepit and short-sighted old man. He enters in a woefully ragged suit, carrying a crooked bow and misshapen arrows. He totters into the dance space, where he stumbles on a yucca plant and howls with pain. In his effort to find it, he lacerates himself thrice more, complaining in a weak shaky voice. When he has marked the spot and the way back to it, in an exaggerated imitation of the old Indian way of doing things, he goes off to find "his woman" and brings her back to pick the yucca fruit. Soon he returns with a tall, stalwart man, dressed to represent a hideous, absurd-looking old granny.[598]

The Southwestern clowns are strongly addicted to gluttony; in fact, the Hopi *kachina* Paiakyamu is called the "Hano glutton",[599] and the Jicarillo Apache clown wears festoons of bread around his neck.[600]

The California Maidu clown is represented as a lazy, stupid person. During the dance two men representing hunters enter. They ask the clown whether he has seen any deer. He answers that they may have gone by when he was asleep. At another time [196] this clown pretends blindness, which leads to absurd episodes. On still another occasion be staggers in with a bundle of splinters which he carries with prodigious effort, grunting and staggering. He spears a fish with so much vigor that the spear is driven entirely through it and then ten men are required to land it.[601]

On the Northwest Coast, the ceremonial perverseness of the Kwakiutl Fool dancer gives him something of a destitute character. He wears a costume of rags, but this is said to be because he dislikes clean and beautiful things, which he always attempts to destroy.[602]

In the Plains and East Woodland, rags were the common garb of the ceremonial buffoon, and begging a favorite amusement. The Cheyenne Contrary Society dressed in tatters.[603] The Winnebago clowns, shabbily clothed, begged for food, pretending to be impoverished and destitute.[604] The clowns of the Plains Cree, Plains Ojibway and Assiniboine were characteristically represented as poor and in need.[605] Even the Iroquois False Face Society dressed in rags and made begging tours.[606]

It is reported that in Central America the Aztec comedians commonly mimicked and ridiculed the deaf, lame, blind, deformed and ailing,[607] and during the feast to Tlaloc priests

---

[596] Goldfrank, 1927, pp. 53-55, 90-91, 93.

[597] Thompson, 1889, pp. 353-355.

[598] Matthews, 1887, pp. 440-443.

[599] Fewkes, 1903, p. 120, Pl. LVIIL.

[600] Russell, 1898, p. 371.

[601] Dixon, 1905, pp. 298, 304; Powers, pp. 310-312.

[602] Boas, 1897, pp. 469, 516.

[603] Grinnell, 2: 206.

[604] Radin, 1923, p. 384.

[605] Skinner, 1915, pp. 528-529; 1914, pp. 494-504; Lowie, 1909, pp. 62-66.

[606] Skinner. 1914, pp. 494-504; Smith, 1888, pp. 184-193.

[607] Bancroft, 2: 201-292.

"dressed like merry-andrews," went from house to house begging food.[608] The "Pilatos" of the Totonac festival of Corpus Christi, like the "old man" of the dances of the northern part of Mexico, represents himself as poverty-stricken. He wears rags, a black derby and a wooden mask.[609]

4. *Burlesque of strangers*

The humorous quality of burlesque of foreigners lies in incongruity. It is a pleasurable break from conventional patterns which is not restrained by emotions of sympathy. These are usually [197] directed against white men who are ordinarily the subjects of greatest emotional feeling, whether fear, envy or contempt.

A characteristic Santo Domingo theme is the "bull and horse" ceremony, which depicts the first arrival of the white men, missionaries and traders, in ludicrously ragged costumes. A mock bull fight is held, followed by songs of "London Bridge is falling down" and "Good Night Ladies." At the end the "traders" produce a suitcase and the Indians buy from them with paper money.[610] A Santa Clara fiesta enacts the arrival of the United States soldiers in a covered wagon, their drunkenness, and finally their fight with the Navajo, in which they are worsted until Utes come to the rescue.[611] A Hopi Powamu ceremony of 1928 caricatured American white girls. The "*kachina* girls", impersonated by men, were dressed in an incongruous attire of skirts, riding boots, sombreros and six-shooters, and they carried vanity-boxes. The Navajo buffoon furnishes great amusement simply by wearing a great false mustache and an exaggerated imitation of spectacles and other belongings of the white neighbors.[612]

The California clown had less leaning toward this type of humor, but we must note that the Yurok burlesque of a Karok fleeing from vengeance after eloping with another man's wife is of this order,[613] and so is the custom of the Southern Maidu of burlesquing the dance of their northern neighbors.[614]

The best illustration from the Northwest Coast comes from the Kwakiutl. An interlude in a potlatch ceremony introduces four men dressed as police officers. They set up an American court, one acting as judge. A woman is arrested for being absent from the preceding part of the ceremony, tried and fined $70 worth of blankets, which is afterward distributed in her name as potlatch gifts. This episode was introduced in 1865 and had been continued up to the time of Professor Boas' visit in 1897.[615]

Of similar cast is the Winnebago dance in which buffoons caricature white men,[616/68] and the Iroquois New Year dance, in which [198] there are imitations of white men skating, locomotives, and the like.[617/69] The same theme was common in Central America.[618]

CULTURALLY DETERMINED HUMOR

[608] Bancroft, 3: 334-335, 339.
[609] Nunez, pp. 191-199.
[610] Gaastra, p. 67.
[611] *El Palacio,* 10:12,1921, anonymous.
[612] Matthews, 1902, p. 433.
[613] Kroeber, 1925, pp. 58-60.
[614] Ralph Beales, personal communication.
[615] Boas, 1897, pp. 562-563.
[616] Chandler, personal communication.
[617] Smith, 1888, pp. 181-103.
[618] Bancroft, 2: 285-286.

That there should be some cultural differences, even within cultures, in what is laughable, is to be expected. For while the type stimuli to laughter — the pleasurable relief, the incongruous, the caricature, etc. — are forms which are not dependent upon cultures, the concrete situations into which they are set vary a great deal. The incongruous, for example, depends upon local cultural traits and patterns. The native African chief bedecked in a top-hat is ludicrous to the European; to his African subject he is the personification of magnificence. For the European has been so conditioned to top-hats that this constitutes an incongruity, a conflict of meaning. The African is not so conditioned.

In general, however, the points in which laughter varies among groups of men are not so far reaching as those themes which are shared by all. It has been shown empirically that the universal themes of humor concern matters of greatest emotional interest, and these do not differ materially with culture. Humor that differs with culture is more likely to concern folk-ways and things of material culture.

A further factor, however, making for cultural difference in the humor which is expressed through the clown is that the clown is seldom purely a comedian. His non-comic duties have frequently affected his comic behavior. For he is in addition to comedian a member of some society whose duties may entail important curing, fertility or military functions. The influence of such factors will be elucidated in the following discussion.

The Southwest phallicism

It has already been demonstrated that phallicism and obscenity constitute universal themes of humor. It must be recognized, however, that these themes, which are particularly emphasized in the Southwest, are more prominent among American Indians than, for example, in our own Euro-American culture. [199]

Obscenity and scatology are carried to the extreme in the Koshare, Newekwe, Wowochim and Manzrau societies of the Southwest, and, to judge from their frequency, are major sources of humor. Funny as these are to the natives, however, they have elicited only emotions of repugnance and disgust from even the ethnologist. Here clearly is a definite cultural difference in humor, and the reason is not obscure.

The concept of fertility is, as Haeberlin[619] has shown, prominent in Pueblo thought and ceremonialism. Fertility has been essential to the very survival of the villages; the keynote of their ceremonies is taken from this necessity. As humor is likely to strike at those things which are of greatest importance, this has come to be the dominant note of Southwestern humor. Moreover, the foremost and oldest clowning societies, the Koshare and its derivatives, are concerned in their sober moments with fertility and rain-making rites. It is not surprising, then, that as clowns these societies repeat the serious themes in clowning fashion.

California

In California distinctive comic differences may also be attributed to general cultural differences. These depend upon the conditioning occasioned by the differences in the ceremonial functions of the clown and are shown for instance in the contrast between the clown

---

[619] 1916.

of the Northwestern Maidu and Patwin and that of the Pomo and Yuki, or, in other words, between those tribes which had the Hesi ceremony and those which lacked the Hesi and stressed the secret or ghost society. In the former the clown served as speaker to the chief and was purely a mundane personage, not even resorting to disguises for his comedy. Among the Pomo and Yuki clowning was not set aside for special personages, but was carried on by men who were primarily ghost impersonators, secondarily comedians, and whose humorous aspect was merged with an unworldly character. The Patwin and Maidu clowns' performances seemed frankly ludicrous, avowedly for sheer entertainment. Among the Pomo and Patwin the clown was primarily an anti-natural being, a ghost, and the grotesque dress, strange behavior [200] and contrary nature were as much an attempt actually to represent such a being as to produce a ludicrous impression. Moreover, within these tribes an atmosphere of sacred unnaturalness, even in regard to the buffoonery of the clowns, is attested by the fact that the audience was prohibited from laughing.

The traits of the Coyote type of clown are mainly to be attributed to Southwestern influence. In large measure, however, this portrayal has been exaggerated by the tricky, obscene characteristic of Coyote, which in western mythology has served to make coyote tales subjects of constant amusement. The Coyote clown represents, then, to a minor degree a cultural difference.

The Northwest Coast

The Northwest Coast has imposed a virile cultural pattern upon the activities of its clowning societies. The Kwakiutl Fool dancers arc primarily a hereditary society, the members of which are possessed during the winter dance season by their spirits. This possession causes excitability, madness, unnatural behavior, and it is provoked by the members of the opposing moiety.[620] The behavior of possessed individuals causes general excitement rather than specific laughter. There is, however, some difference in the character of the madness of the various societies. The Fool dancers tend more toward the comic than the others, although it is not their chief aim. They, as well as the Cannibals and Bear dancers, are closely associated with war, and they carry weapons of war — a lance, knife and club. Their military character is also evident in their behavior. When supcrnaturally excited they attack people by throwing stones, hitting them with sticks, and, in serious cases, stabbing and killing them.[621] This of course is beyond the bounds of humor. In a sense it represents the trait of practical joking carried to a serious extreme, and this extreme follows from their character as a "possessed" military society.

There is, however, a certain humorous turn to the characterization of the Fool dancers. They are represented with enormous noses, in which lie their personalities and their power; Neophytes [201] to the society are initiated by being rubbed with mucous.[622] They possess a real Cyrano de Bergerac complex in regard to this organ. Any allusion to noses irritates them and to have their noses struck causes them to go out of their heads. When in a fury they do not dance, but run about like madmen, throwing things about, striking people and breaking things.[623] People irritate them by pulling or spitting on their noses.[624]

The Haida persons, who are "made *gagixit,*" exhibit a madness comparable to that of the

---

[620] Boas, 1897, p. 420.

[621] *Ibid,* pp. 468-471.

[622] *Ibid,* pp. 468-469.

[623] *Ibid.*

[624] *Ibid,* pp. 523, 545.

Kwakiutl Fool dancers. They rush about town, rolling over, running through people's houses, making fun of their canoes and crying through the woods. People do not venture out, and if anyone is caught in the woods, his clothes are torn off and his person ridiculed. They may pull canoes out of the water and break them. The *gagixit* may be caught. For example, on one occasion an inflated seal stomach was hung up and he was called. He came crying, "A ha, ha, ha," rolled under the stomach and went away. When he returned he was seized and taken to the dance house, where he later danced accompanied by spirit songs. At least part of the function of such individuals is to destroy property which the potlatching chief afterward pays for.[625]

The Plains: contrary behavior

In many respects the ceremomalism of the Plains stands in sharp contrast to that of the other areas considered in this paper. As the Plains tend more toward individual rites and interests, this important ceremonial setting does not permit the type of clown found elsewhere. Societies joined through visions, for example, had their private ceremonies. Public, communal ceremonies were less common. These rituals were in fulfilment of private promises, or to gain personal ends. They centered largely around visions in which the individual rather than the community sought benefits.

With such latitude in behavior and regalia as was permitted by the lack of rigid patterns in the Plains, it might seem that a great range of comic devices would have been possible. As a matter of [202] fact, the Plains clown was dominated and characterized by contrary speech and action, This is generally rationalized as the result of a vision, chiefly of thunder or lightning, which causes one to behave in an unnatural manner. The strength of this association with a vision and the peculiar nature of contrary speech and action brought this into great vogue as a comic device. At the same time the individualistic nature of Plains ceremonialism made it possible that it should also develop into aberrant forms in the military societies. For Plains ceremonialism permitted indefinite variations and vision-given ritual constantly recombined old elements.

Typical features of Plains ceremonialism are exhibited in the Dakota Heyoka society. This society was joined by a vision of thunder or of *Wakinyan*, and such a vision made one *heyoka,* or antinatural,[626] and largely governed his subsequent behavior.

The peculiar traits of the Heyoka have been explicitly and fully described for the Dakota. The desires and experiences even of the Heyoka deities are all contrary to nature. In the winter they stand on the open prairie without clothing; in the summer they sit on knolls wrapped in buffalo robes and yet they are freezing." The initiation ceremony to the Heyoka society is somewhat stereotyped, but the outstanding feature is an antinatural trick, the boiling-water performance. In drawing meat from boiling water the performers hand is protected by certain roots, probably the mallow. During the initiation ceremony the Heyoka members are present dressed as clowns and must act in a contrary manner.[627] Besides the boiling water trick, the Heyoka may splash boiling water on their backs and legs, complaining that it is cold.[628] They exaggerate the unnatural atmosphere by singing individually and discordantly.[629]

---

[625] Swanton, 1909, p. 173.
[626] Wissler, 1912, pp. 82-85.
[627] *Ibid.*
[628] Dorsey, 1894, p. 469.
[629] Lowie, 1913, pp. 113-116.

The prominence of contrary behavior threw other comic devices into the background, but the essential point is that the members of the Heyoka were in grave danger of thunder and lightning if they did not perform these contrary ceremonies, so that they were clowns by the direst necessity, by the imperative demand of a vision.

Examples from other tribes will illustrate the predominance of [203] the contrary concept in Plains humor. The Ponca Heyoka were quite similar to those of the Dakota, but the *Thanigratha*, "Those-who-imitate-madmen", also contrary, were more purely clownish. They might, for example, ford a stream by stripping one leg and hopping across on the leg which was clad.[630]

The Cheyenne Contrary society is also controlled by this concept. Like the Heyoka, it is joined by people who fear thunder and lightning. The society lodge is constructed with the skin wrong side out and the poles outside the skin; the pipe used in the ceremony is assembled incorrectly; the members dress in rags, walk backward, reverse the sitting posture by lying on the ground with their feet up, and say the reverse of what they mean; they tumble about and dance clumsily.[63183] They carry red bows and arrows which they use in reverse manner, and they dart about in an eccentric way "like lightning in a storm," for it is said that the "thunderstorm has with him people who act this way".[632]

The Plains Ojibway clown-doctors, *Windigokan*, combined the serious and humorous aspects of contrary behavior. They were contrary in their play, their warfare, and even in their curing. They too were foolhardy in war. On one occasion twelve of these clowns assembled with their leaders who said: "I am not going to war. I shall not kill Sioux. I shall not scalp four and let the rest escape. I shall go in the daytime." They departed that night and soon met a large body of Sioux. Instead of fleeing they danced until the Sioux, thinking them deities, made offerings to them. Suddenly they drew their weapons and killed four of the Sioux, frightening the remainder. After scalping the four enemies, the leader said: "Now my old men [they were all youths] you must not run home as fast as you can." On another occasion they performed as clowns, being terrified at stumps, fleeing from dogs and being thrown into spasms at drum beats.[633]

Summary

Those differences which exist between the comic practices of the various American Indian clowns follow in part from the differences [204] set up through different cultural values, in part from purely historical accidents. The emphasis in the Southwest on sex, obscenity and scatology arose from the supreme importance in this area of the concept of fertility. The unusual prominence of the same things among the nomads of the Southwest and tribes of California arose largely from a cultural connection with the Pueblo tribes. The importance of ceremonial madness on the Northwest Coast was the upshot of a peculiar turn of development and determined the basic character of the clown in that area, while the assignment of clowning to a military society further exaggerated the clown's obstreperous and violent behavior. In the Plains, the association of clowning with societies born of visions gave the organizations a typical Plains cast, while a historical accident which originated contrary behavior — probably in a single group — lent the societies their characteristic flavor.

---

[630] Skinner, 1915fl, p. 789.
[631] Grinnell, 2: 204-210.
[632] *Ibid*, p. 329.
[633] Skinner, 1914, pp. 500-505.

CONCLUSIONS

The high degree of "psychic unity" of man in regard to things laughable is explainable in terms of similar conditioning under different cultures of an innate response. There is no evidence to demonstrate any differences between races in the unconditioned stimuli which produce laughter. All indications point to laughter as an innate response to pleasurable stimuli. To the extent, then, that different cultures find similar things comical, there has been a similar conditioning to things painful and pleasurable. This means simply that sickness, misfortune, poverty and the like, and physiological necessities affect all groups of men alike. They are equally charged with emotional interest and pleasurable or comic relief from them is everywhere sought.

UNIVERSITY OF MICHIGAN

Julian Haynes Steward (1902 - 1972) was born in DC, at 16 enrolled at Deep Springs Preparatory School in the Great Basin, setting his life goals, started college at UC Berkeley but a year later switched to Cornell for degrees in zoology and geology, then returned to Berkeley for his 1929 PhD on Buffoons, an anomaly in a career devoted to cultural ecology and evolution. He did archaeology on the Columbia River, fieldwork in well-watered Owen's Valley (1933), began anthropology at Michigan (1928), again at Utah (1930), taught at Berkeley (1934), Columbia (1946-52), and finally Illinois (1953-68). His surveys of the Basin (1935) were funded by Kroeber, land claims (1953) and BAE (1935-45), where he also directed Handbook of South American Indians. Michigan published Buffoons and BAE, Bulletin #120 *Basin-Plateau Aboriginal Sociopolitical Groups*; *Steward Journal of Anthropology* continues his legacy.

LITERATURE CITED

BANCROFT, H.H 1876. Native Races of the Pacific States. 5vols. New York. [205]

BANDELIER, ADOLF F 1890. The Delight Makers. New York.

BARRETT, S.A 1919. The Wintun Hesi Ceremony. Univ. Cal, Publ Am. Archaeol and Ethnol, 14: 437-488.

BOAS, F 1892. Eighth Rep. on the Indians of British Columbia. Brit. Assn. Adv. Sci, meeting of 1891, pp. 408-474.

——— 1897. The Social Organization and Secret Societies of the Kwakiutl Indians. US Nat. Mus. Rep. for 1895: 311-738. Washington.

BOURKE, JOHN G 1891. Scatalogic Rites of All Nations. Washington.

BRINTON, DANIEL G 1883. The Güegüence; a Comedy Ballet in the Nahuatl-Spanish Dialect of Nicaragua. Philadelphia.

CHAMBERS, E.K 1903. The Mediaeval Stage. 2 vols. Oxford.

CUSHING, FRANK H 1920. Zuñi Breadstuff. Ind. Notes and Monogr., 7:1-673.

DIXON, ROLAND B 1905. The Northern Maidu. Am. Mus. Nat. Hist., Bull. 17.

DORSET, J.O 1894. A Study of Siouan Cults. Bur, Am. Ethnol, Rep, 2:351-544.

FEWKES, J.W 1808. The Growth of Hopi Ritual. Journ. Am. Folk-Lore, 11:173-194.

——— 1900. The New Fire Ceremony at Walpi. Am. Anthropol, New Ser. 2:80-138.

——— 1903. Hopi Katcinas. Bur. Am. Ethnol, Ann. Rep., 21:13-126.

GAASTRA, MRS. T. CHAS 1925. Santo Domingo "Bull and Horse" Ceremony. El Palacio, 18 (No. 4): 67-69.

GOLDFRANK, E.S 1927. The Social and Ceremonial Organization of Cochiti. Mem. Am.

Anthropol Assn., 33.

GRINNELL, GEO. B 1923. The Cheyenne Indians. Their History and Ways of Life. 2 vols. New Haven.

HAEBERLIN, H.K 1916. The Idea of Fertilization in the Culture of the Pueblo Indians. Am. Anthropol Assn., Mem. 3:1-55.

KROEBER, A.L 1907. The Arapaho. Am. Mus. Nat. Hist., Bull. 18:1-230; 279-454.

—— 1925. Handbook of the Indians of California. Bur. Am. Ethnol, Bull. 78.

LOWIE, ROBERT H 1909. The Assiniboine. Am. Mus. Nat. Hist., Anthropol Papers, 4:1-270.

—— 1913. Dance Associations of the Eastern Dakota. Ibid, 11: 101-142. [206]

LUMHOLTZ, CARL 1907. Symbolism of the Huichol Indiana. Ibid, Mem. 3 (Whole Series): 1-228.

MASON, J ALDEN 1920. The Papago Harvest Festival. Am. Anthropol., New Ser., 22: 13-25.

MATTHEWS, WASHINGTON 1887. The Mountain Chant, a Navajo Ceremony. Bur. Am. Ethnol, Ann. Rep., 5: 385-168.

—— 1902. The Night Chant, a Navaho Ceremony. Am. Mus. Nat. Hist., Mem. 6: 1-332.

MEAD, MARGARET 1928. Coming of Age in Samoa. New York.

NUNEZ Y DOMINGEZ, José PE J 1927. Corpus Christi in My Native Region. Mexican Folkways, 3: 191-202.

PARSONS, ELSIE CLEWS 1917. Notes on Zuñi. Am. Anthropol. Assn., Mem. 4:151-327.

POND, G.H 1889. Dakota Superstitions. Minn. Hist.Soc. Coll., 2: 215-257.

POWERS, STEPHEN 1877. Tribes of California. Contrib. North Am. Ethnol, III. Washington.

RADIN, PAUL 1923. The Winnebago Tribe. Bur. Am. Ethnol, Ann. Rep., 37:35-560.

REAGAN, ALBERT B 1915. Masked Dancers of the Jemez Indians. *The Southern Workman*, Aug, 423-427.

ROBINSON, DAVID M ?? "Greek Drama" in J. Hastings, Encyclopaedia of Religion and Ethics.

RUSSELL, FRANK 1898. An Apache Medicine Dance. Am. Anthropol., 11:367-372.

SAPIR, EDWARD 1911. Some Aspects of Nootka Language and Culture. Am. Anthropol., 13: 15-28.

SKINNER, ALANSON 1914. Political and Ceremonial Organization of the Plains-Ojibway. Am. Mus. Nat. Hist., Anthropol, Papers, 11: 475-511.

—— 1915. Societies of the Iowa. Ibid, 11: 679-740.

—— 1915a. Ponca Societies and Dances. Ibid, 11: 777-801.

SMITH, DE COST 1888. Witchcraft and Demonism of the Modern Iroquois. Journ. Am. Folk-Lore, 1: 184-193.

SPECK, FRANK G 1907. The Creek Indians of Taskagi Town. Am. Anthropol. Assn, Mem. 2: 99-164.

—— 1909. Ethnology of the Yuchi Indians. Univ. Pa. Museum, Anthropol. Publ, 1: 1-154.

—— 1911. Ceremonial Songs of the Creek and Yuchi Indians. Ibid., 1: 155-245. [207]

STEVENSON, MATILDA C 1904. The Zuñi Indians; Their Mythology, Esoteric Societies and Ceremonies. Bur. Am. Ethnol, Ann. Rep. 23.

STRONG, WILLIAM D 1929. Aboriginal Society in Southern Calif. Univ. Cal, Publ. Am. Archaeol. and Ethnol, 26: 1-249.

SWANTON, JOHN R 1905. The Haida of Queen Charlotte Islands. Jesup North Pac. Exped., vol. 8, pt. 1.

—— 1909. Contribution to the Ethnology of the Haida. Am. Mus. Nat. Hist., Mem. 8, pt. 1.

—— 1928. Religious Beliefs and Medical Practices of the Creek Indians. Bur. Am. Ethnol, Ann. Rep., 42: 473-673.

THOMPSON, GILBERT 1889. An Indian Dance at Jemez, New Mexico. Am. Anthropol, 2: 351-355.

WISSLER, CLARK 1912. Societies and Ceremonial Associations in the Oglala Division of the Teton-Dakota. Am. Mus. Nat. Hist., Anthropol Papers, 11:1-99.

index

* = key entry   f = span of 5 pages, usually forward   #0 = span of 10 pages forward

A

Aa'ni = ʔɔɔʔɔ́ɔ́niinénɔh ~ Gros Ventre, 2
Abenaki, 39
Achilles, 60
Achumawi, 22, 35
acorns, 15*, 30; meal = *pinole*, 51f; soup, 28
Charlie Anderson, 45
Annikadel, 22
antics, 78f, 83, 92, 99, 105f
anti-natural, 71f, 77
antithesis, 3, 26
Apache, 28f, 48; Plains, 118
ayelkwi = power 21, 38 Luiseño
Aztalan, 49

B

backward speech, 80, 92, 110, 117, = *nanoma ponait*
Bear, 5f, clan, 9; Midé, 32; moiety, 12
bear, 4f, claws, 9; Cut Foot, 13; circumlocutions, 6f; crazy, 121; grease, 122; healing, 5, 9, 30; grease, 122; grizzly, 48; grizzly wife, 10; mediator, 5, 13f; polar, 17; respect, 15; rite, 14; skin, 11; skulls, 15; spouse, 6; suit, 19; welcome, 8f, 15
Bear Butte, 26
Bear Doctors, 9, 13
Bear Gulch, 131
Bear sib, 12
beetle, 53
begging, 95, 155f
berdache, 4ff, 29f, 36, 40, 100, 107f
William Beynon, 55
bison, 2, 15, 77f, 82, 124
black, 11, 26, 34, 60, 66f, 73f, 94, 113, 122, 136, 144f
Blackbird, 113
Black Butte = Wiespa, 53
Black Elk, 100
Black Raven, 133
Blackfeet, 11f, 29, 56, 72f, 82f, 115
Blood tribe, 83
blood, 19f, 24f, 37f, 48f, 133, 56, 44, 52,

139; = *humukw*, 14; shed, 134
Karl Bodmer, 116
Buffalo Calf Road Woman, 29
Bull Dance, 121
bundles, 11, 28f, 41, 108
Bushyhead mask, 20
Buzzards, 49

C

Cahuilla, 47
Carrier = porteur, 40
chastity, 25, 27, 29
Chemehuevi, 31
Cheyenne, 24f, 38, 49, 90f, 97f, 104f, 111, 95, 121, 123
Chief Dogs, 118
Christmas tree, 62
Chungishnish, 53, 56
circle of life, 26
Coeur d'Alene, 68f, 72f
cosmos, 4f, 12f, 22f, 58
cowry, 35, 37
Cowry, 13
Coyote, 63, 159
crazy, 26, 80f, 90, 96f, 105f, 114, 123, 127f, 132f, 137f, 142f, 147f
Crazy Dogs, 82f, 90, 115, 119
Crazy Lodge = 98f, 127* = *hohooko 'oowu'*
Crazy-Dogs-Wishing-to-Die, 119f
Cree, 4, 18, 25f, 75, 80f, 90, 96, 102, 105f
Cry, 51f
crystals, 29, 35
Cutfoot, 13

D

dearly-loved child, 134
deer hoof rattles, 80, 103, 119, 142f
dicta = enchantments, 46
Henry Dobyns, 23
Dogs, 78, 82f, 90, 116f, 130f, 133, 138, 155; Crazy, 82f, 119; dances, 135; Real, 87, 116, = *macukaike*; Yellow, 117
dogs, 16f, 99, 103, 117, 128; judge, 34; meat, 100, 105, 141; wood, 113
drum, 32, 60, 88, 101, 135f, 142; dance,

131f

F

Flat Pipe, 132, 134, 136, 138
Foolish Ones = *sakhunu*, 112
Forty-Four Chiefs, 26
forty-four manito, 13
Four Holy Beings, 135
Frankenstein's catle, 48
Leo Frobenius, 5
Frog, 6, 39f, 44
frogs, 30, 43, 109
fur robe, 76, 94

G

gaan, 55 ~ Tlingit
gagixit, 159f
gambling, 133, 137, 143
gɔl, 16 ~ Tsimshian
ghats = cremation grounds, 58
Gilcrease Museum, 43
Gosiute, 55
gourd masks, 20
grandfathers, 14, 86, 97f, 127f, 132f, 137f, 142f, 148
grotesquesness, 77, 89, 92
Gwich'in, 26

H

herbals, 14, 98f,
herbalists, 5, 87f
Robert Hertz, 47
Hesi, 153, 159
heyoka, 4f, 40, 72, 79f*, 88, 97f, 102f, 107f, 112f, 122f, 155, 160
Hidatsa, 2, 18, 28f, 72, 81f, 87f, 116f
Hollywood, 95, 112
Holy Woman, 122
Holy Woman Above, 30
Hot Dancers, 88
Hot Dances, 72, 84f*, 90, 98
human hairs, 33, 45
Huron, 41, 49, 87f, 92
Huskfaces, 19
hysteria, 60

I

inclosive, 5, 17
Inuit, 21f, 39, 96
inverse speech, 75f, 94f, 103f, 116f
inversion, 76, 83, 97, 130
inyăs, 67
Iowa, 74, 87f; Ioway, 28f, 35
Iruska, 72, 85f, 89f, 113

J

jesters, 153f
Jicarilla, 28, 35

K

kachina, 34, 152f
Kamia, 53*
Kashaya Pomo, 48
Kennewick, 47
Kickapoo, 23f, 35
Kiowa-Apache, 101, 116f
Kittitas, 65
Klintidie, 118f
Konds, 153
Koshare, 154f
Koyemsi, 152f
kulturkreis, 18

L

Labrets, 27
Lakota, 2f, 22f, 29f, 38f, 96f, 107f, 115f, 123
Ruth Landes, 13f, 31f
left, 4ff, 23, 27, 32f, 50, 110, 146f
Claude Levi-Strauss, 5, 16
Lewis and Clark, 115
Liaik, 8
liatəd = probe, 45
libido, 155
Lime-Crazy, 99, 129
Łlingit, 54 = Tlingit
Lone Man, 122
Lonewis, 41, 51, 54
Low Horn, 56
Lozen, 29
Luiseño, 21, 38, 52f*
lunar cycle, 16
Lushootseed, 32, 38

M

Mafia, 43f
Ma'heo'o, 24
Maidu, 51*, 156
Makah, 35
Laura Makarius, 19
Manabus robe, 29
manitu, 29
Manzrau, 158
Marmes, 47
Masing, 19
Massaum, 104f, 121
maxpe, 57
meeters, 30
megis, 33f
Menominee, 25, 32f; Menomini, 87f
Metamorphosis, 66f
Miami, 31
Midewiwin, 5, 13f, 32f
Milky Way, 34, 49
Mind, 5, 14f, 25, 31, 41, 43, 63, 86, 145; mindful, 12
misfortune, 41, 63, 82, 109, 135f, 141, 152f, 162
Miwok, 51, 153
Modoc, 50
moieties, 12, 18f, 25, 39
moon, 12, 22
James Mooney, 127
Lawwrence Morgan, 7
Mosquitos, 83f
mosquitos = snowflakes, 109
moth = *hohookehe'* = 'little crazy', 128
mother earth, 86
mushroom, 142, 146
Mvskogi = Creeks, 32

N

Navajo, 21f, 24f, 34f
necklace, 9, 52
Newekwe, 152f
Night Chant, 152
nookohookee = 'white crazy man', 99, 127

O

obscenity154f
Offerings Lodge, 129

Ojibwa, 4, 13f, 22f, 27f, 38, 72, 77f, 85f, 92; Plains, 99, 103, 124
Okipa Fool = *Okeheede*, 122f*
Omaha, 13, 22, 33, 85, 116
omotome = breath, 24 Cheyenne
Oshara, 6
Oto, 25f, 29
Ottawa, 23, 87
ʔɔɔʔɔ́ɔ́ɔ́niinénɔh = Aa'ni, 2
owl feathers, 77, 82f, 131
Owl-Man, 120 Plains Apache

P

Paiakyamu, 156
paiduma, 5
Pamunkey, 43
pantomimes, 102f
Parry Island, 30, 89f
Pawnee, 28, 35f, 72, 85f, 94f, 108f, 114*, 124
Penobscots, 40
"people", 4f, 17
pet, 24, 110
phallus, 123
pinole, 51
pipe, 84, 91, 103f, 119, 132f, 147; Flat, 133f
pipestems, 11, 35
Plains Cree, 77f, 92, 99, 103*
Plains Ojibwa, 77f, 91, 99, 103*
polarities, 5, 10, 32
police, 13, 115f, 128f, 157
Ponca, 35, 72, 79f, 99, 106f*
Popul Vuh, 44
Potawatomi, 25f, 31, 87
Powamu, 157
probe = *liatəd*, 45
pukutsi, 115 Comanche

Q

quasquay = Bluejay, 60f, 69
Quechan, 23, 30
Quileute, 34

R

rattles = *θaθanas*, 141
Real Dogs, 85
Real Dogs, 82f, 117 = *macukaike* Hidatsa

right ~ side, 5f, 23, 33, 50, 85, 111, 141, 149
right ~ legal, 28, 32f, 77, 111, 140
right ~ OK, 41, 116, 129f, 139, 143f
ritualists, 46, 73, 80, 88f
rowdyism, 154

S

sacrifices, 46, 58f, 91, 121, 131f, 144; dance, 139f, 142f
Sarsi, 84
Saturnalia, 61
Sauk, 24f, 32f, 87f
sekwitsit puhitsit = mud men, 115 #485 Comanche
semen, 59
semen = bone, 39
semi-moieties, 18
Seven Old Men, 128
Shawnee, 23, 31f
Shibalba, 44
Shiva, 58
"shorts", 139f, 148 Aa'ni team
sibs, 12
sipiniit, 24 Inuit
Skeleton Being = *paguk*, 102
Sora rails, 45
spartan, 55
St Ignatius mission, 62
Stars, 6
Stars, 128, 141, 143, 144, 146, 147, 155
Stars, 133, 137f, 142f, 149 / vs Wolves
stars, 35
struckon, 4
Stump Horn, 113
stunts, 102, 107
sumesh, 60f, 69
sumi'x, 69
summer, 5, 18f, 35, 68, 110, 119, 138
Sutaio Sacred Hat, 26
sweathouse, 31
Sweet Medicine, 26, 106

T

taboos, 17f, 25, 30, 39f, 56, 123, 133
tabus, 68, 74
Tacitus, 56
"talls", 138f, 147f

teaching, 32, 46
Tewa, 10
θaθanas = rattles, 141
Thunder, 40, 78f, 89f, 104f; Winged One, 107
Thunderers, 26, 32, 100
Thunderbirds, 28, 108
Thunderbird sib, 21
Thunder-Bow, 111f, 116, 117, 123
Tih-pik-nits' Pahn, 54
Tillamook, 23, 49
Tlaloc, 156
Tlingit, 18f, 27, 39, 54, 56; see Łingits
Tohono O'Odham, 27, 29, 35, 50
toloache datura, 52
totemism, 8, 16
Totonac, 157
toy bow, 23
Tsimshian, 4, 16f, 28, 42, 46f, 53f
Tutelos, 35

U

Underwater Panther = *piasaw*, 43

V

virgin dorms = ieouinnon, 26
Vishnu, 58
vower, 132ff, 142f

W

Wabano, 83f, 87
wakan, 30, 100, 109f
Wakashan, 6
Wakinyan, 160
wankech, 53
web, 21, 36
webbing, 5, 43
White Ear, 113
"white fool" = *nankhahankan*, 99
"White Painted Fool" = *haaatinahankan*, 99
White Stone, 44
wild rice, 15, 23
Windigokan, 161
Windover, 44f
winter, 5, 18, 35, 43, 62, 65f, 82, 96, 116, 128, 136; food, 122; Midwinter, 92
winter counts, 110

winter dance, 65f, 71f
winter storms, 109
Wintun, 153
Without Fires, 38 #216
Wiyot, 21, 53
Wolf Chief ~ William Beynon, 55
Wolves ~ soldiers, 132, 137f, 148 / vs Stars
wolves, 40, 85
World Heart, 22
Wowochim, 158
wristlets, 24
Wyandot, 25

X

Xgyet, 53

Y

Ya'ukwekam, 44
Yellow Noses, 117
Yuchi, 23
Yuki, 159
Yup'ik, 37
Yurok, 27, 31
Yuwipi, 38

* = key entry   f = span of 5 pages, usually forward   #0 = span of 10 pages forward

Please Help Wipe Out Typo-Gnomes by Reporting them. Corrections Welcome!

9 798652 137656